MORE WOMEN OF WONDER

MORE WOMEN OF WONDER

SCIENCE FICTION NOVELETTES
BY WOMEN ABOUT WOMEN

EDITED, WITH AN
INTRODUCTION AND NOTES, BY

PAMELA
SARGENT

VINTAGE BOOKS
A Division of Random House, New York

A Vintage Original, August 1976
First Edition
Copyright © 1976 by Pamela Sargent

ACKNOWLEDGMENTS

"Jirel Meets Magic," by C. L. Moore. Copyright 1935, ©
1962 by C. L. Moore, reprinted by permission of the
Harold Matson Company, Inc.

"The Lake of the Gone Forever," by Leigh Brackett. Copyright 1949 by Standard Magazines, Inc. Originally appeared in *Thrilling Wonder Stories*. Reprinted by permission of Lurton Blassingame, the author's agent.

"The Second Inquisition," by Joanna Russ. Copyright ©
1970 by Damon Knight. Originally appeared in *Orbit 6*.
Reprinted by permission of the author.

"The Power of Time," by Josephine Saxton. Copyright ©
1971 by Robert Silverberg. Originally appeared in *New
Dimensions 1*. Reprinted by permission of the author and
her agent, Virginia Kidd.

"The Funeral," by Kate Wilhelm. Copyright © 1972 by
Harlan Ellison. Originally appeared in *Again, Dangerous
Visions*. Reprinted by permission of the author.

"Tin Soldier," by Joan D. Vinge. Copyright © 1974 by
Damon Knight. Originally appeared in *Orbit 14*. Reprinted by permission of the author.

"The Day Before the Revolution," by Ursula K. Le Guin.
Copyright © 1974 by Ursula K. Le Guin (first appeared
in *Galaxy*); reprinted by permission of the author and
her agent, Virginia Kidd.

Library of Congress Cataloging in Publication Data
Main entry under title:

More women of wonder.

Bibliography: p.
CONTENTS: Moore, C. L. Jirel meets magic.—
Brackett, L. The lake of the gone forever.—Russ, J.
The second inquisition. [etc.]
1. Science fiction, American—Women authors.
2. Women—Fiction. I. Sargent, Pamela.
PZ1.M818 [PS648.S3]   813'.0876   76-13239
ISBN 0-394-71876-3

To the memory of
JANET KAFKA,
who made it possible

CONTENTS

INTRODUCTION
PAMELA SARGENT

I

In a previous collection of stories, *Women of Wonder*, I discussed the role of women in science fiction mainly from a historical perspective. I mentioned some of the achievements of women sf writers, the treatment of female characters in some science-fictional works, and the relationship between feminist concerns and serious futuristic thought.

Although women have been represented both as writers and as characters in science fiction, they have played a minor role in the genre until recently. Female writers such as Francis Stevens, C. L. Moore, E. Mayne Hull, and Leigh Brackett, who wrote for the predominantly male-oriented magazines during the first half of the century, were notable exceptions, but for the most part, the writers and readers of science fiction were males. This is still the case today, although there are signs that this is changing.

The mode of literature is that of an indirect interpretive experience. Through a novel or story, one can simulate living through experiences not normally part of one's existence. One can gain insights into various human problems and types of behavior by observing and coming to know fictional characters as they interact with one another and with their environments. These insights may influ-

ence the reader's attitudes and behavior. If a novel
is truly influential, it becomes a part of the culture,
thus influencing even those who may never have
read it. The fictional experience at its best carries
an emotional impact that the factual recounting of
an experience may lack. The creation of characters
with whom the reader can identify, or come to understand, or for whom he or she can feel sympathy,
is an important part of this process. Literature has
the tacit aim of improving us through imagination
and understanding, by creating in our minds what
we could not otherwise observe. In serious science
fiction, in which the writer questions past values
and future alternatives, science and technology
exist against the background of a moral tradition.

Science fiction conveys conditional, hypothetical,
or "lived-through" futures. The futurist can present
various future possibilities or scenarios, the jour-
nalist can speculate about possible results in a serious or playful manner, while the science fiction
writer can show how these future worlds might
feel. Once the reader becomes, even if only for a
short time, a part of the world he or she reads
about, a psychological acceptance of certain future
possibilities is created. The reader's attitudes may
be influenced to some degree. Various scientists and
astronauts have admitted reading science fiction as
young people, and it is safe to conclude, as many
of them have, that it has had some effect on their
career choices.

Herman Kahn and Anthony J. Wiener, in discussing organized efforts to study the future, have
written:

These efforts are hardly likely to replace individual visions of the future of the kind we already know, such as those of H G. Wells, Aldous Huxley, and George Orwell, to take only the best-known recent examples in English. Such personal works of imagination—nearly all of them in fact passionately aimed at changing the future—are likely to prove more influential than more systematic and "reasonable," but correspondingly more prosaic, efforts.[1]

One science fiction novel which few people today have actually read has had an obvious effect: Mary Shelley's *Frankenstein*. The title alone connotes one of the central mythic attitudes of our time, the fear that our technology will (or has) become a monster that will destroy us. Science fiction, or notions derived from it, can create the relevant myths of our age. Thus the literature shapes attitudes toward future possibilities even in the minds of those who have not read it.

Any worthwhile literature reflects its time, and science fiction is no exception. Though science fiction writers have often prided themselves on being able to entertain an unlimited number of exotic possibilities, the fact is that the genre, which is uniquely part of the twentieth century, reflects our century's attitudes. Often future societies are seen as monarchistic, capitalistic, militaristic, or, in the case of post-holocaust stories or tales about the settlement of other planets, primitive. Since these

[1] Herman Kahn and Anthony J. Wiener, *The Year 2000* (New York, Macmillan, 1967), p. 4.

"future" societies are often modeled on past or present societies which have little regard for women, female characters are of little importance except in their traditional roles.

I do not believe that science fiction can be considered a truly serious literature unless it deals more thoughtfully with women and the concerns of women. These concerns should of course be of interest to everyone; the division of various pursuits into "masculine" and "feminine" activities limits all people. Writers of adventurous science fiction, and those who use science-fictional ideas metaphorically rather than realistically, can improve their work by more thoughtful characterization. As more women writers enter the genre, and as more men deal thoughtfully with their female characters, science fiction will hopefully become a more androgynous and human literature.

II

The history of women in science fiction begins with Mary Shelley, the author of *Frankenstein*. In addition to this novel, which can be considered the first work of science fiction, Shelley was also the author of *The Last Man* (1826), a novel in which a plague is responsible for the death of humankind. The post-holocaust story has since become a permanent fixture in science fiction. The disaster depicted can be an atomic war, an ecological disaster, or anything else about which the author is particularly fearful. But at the time Shelley wrote, the possibility of humanity's extinction seemed more fanciful. *The Last Man* was unpopular among Shelley's contemporaries, who regarded the events of the novel as impossible.

Thus Shelley can be credited with two of science fiction's most enduring themes: the destruction of an individual or a society by its technology, and the destruction of all humans by forces beyond our control. These two themes can often be wedded together in the same work, as they are in novels and stories about the results of world-wide nuclear war.

Hugh J. Luke, Jr., in his introduction to a modern edition of *The Last Man*, mentions some of the flaws of this novel, among them the flowery and "exalted" language and the somewhat excessive length of the book. But he goes on to say:

. . . anyone who has lived with the possibility of instantaneous and complete obliteration of human society—that possibility, in Falkner's phrase, "so long sustained by now that we can even bear it"—can hardly dismiss the theme of *The Last Man* as a merely grotesque one.[2]

The next important female writer of science fiction was Francis Stevens. She was born Gertrude Barrows in 1884. Her novel *The Heads of Cerberus*, possibly the first science fiction novel to deal with the theme of parallel worlds, was published in 1918.

One story by Stevens, "Friend Island," published in *All Story Weekly* in 1918, is of particular interest. Here Stevens uses as her background a world in which women are regarded as the superior sex.

[2]Hugh J. Luke, Jr., in his introduction to Mary Shelley, *The Last Man* (Lincoln, University of Nebraska Press, 1965), p. viii.

The narrator of the story is a retired woman sea
captain who relates her tale to a deferential man.
Within the context of the story, the captain remarks
on the position of men in her world:

> There's too much preached nowadays that man
> is fit for nothing but to fetch and carry and do
> nurse-work in big child-homes. To my mind, a
> man who hasn't the nerve of a woman ain't fitted
> to father children, let alone raise them.[3]

The captain tells her story: when she was young,
she survived a shipwreck and was washed up on
the shore of a pleasant island. There she finds a
message on a piece of board telling her that the
island is dangerous. She ignores this warning and
discovers that the island is a lovely spot, but has
the peculiar ability to reflect her moods. When she
is lonely, the weather becomes cloudy or stormy.
When she treats the island with some consideration,
it responds with pleasant weather and enough food
and water for survival.

Evenually the man who left her the danger warning, Nelson Smith, reappears. He is adrift on a
small floating island that has carried him back to
the island from which he had fled. He and the captain manage to escape together, but not before the
island, enraged by Smith's insulting behavior, has
almost killed them both.

[3]Francis Stevens, "Friend Island," in *Under the Moons
of Mars: A History and Anthology of "The Scientific Romance" in the Munsey Magazines, 1912–1920*, Sam Moskowitz, ed. (New York, Holt, Rinehart & Winston, 1970),
p. 127.

The captain finds out why Smith had left the island before. He had cursed at it and insulted it, and the sentient island responded in kind. The captain is sorry about all of this; she was thinking of marrying Smith until she became disillusioned by what she calls his "mannishness." As she puts it: "Some folks never knows a lady till she up and whangs 'em over the head with a brick. A real, gentle, kind-like warning . . . you would not heed!"[4]

The next woman to make a mark in science fiction was C. L. Moore. Her first story, "Shambleau," was published in *Weird Tales* in 1933. The hero of that story, Northwest Smith, saves an alien woman from a mob seeking her death. He later discovers that she is a psychic vampire, and narrowly misses falling under her spell. The noted science fiction writer Lester del Rey says about this story:

> It is probably impossible to explain to modern readers how great an impact that first C. L. Moore story had.
> Here, for the first time in the field, we find mood, feeling, and color. Here is an alien who is truly *alien*—far different from the crude monsters and slightly-altered humans found in other stories. Here are rounded and well-developed characters . . . And—certainly for the first time that I can remember in the field—the story presents the sexual drive of humanity in some of its complexity.[5]

[4]Stevens, p. 135.
[5]Lester del Rey, "Forty Years of C. L. Moore," in *The Best of C. L. Moore* (New York, Ballantine Books, 1974), pp. 1–2.

Moore also wrote stories with memorable female protagonists. During the 1930s she wrote a series of stories about Jirel of Joiry, a woman who was a ruler and warrior. "Black God's Kiss," the first of these stories, appeared in *Weird Tales* in 1934. As Lester del Rey puts it:

> In those days, the sf magazines were all intensely male oriented. Most of the readers were male, and the idea of sexual equality had never been considered—certainly not for the protagonist of an adventure story. For such fiction, it followed axiomatically, one used a male hero. But in "Black God's Kiss" the intensely feminine Jirel was a woman equal in battle to any swashbuckling male hero who ever ruled over the knights of ancient valor.
>
> Jirel of Joiry was no imperturbable battler, however. She loved and hated, feared desperately to the core of her superstitious heart—and yet dared to take risks that no man had ever faced. Every male reader loved the story, forgot his chauvinism, and demanded more stories about Jirel.[6]

In spite of Moore's success with Jirel, science fiction or fantasy adventure stories to this day almost always have male protagonists. During the 1960s two other writers of sf, Joanna Russ and Rosel George Brown, again wrote adventures with heroines; Brown created the character of Sibyl Sue Blue, an intergalactic policewoman, while Russ wrote about Alyx, a woman of the distant past. In spite of the success of Jirel years earlier, both Russ and

*Del Rey, pp. 2–3.

Brown had to combat the notion that only men could be the heroes of adventure stories.

Leigh Brackett, who did much of her science fiction writing during the 1940s and early 1950s, became a popular writer of adventurous sf stories. It did not seem to matter to Brackett's readers that she was female; her colorful stories, filled with action and set in exotic settings on other planets, were well-liked. A vigorous "masculine" style and tough aggressive heroes are characteristic of her work. Her most recent sf novel, *The Ginger Star* (1974), features Eric John Stark, a strong hero who appeared in some of her earlier work.

Much early American science fiction, written for the pulps, concentrated on adventure involving larger-than-life characters. There was usually a minimum of scientific accuracy; many stories were actually closer to fantasy than science fiction. This began to change during the late 1930s, when John W. Campbell, Jr., took over the editorship of *Astounding* magazine.

Campbell, trained as a nuclear physicist but unable to find work in his field during the Depression, had little patience with capricious or deliberate scientific errors in stories. He insisted that his writers think seriously about the ideas and devices used in their fiction, and that they pay attention to the implications of scientific ideas and advanced technology. He was interested in realism. He had an incalculable effect, as an editor, on such well-known writers as Isaac Asimov, Lester del Rey, Robert A. Heinlein, Theodore Sturgeon, and Poul Anderson.

Campbell was responsible for encouraging more serious, less fanciful science fiction. Serious extrapolation was encouraged, though much of it was technical rather than social. He wanted to give his readers, who were primarily technically trained or scientifically oriented males, stories which would not needlessly violate what they knew to be facts. On several occasions he even urged engineers and scientists to write stories for him.

As a result, more stories appeared with scientists or engineers, rather than men of action, as heroes. The characters were more recognizably human. The reality of research and development was reflected by authors in their fiction. But the scientific and technological world, then as now, was dominated by men. The realism desired by Campbell resulted in stories that did in fact mirror the world around them. Women were of little importance.

There were exceptions; writers Katherine Mac-Lean, C. L. Moore, Pauline Ashwell, and later Anne McCaffrey appeared in the pages of *Astounding* or *Analog* (*Astounding*'s later title). Moore's fine short novel "No Woman Born" was published by Campbell in 1944. Its heroine, a dancer named Deirdre, has her brain transplanted into a metal body after she is nearly killed in a fire. The problems of Deirdre's adjustment to this body are sensitively portrayed; at the story's conclusion, we realize that Deirdre will have many difficulties and that there is a possibility she may become estranged from other humans. But Deirdre is aware of these problems and may, the reader can hope, overcome them; Moore leaves this possibility open.

Other memorable stories by women published in *Astounding* include Judith Merril's first science fiction piece, "That Only a Mother," and Wilmar

Shiras' "In Hiding," both appearing in 1948. Some memorable female characters were portrayed in stories by Isaac Asimov, Robert A. Heinlein, and others. But the emphasis on realism, ironically, did little to enhance the status of women in science fiction.[7]

During the 1950s, more science fiction stories by women began to appear. Several of these writers, such as Katherine MacLean, Marion Zimmer Bradley, and others, were adept at writing solid science fiction involving male and female characters, good plotting, and interesting ideas. Others specialized in stories involving women in traditional roles as heroines.

The underlying assumptions of many such stories were that women are instinctual, emotional, concerned mainly with their households and children, and uninterested in science and technology except for their most trivial applications. Alfred Bester, a gifted writer of science fiction, made the following ambivalent observation in a review of a collection of short stories published in 1960:

It's been suggested that most women fail to write significantly because the female mind is visero-

[7]Anne McCaffrey, in her essay "Hitch Your Dragon to a Star: Romance and Glamour in Science Fiction" (which appeared in *Science Fiction: Today and Tomorrow*, Reginald Bretnor, ed. [New York, Harper & Row, 1974]), discusses what Campbell told her about a character in one of her stories: "I wanted Ruth [her character] to be a 'liberated woman.' John Campbell asked me to define her in terms of a customary womanly role . . . Essentially, he told me, man still explores new territory and guards the hearth; woman minds that hearth whether or not she programs a computer to dust, cook, and rock the cradle." (p. 282)

tonic, and occupied almost exclusively with the moment-to-moment reality of emotions. If this is true, literature's loss is science fiction's gain, for *Out of Bounds*, Judith Merril's collection of short stories, is a warm and colorful rendering of the minutiae of the future.[8]

Bester, of course, was not making a statement of fact but offering a hypothesis; his only assertion is that the story collection is a good one. Others looked at the matter somewhat differently. Sf author and editor Damon Knight, in a review of a novel by a woman he found particularly saccharine, wrote: "Is this the 'woman's viewpoint'? I don't believe it; I think it is the woman's-magazine viewpoint, from which God preserve us."[9]

The 1960s saw the development of stylistic innovations in science fiction. There was also a growing concern with the psychological effects of technology on people. Some authors wished to reject certain "genre" features of sf, such as adventure plots, mighty and triumphant heroes, "pulpy" writing, or a concentration on strange gadgets. Others wished to concentrate on themes that the genre had not emphasized. There was talk at this time of exploring "inner space" rather than "outer space."

Many important female writers of science fiction, among them Ursula K. Le Guin, Carol Emshwiller, Joanna Russ, and Josephine Saxton, began to publish fiction. This was not the result of a willingness

[8]Alfred Bester, in *Fantasy & Science Fiction*; reprinted in Judith Merril, *Out of Bounds* (New York, Pyramid Books, 1960).
[9]Damon Knight, *In Search of Wonder*, 2nd ed. (Chicago, Advent Publishers, 1967), p. 105.

to publish stories reflecting "women's concerns," nor of a conscious desire on the part of editors to publish more stories and novels by women. Some writers, however, women as well as men, may have felt that the field was more receptive to the kinds of stories that they wished to write. It should also be noted that many of these writers began by writing more traditional science fiction. But perhaps the emphasis on innovation encouraged more women to enter the field and to write stories that were neither traditional nor limited to the "housewife" genre of sf.

Present-day writers, both male and female, have certain advantages over those of the past. They can deal with feminism, having had it brought to their attention by the women's movement. In addition, more women are writing science fiction now; among the writers whose first published works appeared during the 1970s are Vonda N. McIntyre, Suzy McKee Charnas, Joan D. Vinge, Marta Randall, Eleanor Arnason, Lisa Tuttle, Brenda Pierce, and Joan Bernott.

This, of course, does not ensure that the genre will become more progressive. Action-adventure stories with strong male protagonists are still popular; characters in traditional roles are still present in many sf stories. But one cannot expect people to shrug off ingrained attitudes overnight, nor to abandon forms that may have served them well in the past.

Four recent science fiction novels are of particular interest. They reveal some of the ways in which the role of women is being explored within the genre. Ursula K. Le Guin's *The Dispossessed* (Harper & Row, 1974) is a critical utopian novel which explores the differences and the conflicts between two human societies in another planetary system. One planet, Urras, is dominated by a capitalistic, wealthy, and technologically advanced society. Anarres, the moon of Urras, has been settled by members of an anarchistic revolutionary movement. Both societies, and the problems that result from the political philosophies of each, are seen through the eyes of a physicist, Shevek. He has grown up on Anarres and is the first member of his society to visit Urras in two hundred years. Among other things, the novel contrasts the role of women in both worlds. On Urras, women are wives, mothers, and sex objects. On Anarres, no distinction is made between the sexes; as a result, women and men are equally represented in every area of life. The reader also learns that the political philosophy which resulted in the society of Anarres was that of a woman, Odo.

Joe Haldeman's *The Forever War* (St. Martin's, 1974) is modeled on traditional science fiction works. The plot is also traditional. We see a future interstellar war through the eyes of one soldier, William Mandella. Unlike many science fiction novels about the future of warfare, this book does not glorify an ultimately purposeless venture, although bravery on the part of individual soldiers exists. The combat troops depicted are draftees, not volunteers. Both men and women are seen in combat, and homosexuals of both sexes are present as characters, though Mandella himself is heterosexual. The even-handedness of the author's treatment of both sexes is remarkable, and a poignant element

is added to the war story as Mandella falls in love
with a fellow soldier, Marygay Potter. Regardless
of one's attitudes toward war, the realistic portrayal
of female combat troops and the psychological acceptance of such a future possibility by readers
will no doubt alter the image of women.

Le Guin's novel shows us men and women becoming more like one another, each gender having
characteristics of both sexes, while Haldeman's depicts women who have become as tough as any
male soldier. Joanna Russ's *The Female Man* (Bantam, 1975) is an explicitly feminist novel which
utilizes innovative writing techniques in telling of
four women, each a version of the same character,
from four alternate worlds. Here science-fictional
elements are used in order to show various female-
oriented power fantasies: a woman from a world
in which there are no men calmly disarms a boor-
ish man at a cocktail party in our world; another
character, genetically altered (she has, among other
characteristics, retractable claws), kills a man of
her world, where the sexes are openly at war. There
is an undercurrent of rage throughout the novel.

One of the most interesting of the many elements
in *The Female Man* is the following description of
an all-female world and the type of society it might
develop:

> On Whileaway they have a saying: When the
> mother and child are separated, they both howl,
> the child because she is separated from the
> mother, the mother because she has to go back
> to work . . . At the age of four or five these inde-
> pendent, blooming, pampered, extremely intelli-
> gent little girls are torn weeping and arguing

from their thirty relatives and sent to the regional school, where they scheme and fight for weeks before giving in . . .

Whileawayan psychology locates the basis of Whileawayan character in the early indulgence, pleasure, and flowering which is drastically curtailed by the separation from the mothers. This (it says) gives Whileawayan life its characteristic independence, its dissatisfaction, its suspicion, and its tendency toward a rather irritable solipsism.[10]

Thomas M. Disch's *334* (Avon, 1974) takes place in the decaying New York City of the early twenty-first century. It could be called a futuristic novel of manners; the story concerns itself with the day-to-day problems and lives of several citizens in a drab welfare state which seems to be breaking down, yet somehow goes on. Among the women characters in this novel are Shrimp, a Lesbian whose sexual fantasies focus on bearing children by artificial insemination, and Milly, a high school sex demonstrator whose husband Boz desperately wants a child. He finally has one, brought to term in an artificial womb, and has an operation giving him breasts so that he can nurse the infant.

All these very different works have one thing in common; they are serious works which attempt to deal intelligently with women. *The Female Man* is the most explicitly feminist, although *The Dispossessed* also touches on some feminist concerns. Neither *334* nor *The Forever War* can be called "fem-

[10]Joanna Russ, *The Female Man* (New York, Bantam Books, 1975), pp. 49–52.

inist," but both novels, because of their attempt to write about the future seriously, take some care with their female (and male) characters.

Although it is likely to be in serious sf works that we will find a concern with women, the role of the adventure novel or story should not be overlooked. An adventure story set in an exotic or fantastic setting with larger-than-life characters can provide interesting characterizations of women. Such a story often concerns itself with an ideal; a character stronger or braver than most of us is facing problems that would, in the real world, be too great for most of us to handle. Strong, idealized women figures can be presented in such works. In fact, "realistic" science fiction works of the past, which often extrapolated their futures from the world contemporaneous with the author, restricted their female characters more severely than some of the works of A. E. van Vogt (who could show an empress, Innelda, ruling an interstellar empire), Stanley G. Weinbaum (who created the Red Peri, a female space pirate), C. L. Moore (in her Jirel of Joiry tales), or comics which featured the exploits of characters such as Wonder Woman or Supergirl.

III

Although most science fiction has been written by men, and most sf writers today are male as well, it would be incorrect to assume that a woman trying to publish sf would always run into insurmountable difficulties. C. L. Moore writes about the sale of her first story, "Shambleau":

This story was *not* rejected by every magazine in the field before it crept humbly to the doorstep of *Weird Tales*. My own perfectly clear memory tells me that I sent it first to *WT* because that was the only magazine of the type I knew well, and that an answering acceptance and a check . . . arrived almost by return mail.[11]

There also seems to be little evidence that Leigh Brackett, E. Mayne Hull, and Marion Zimmer Bradley have suffered unduly for being female writers. Of course, a reader might assume that the stories under these bylines were written by men; there was nothing overtly feminine about the names. But most readers did eventually learn that Brackett, Moore, and Bradley are women.

It is, however, necessary to point out some of the problems female writers did encounter. Andre Norton, the writer of many books primarily for young readers, has said:

When I entered the field I was writing for boys, and since women were not welcomed, I chose a pen name which could be either masculine or feminine. This is not true today, of course. But I still find vestiges of disparagement—mainly, oddly enough, among other writers. Most of them, however, do accept one on an equal basis. I find more prejudice against me as the writer of "young people's" stories now than against the fact that I am a woman.[12]

[11] C. L. Moore, "Afterword: Footnote to 'Shambleau' . . . and Others," in *The Best of C. L. Moore.*
[12] "An Interview with Andre Norton," in *Luna Monthly*, No. 40 (September 1972), p. 4. The interview was conducted by Paul Walker.

This last line is indicative of the way in which children are regarded by many. Some consider it more important to write for adults, in spite of the fact that a young person may be more affected or influenced by a work than an adult could be. It is too bad that sf writers, many of whom have written good books for younger readers, should sometimes be ashamed of this. Some writers, of course, resent the fact that in many circles, *all* sf is considered "children's literature."

A look at Norton's long list of works, which includes more than forty novels, will show that in most of them she has used male protagonists, although recently she has written books with heroines. She was no doubt discouraged from using heroines by publishers who believed, accurately, that most young readers of sf were boys. Young girls were thus discouraged from reading science fiction, which seemed to have little of interest to them, and the situation was perpetuated.

Other women, particularly those writing during the 1950s, solved the difficulties of publishing sf in a different way. Those who wished to write stories about women found themselves, with few exceptions, limiting their characters to the "socially acceptable" female roles. Judith Merril, whose first story was published in 1948, became prominent during the 1950s. Later, during the late 1950s and early 1960s, she became even more important as an editor; her collections of science fiction remain classic anthologies.

Merril, who wrote an overtly feminist story, "Survival Ship," an experiment in writing a story with no gender pronouns, became much better known during the 1950s for works which disparaging critics called "wet-diaper" science fiction. Many of them emphasized the roles of childbearing and child rearing, or the love of the heroine for her man. Some were well-written, compassionate tales; others lapsed into sentimentality. Other writers, among them Margaret St. Clair, Mildred Clingerman, and Rosel George Brown, also wrote some stories with "traditional" heroines. One wonders if some of these writers sensed that they were in a paradoxical position; sneered at when they published stories with traditional heroines, replete with all the old assumptions about the abilities of women, but turned down when they tried to publish stories with more innovational heroines.

One should look at such stories within the context of the times in which they were written. Judith Merril, in an afterword to one of her stories, wrote:

> I grew up in the radical 'thirties. My mother had been a suffragette. It never occurred to me that the Bad Old Days of Double Standard had anything to do with *me*.
> The first strong intimation, actually, was when the editors of the mystery, western, and sports "pulp" magazines, where I did my apprentice writing, demanded masculine pen-names. But of course they were pulps, oriented to a masculine readership, and the whole thing was only an irritation: as soon as I turned to S-F, the problem disappeared.
> At the end of World War II, the wonderful working-mothers' day-care centres all closed down, and from every side the news was shouted that Woman's Place was after all In The Home.

Newspapers, magazines, counseling services told us firmly that children who had less than constant attention from their *very own* mothers were doomed to misery and delinquency; the greatest joy available to the "natural woman" was the pleasure of Building Her Man's Ego. (There were not enough jobs for returning veterans till the ladies went home.)

There was a lot of pressure; one couldn't help wondering. Could it be true? I didn't think so; neither did my returning husband. We were 'thirties radicals, after all, so what if it was the 'forties? But I was beginning to get a little bit of attention as a writer: and even he—and even I—found the resultant situation a bit embarrassing, a little uncomfortable.

Ten years later, I had a growing "name" as a writer, a lot of good colleague/friends, and two divorces. Complicated. One worried, and kept trying to figure things out.[13]

Male sf writers have been know to defend their past lapses on the grounds of societal assumptions and influences. I too am willing to assert that these ingrained attitudes, rather than a conscious intent to bar women from the field, were the cause of science fiction's predominantly male orientation. One only hopes that some of these people might show the same understanding of the lapses of their female colleagues.

There were writers who managed to escape both the "wet-diaper" genre and its opposite, the "superior male" type of science fiction. Stanley G.

[13]Judith Merril, *Survival Ship and Other Stories* (Toronto, Kakabeka Publishing Co., 1973), p. 32.

Weinbaum created Black Margot and other strong female characters. Isaac Asimov created Dr. Susan Calvin, as well as male characters whose strength was in their minds rather than in their bodies. Robert Heinlein, who wrote of competent men, also showed women engineers, mathematicians, doctors, and soldiers; in his short novel *The Unpleasant Profession of Jonathan Hoag*, he depicted a married couple whose relationship was based on mutual respect, friendship, and love. C. L. Moore, Katherine MacLean, and others avoided the "housewife" stereotype. But because some writers avoided the trap does not mean that science fiction, whether unintentionally or not, was not discriminatory. Because a few people can transcend limitations does not mean that the limitations are absent. The test of any human enterprise is not what it allows the strong, but the opportunities it provides for everyone else, with merit being the only measure.

Women, of course, were not the only ones suffering some form of discrimination in science fiction. In the "pulp" days, Northern Europeans were most acceptable as heroes and perhaps as writers. Horace L. Gold, a skilled sf writer who had an important effect on the genre as editor of *Galaxy* during the 1950s, used the byline "Clyde Crane Campbell" during the early 1930s. Gold gives the reason:

> Nazism's anti-Semitism had spread all through the world and it permeated Street and Smith [publishers of *Astounding*], so I knew better than to write under my own name.[14]

[14]Horace L. Gold, "Looking Aft," in *Galaxy*, Vol. 36, No. 9 (October 1975), p. 22.

Stock characters in pulp tales often included villainous Asians, evil Germans or Russians (depending on the political situation and the author's sympathies), and primitive, superstitious black people. This xenophobia carried over to depictions of aliens as well. Aliens were often seen as threatening or cruel, almost the embodiment of our own racism. It was right to fight them, or even wipe them out.

This situation was somewhat altered by Stanley G. Weinbaum, who published his first story, "A Martian Odyssey," in 1934. Weinbaum used his own name as a byline, readers loved the story, and anti-Semitism vanished at Street & Smith. When John Campbell took over *Astounding* in 1938, he encouraged writers like Gold and, later, Isaac Asimov, to use their own names. Weinbaum's career was tragically short; in 1935, he died at the age of thirty-three. But in his treatment of alien characters, he has had a lasting effect on science fiction. Isaac Asimov has written:

> There were, to be sure, extra-terrestrial creatures in science fiction long before Weinbaum. Even if we restrict ouselves to magazine science fiction, they were a commonplace. Yet before Weinbaum's time, they were cardboard, they were shadows, they were mockeries of life.
>
> The pre-Weinbaum extra-terrestrial, whether humanoid or monstrous, served only to impinge upon the hero, to serve as a menace or a means of rescue, to be evil or good in strictly human terms—*never* to be something in itself, independent of mankind.
>
> Weinbaum was the first, as far as I know, to

create extra-terrestrials that had their *own* reasons for existing.[15]

In addition to his characterization of aliens, Weinbaum was also more innovative than others in his treatment of female characters. "The Red Peri," published in *Astounding* in 1935, has as its main character a female space pirate. "The Adaptive Ultimate," also published in *Astounding* in 1935, was the story of a young woman, Kyra Zelas, who is dying of tuberculosis. A young doctor, Daniel Scott, gives her an injection of a new serum never before used on humans. She recovers and becomes incredibly strong, with powers enabling her to adapt physically and mentally to almost any situation. She becomes obsessed with the desire to rule the world, and Scott, who has fallen in love with her, realizes she is dangerous. Scott and his colleague, Herman Bach, trick Kyra so that they can rob her of her powers by surgery. They succeed; Kyra is once more only a sick young woman who will die of tuberculosis. But Scott is filled with remorse and regrets the action. He had loved the strong, capable woman Kyra had been.

The relationship between the treatment of aliens, other cultures, and women in science fiction is made clear by Ursula K. Le Guin. In a recent essay she compares the treatment of women to that accorded aliens:

The question involved here is the question of The Other—the being who is different from your-

[15]Isaac Asimov, "The Second Nova," in *The Best of Stanley G. Weinbaum* (New York, Ballantine Books, 1974), p. x.

self. This being can be different from you in its sex; or in its annual income; or in its way of speaking and dressing and doing things; or in the color of its skin, or the number of its legs and heads. In other words, there is the sexual Alien, and the social Alien, and the cultural Alien, and finally the racial Alien . . .

If you deny any affinity with another person or kind of person, if you declare it to be wholly different from yourself—as men have done to women, and class has done to class, and nation has done to nation—you may hate it, or deify it; but in either case you have denied its spiritual equality, and its human reality. You have made it into a thing, to which the only possible relationship is a power relationship. And thus you have fatally impoverished your own reality. You have, in fact, alienated yourself.[16]

---

[16]Ursula K. Le Guin, "American SF and the Other," in *Science Fiction Studies*, #7, Vol. 2, Part 3 (November 1975), pp. 208–209. Le Guin also makes the following points:

Male elitism has run rampant in SF. But is it only male elitism? Isn't the "subjection of women" in SF merely a symptom of a whole which is authoritarian, power-worshipping, and intensely parochial? . . .

Well, how about the social Alien in SF? How about, in Marxist terms, "the proletariat"? . . . Are they ever *persons*, in SF? No. They appear as vast anonymous masses . . .

What about the cultural and the racial Other? This is the Alien everybody recognizes as alien, supposed to be the special concern of SF. Well, in the old pulp SF, it's very simple. The only good alien is a dead alien . . .

Then there's the other side of the same coin. If you hold a thing to be totally different from yourself, your fear of it may come out as hatred, or as awe—reverence. So we get all those wise and kindly beings who deign to rescue Earth from her sins and perils. The Alien ends up on a pedestal in a white nightgown and a virtuous

In this context, we can see science fiction reflecting the attitudes of much of the white middle-class audience which makes up most of its readership in the United States. Rather than consider future possibilities, both scientific and societal ones, rigorously, the genre has often catered to the prejudices of its audience.

The ultimate failure of much science fiction lies in the fact that it has not been seriously concerned with the future. Australian novelist and critic George Turner has said:

smirk—exactly as the "good woman" did in the Victorian Age.

In America, it seems to have been Stanley Weinbaum who invented the sympathetic alien . . . via people like Cyril Kornbluth, Ted Sturgeon, and Cordwainer Smith, SF began to inch its way out of simple racism . . . As the aliens got more sympathetic, so did the human heroes. They began to have emotions, as well as rayguns . . .

. . . The only social change presented by most SF has been towards authoritarianism, the domination of ignorant masses by a powerful elite—sometimes presented as a warning, but often quite complacently. Socialism is never considered as an alternative, and democracy is quite forgotten. Military virtues are taken as ethical ones. Wealth is assumed to be a righteous goal and a personal virtue. Competitive free-enterprise capitalism is the economic destiny of the entire Galaxy. In general, American SF has assumed a permanent hierarchy of superiors and inferiors, with rich, ambitious, aggressive males at the top, then a great gap, and then at the bottom the poor, the uneducated, the faceless masses, and all the women. The whole picture is, if I may say so, curiously "un-American." It is a perfect baboon patriarchy, with the Alpha Male on top, being respectfully groomed, from time to time, by his inferiors . . .

. . . I would like to see the Baboon Ideal replaced by a little human idealism, and some serious consideration of such deeply radical, futuristic concepts as Liberty, Equality, and Fraternity. And remember that about 53% of the Brotherhood of Man is the Sisterhood of Women. [pp. 208–210]

The realities of the myths and the limitations
of the sf writers can be brought home very
strongly by reading the popularisations of science
written by such people as Gordon Rattray Taylor
. . . you'll discover that the things the scientists
are talking about in their common laboratory talk
from day to day are far beyond anything that sf
writers have dreamed up yet . . .

. . . sf couldn't care less about tomorrow. I
don't think the fans [readers of science fiction]
do either; the fans want to be amused.[17]

This also has been science fiction's failure as far as
women are concerned. It was easier to write tales
of scientific problems which had no bearing on the
society at large. It was more fun to write wishful-
filling fantasies or even satires on aspects of modern
life. The feature most distinctive of science fiction
—the fictional development of possible future worlds
using ideas derived from physical, biological, and
social sciences—was the one most undeveloped.

Science fiction is supposed to be a literature of
ideas. Alone among our present genres it can show
us a world which does not exist, has not existed, but
which could come into being. It can show us alternatives, many of which might be antithetical to our
presuppositions. It can mirror our thoughts, fears,
and hopes about the future in terms of literary experience. It might even be able to show us possible
alternate roles for both women and men without
using either the "role-reversal" sort of idea, in which

[17]George Turner, "Back to the Mainstream," in *SF Com-
mentary* 41/42, 1975, edited by Bruce Gillespie, p. 60. This
was a speech given in Melbourne, Australia, in the spring
of 1973, and transcribed by Tony Thomas for *SF Commen-
tary.*

women and men simply change places, or the models of past societies.

IV

When one considers the impact that technology has had on human life throughout human history, it is surprising that more writers have not considered the effect such technical tools might have on women's lives. There are a vast number of science fiction stories which show the impact of labor-saving devices, computers, space travel, increased communications, and new scientific ideas on men. About all such things seem to accomplish for women, however, is to give them more leisure time in which to worry about their children, lounge about their residences in futuristic fashions, oversee robotic or computerized "servants," gossip with friends, choose from a cornucopia of exotic drugs and liqueurs, and worry about retaining the affections of their husbands. In more "modern" works they may have love affairs, be respected rather than scorned prostitutes, seek power through their men, or even pursue a career which is abandoned after marriage or subordinated to the relationship. On other planets, where conditions are usually more primitive than those on Earth, they often quickly become involved primarily in childbearing.

Those who assert that men have dominated in the past because men have greater muscular strength than women, and women are limited by pregnancy, should consider the impact of technology more seriously. Does muscular strength matter if machines do most of the physical work? Women can wear exoskeletons, push buttons, program computers, or pilot spaceships as easily as men. Does pregnancy and its supposed limitations matter if women can control their bodies and choose the conditions of birth?

Concerning childbearing, science fiction has generally been less than innovative. The use of artificial means of reproduction is often seen as dehumanizing; Aldous Huxley's classic *Brave New World,* in which artificial wombs are used in the production of needed human types, is one of the most famous illustrations of this approach. In some sf novels, female characters go to other worlds so they can breed freely; other women, who may dwell on an overpopulated Earth, feel deprived of purpose when not allowed to have children. Science fiction has often asserted that childbirth is a necessary experience for women; that it is a woman's primary function.

The temptation, in the light of all this as well as the historic and present-day realities of childbirth, is to move to a completely different point of view and assert, as Shulamith Firestone does, that "pregnancy is barbaric."[18] R. C. W. Ettinger has also dealt with this subject harshly:

> . . . it is a little hard to see why suckling or carrying a child should produce a special bond, any more than in other forms of parasitism. Does one feel special tenderness toward his tapeworm?
>
> Certainly breast feeding is on the way out, despite occasional flurries of fashion. It must go be-

[18]Shulamith Firestone, *The Dialectic of Sex* (New York, Bantam Books, 1972).

cause in too many ways it degrades the woman.
It reduces her to a biological machine . . .

. . . Many women don't believe it, but I am
convinced ectogenesis will be a nearly unqualified
benefit, and that almost all women will welcome
the chance to be "fathers" instead of mothers. At
first, they will claim their main reasons for ap-
proving of it are that the foetus will receive
greater protection and more reliable care under
controlled conditions, and possibly that husbands
will have less inconvenience, but they won't miss
the swollen bellies and the backaches either.[19]

This point of view, however understandable, does
not, as Adrienne Rich puts it, take account of "what
biological pregnancy and birth might be in a wholly
different political and emotional setting."[20] As she
points out, adverse reaction to childbirth grows out
of the fact that women, now and in the past, have
been victimized by it. Poor women have to contend
with pregnancy in a context of malnutrition, pov-
erty, inadequate medical care, and often desertion
by the father. Middle-class women in the United
States involved in "natural" childbirth are reacting
against what can be seen as an overtechnologized
and alienating approach to the process. Rich con-
cludes:

Ideally, of course, women would choose not
only whether, when, and where to bear children,

[19]R. C. W. Ettinger, *Man Into Superman* (New York, St.
Martin's Press, 1972), pp. 106–107.
[20]Adrienne Rich, "The Theft of Childbirth," in the *New
York Review of Books*, Vol. XXII, No. 15 (October 2, 1975),
p. 26.

and the circumstances of labor, but also between biological and artificial reproduction. But I do not think we can project any such idea onto the future—and hope to realize it—without examining the shadow-images we carry in us, the magical thinking of Eve's curse, the social victimization of women-as-mothers . . .

If motherhood and sexuality were not wedged resolutely apart by male culture, if we could *choose* both the forms of our sexuality and the terms of our motherhood or non-motherhood freely, women might achieve sexual autonomy (as opposed to "sexual liberation"). The mother should be able to choose the means of conception (biological, artificial, or even parthenogenic), the place of birth, her own style of giving birth, and her birth attendants. Birth might then become one event in the unfolding of our diverse and polymorphous sexuality—not a necesary *consequence* of sex, but one aspect of liberating ourselves from fear and the loathing of our own bodies.

Patriarchal childbirth—childbirth as penance and as medical emergency—and its sequel, institutionalized motherhood, is alienated labor, exploited labor, keyed to an "efficiency" and a profit system having little to do with the needs of mothers and children, carried on in physical and mental circumstances over which the woman in labor has little or no control. It is exploited labor in a form even more devastating than that of the enslaved industrial worker who has, at least, no psychic and physical bond with the sweated product, or with the bosses who control her. Not only have conception, pregnancy, and birth been expropriated from women, but also the deep para-

physical sensations and impulses with which they
are saturated.[21]

Has this complex innovative attitude been reflected in science fiction? Only very rarely; most
sf, when it bothers to deal with childbirth at all,
sees it either as only a regrettable necessity or
the most important thing a woman can do.

One author who has written humanely of childbirth is Ursula K. Le Guin. In her novel *The Dis-
posessed*, the main character, Shevek, assists his
partner, Takver, when she gives birth to their child:

Takver had no time for emotional scenes; she
was busy. She had cleared the bed platform except
for a clean sheet, and she was at work bearing a
child. She did not howl or scream, as she was not
in pain, but when each contraction came she
managed it by muscle and breath control, and
then let out a great *houff* of breath, like one who
makes a terrific effort to lift a heavy weight. Shevek had never seen any work that so used all the
strength of the body.

He could not look on such work without trying
to help in it. He could serve as handhold and
brace when she needed leverage. They found this
arrangement very quickly by trial and error, and
kept to it after the midwife had come in. Takver
gave birth afoot, squatting, her face against Shevek's thigh, her hands gripping his braced arms.
"There you are," the midwife said quietly under

[21]Rich, pp. 26, 29–30. It should also be pointed out that
advanced techniques, and a change in attitudes, would make
more options available to men. "Patriarchal childbirth," as
practiced, alienates many men from this process and does
not allow them to participate in the birth of their children.

the hard, engine-like pounding of Takver's breathing, and she took the slimy but recognizably human creature that had appeared. A gush of blood followed, and an amorphous mass of something not human, not alive. The terror he had forgotten came back into Shevek redoubled. It was death he saw. Takver had let go his arms and was huddled down quite limp at his feet. He bent over her, stiff with horror and grief.[22]

Later, Shevek rests with Takver and their daughter:

The baby and Takver were already asleep. Shevek put his head down near Takver's. He was accustomed to the pleasant and musky smell of her skin. This had changed; it had become a perfume, heavy and faint, heavy with sleep. Very gently he put one arm over her as she lay on her side with the baby against her breast. In the room heavy with life he slept.[23]

Joanna Russ, in her novel *The Female Man*, shows a society composed entirely of women in which the inhabitants must of necessity reproduce differently, aided by technology. Women can choose to be either a "body-mother" (the parent who bears the child) or an "other mother" (the parent who contributes the ovum making up half of the daughter's genetic heritage).

Another possible option is shown by Theodore Sturgeon in his novel *Venus Plus X* (1960). Sturgeon writes of our far future descendants, the Le-

[22]Ursula K. Le Guin, *The Dispossessed* (New York, Harper & Row, 1974), pp. 214–215.
[23]Le Guin, p. 216.

dom, each of whom is both male and female. This
type of physique was a deliberate choice on the
part of these people, who consider one of the most
fulfilling sexual experiences to be when both part-
ners conceive children and bear them. In *Podkayne
of Mars* (1963), Robert Heinlein shows us a world
where women bear their children in youth. The
infants are then "frozen" cryonically. The parents
can then establish themselves in their careers,
"thawing out" the children later when they have
time to raise them.

Another area of science fiction which has paid
little attention to women is the "hard science" story,
or one in which scientific ideas are of central importance. Writers of such works sometimes assert
that the idea is in fact the hero of the story. It could
be argued that in this kind of story, centered around
a particular technical device or scientific idea, there
is really no necessity for including women characters. In fact, the characters need not even be human.

But this sort of argument only betrays the attitude that women and scientific ideas do not "go
together" in the way that men and such ideas do,
that a woman would only interfere with the story
or distract the reader. As it turns out, some "idea"
stories, among them "Omnilingual," by H. Beam
Piper, Isaac Asimov's "robot" stories, and some of
the works of Hal Clement, have women characters who are primarily scientists.

"Omnilingual" (1958) shows us both male and female archaeologists working on Mars. They are
studying ancient Martian artifacts. One of the archaeologists, Dr. Martha Dane, finally solves the

problem of how to translate the Martian language.

What is interesting in this story is that the women's most important characteristic is their role as scientists. The story would have been no different had only male characters been used; the interpersonal relationships and the research depicted would have been much the same. But the fact that Piper used both sexes implies something about his view of the world from which the characters came. We never see the Earth in this story, but one can assume that it is a world where women are represented in many fields. This is something which writers of pure "idea" stories tend to ignore; even though the idea is paramount, the kinds of characters present in the story and the way in which they interact will, by implication, show what kind of future the author foresees.

Another topic rarely covered in science fiction is that of homosexuality. Some writers, perhaps facetiously, have wondered exactly what many all-male adventures implied. Most writers of sf have simply prefered to skirt the issue of homosexuality or ignore it altogether. A few have stereotypical views of gay people and take a condemnatory stance toward such sexual expression in their work. In this, too, science fiction has mirrored society. Homosexuals and Lesbians, as far as most sf was concerned, simply did not exist.

There are some notable exceptions to the rule. Theodore Sturgeon dealt with male homosexuality in his story "The World Well Lost" (1953), in which two humanoids from the planet Dirbanu arrive on Earth. The two aliens are fugitives who have stolen a spaceship. Our world is enchanted with the two and nicknames them "loverbirds," but then their planet asks Earth to return them.

The two Earthmen who must take the aliens back to their own world discover during the course of their journey that the two humanoids are homosexuals and cannot express their love for each other on their own world. They also find out why Dirbanu will have nothing to do with Earth. To the Dirbanu, whose males and females have radically different appearances, the sight of human males and females with their similar physiques is repulsive. Earth to them looks like a planet of homosexuals. Sturgeon makes a plea for understanding at the end of the story; we discover that one of the Earthmen, Grunty, is in love with his captain, Rootes, but he can never express this openly, as Rootes is disgusted by homosexuality.

Samuel R. Delany and Joanna Russ are two writers who have also dealt with characters who are not heterosexual. Delany has dealt with bisexual characters in triple relationships; Russ has written about Lesbians in both *The Female Man* and her short story "When It Changed" (1972). Marion Zimmer Bradley has also depicted male and female homosexuals in some of her work. Shevek, the main character in Le Guin's *The Dispossessed*, comes from a society that accepts bisexuality and homosexuality. Joe Haldeman's *The Forever War* shows a future Earth where homosexuality is commonplace.

Science fiction has rarely dealt with sex at all until fairly recently, so it is not surprising that it has for the most part avoided homosexuality. This is beginning to change. If the genre is to deal successfully with relationships between the sexes and love among human beings, it will have to consider both homosexuality and bisexuality.

V

Several questions come to mind in the assembling of collections such as this one and its predecessor, *Women of Wonder*. The most obvious are: Why do such a collection at all? Should it not be evident to almost anyone that women can and have written fine science fiction?

It is clear to anyone who has read extensively in the genre. But it may be less obvious to someone who is not as familiar with sf, or to someone who may have stopped reading it years ago. If one takes the trouble to look through issues of old magazines, or anthologies reprinting many of the best stories, or a shelf of science fiction novels, one is struck immediately by the overwhelming preponderance of male authors. Most of the anthologies, especially those of earlier decades, have no stories by women in their pages, not necessarily because the editors were discriminating against women, but simply because there were more stories by men from which to choose.

In addition, there is the "masculine" image of science fiction and the fact that it has been for the most part oriented to male readers, often explicitly. John W. Campbell, for example, often addressed his readers with the term "gentlemen." Someone who is exploring the genre for the first time might

easily wind up reading only male authors. In more
recent anthologies, women are more equally represented.[24]

What kinds of stories should be represented in
such a collection? I chose, both in *Women of Wonder* and in this collection, to take an historical approach. I wanted to show good examples of the
various types of science fiction. These range from
science fantasy to straightforward extrapolation. I
tried to include examples of both the "old-fashioned" story and the more "innovative" one.

Because of this approach, some readers might
conclude that the stories are not really feminist.
While editing *Women of Wonder*, I did not include
stories simply because they were feminist in orientation. Instead, I chose stories that would give a
picture of how the role of women in science fiction
developed, and chose to argue for a creative fem-

[24]It is sometimes forgotten that during science fiction's
earlier days, the genre must have seemed very attractive to
the few women who wrote it. In sf, at least, they could
write adventure stories or speculate about science and technology. To some of them, science fiction probably appeared
to offer them a freer rein than other types of writing. Men
may have dominated the field, but then they have dominated many human endeavors because of social condition-
ing and circumstance.

It is also important to remember what in fact limited
some writers. Andre Norton was restricted by publishers
who wanted a male byline (or at least an androgynous one)
on books which had male protagonists; in other words, she
was limited by commercial considerations as well as by
prevailing attitudes toward women. Robert Heinlein was
limited by some of the same considerations; in his successful
series of novels for young people, he could not deal frankly
with sex. Judith Merril, who often limited her female characters to traditional roles, did so at least in part because the
society around her insisted that these roles were proper and
right.

inism in my introduction instead. I have kept that approach in this book as well.

I also did not want to subordinate the purely imaginative function of science fiction to its didactic function. It would of course have been possible to edit a feminist anthology; this has been done by Vonda N. McIntyre and Susan Janice Anderson in their collection *Aurora: Beyond Equality* (Fawcett-Gold Medal, 1976). *Aurora*, which shows what is being done now, complements *Women of Wonder* and *More Women of Wonder*. If it sometimes seems to the reader that past stories do not capture the complexity of our present-day discussions of women, one must also remember when they were written, and give some credit to the authors who tried to deal with women seriously and imaginatively at a time when there was little encouragement on the part of editors and publishers to do so.

Because I have tried to capture both the imaginative and didactic aspects of science fiction in my anthologies, I should address myself to the question of what science fiction should be. I have contended throughout this essay that science fiction has not lived up to its potential; that, in fact, because of the influence of the society of which writers are a part, those writers have often not been as truly speculative as possible.

What can science fiction do? One well-known writer of sf, Gordon R. Dickson, has stated its central purpose eloquently:

. . . the science fiction hard-core audience is interested in the investigation of all possible subjects, whether these happen to be palatable at the moment or not.

Investigation, however, is the key word. Core science fiction does not investigate dark or hitherto unexplored territories simply for the sake of being called explorative . . . The explorations of science fiction are normally for the purpose of testing an idea, a question, or a possibility in the literary laboratory; as opposed to trying it out in the real world, where a botched experiment can mean famine, pestilence, or the bloody slaughter of one people by another.

Science fiction is, in fact, essentially an unstructured think-tank in which authors of differing points of view can paint differing solutions or eventualities suggested by present problems or situations. As a literature it is favorably designed to act as a vehicle for ideas or arguments—to be a seedbag for a philosophical fiction.[25]

This purpose may be overlooked by those exploring science fiction now; as sf author and editor Ben Bova puts it, many scholars place "too much emphasis on the history of science fiction as a literary genre, and not enough stress on the various fields of human endeavor that *make* science fiction: such as scientific research, sociology, politics, history, technological developments, et cetera."[26]

At its best, science fiction should enlist all the faculties of the person writing it. It should incorporate extrapolation, characterization, good writing,

[25]Gordon R. Dickson, in his introduction to *Combat SF*, Gordon R. Dickson, ed. (New York, Doubleday, 1975), p. vii.

[26]Ben Bova, "Teaching the Teachers," in *Analog*, Vol. XCVI, No. 1 (January 1976), p. 6.

attention to ideas, and good storytelling. It has often failed because it is a relatively new form, one which is intimately tied to our recent perception of ourselves as technological beings. But it is also heir to the older tradition of fantasy. There is no reason why it cannot suceed in the future. The role of feminism in science fiction is ultimately a part of a more general desire to see the genre expand its horizons.

As civilization develops, the problem of the emergence of creativity in social as well as artistic matters must be seen as endemic to the struggles of the planetary culture. The problem of women in world societies shows a conflict in which certain forward-looking elements of the society try to utilize the reservoir of skilled and talented people. Those within the women's movement who seek personal gratification show a symptom of the culture's struggle for more efficient use of the talented. The inward personal manifestation of this is seen in the outrage of women and racial minorities who know that they can be useful and valuable and are not permitted to be so in certain fields.

It is not startling, therefore, that science fiction should both mirror and itself contain the deficiencies of the society around it. One hundred years of science fiction shows us a literature becoming more conscious of its possibilities and aims, naturally reflecting the same development in the society around it.

With the entrance of more women writers into the genre of science fiction, and a growing interest in serious scientific ideas, social concerns, and future prospects, it is possible that the literature will be of more interest to women. The images and characters of science fiction stories may affect women's notions about themselves and their role in the future. Women may have shown good sense in the past by not being interested in science fiction. Why read a literature in which the future was often made by men for men? Why be interested in a world which excluded women from any meaningful participation in its activities? But in serious futuristic science fiction, where women are represented both as writers and as thoughtfully portrayed characters, we may find an art that life can imitate.

About this anthology: I had two reasons for doing this book. The first was to include stories that could not be included in *Women of Wonder* because of length limitations. I also wanted to include examples of the science fiction novelette and novella, whose forms are different from the short story or novel with which most readers of sf are familiar. Although this collection can supplement the previous volume, *More Women of Wonder* can also stand alone.

Science fiction writer James Gunn has summarized the problems of the science fiction novel and short story, while pointing out the virtues of the novelette:

The structure of a science fiction novel . . . is almost always the same: 1) a suspenseful situation 2) rising through thrilling incidents to a shattering climax and 3) an anticlimax to a resolu-

tion which cannot ultimately resolve . . . The
science fiction novel starts too high and builds
even higher: when what is at stake is racial survival or the fate of galaxies, a society, a nation,
a city, or even customs, traditions, or beliefs, the
fate of any single individual or group is of relative insignificance.

The science fiction novelette, on the other
hand, can reduce its scale to the manageable.
Length does not compel it to resolve its themes;
the novelette—and its reader—is satisfied with
the problem dramatized, not solved. The single
case stands for many.

I distinguish between the science fiction novelette and the short story because the short story
is too short to encompass an entirely new world.[27]

Some writers, of course, transcend these limitations;
the concluding piece in this volume is a short story.
But the science fiction novelette has proved more
durable than novelettes in other literary forms; novelettes are present in almost every recent issue of
an sf magazine or anthology. The stories which
follow, save one exceptional short story, are successful examples of the science fiction novelette.

[27]James Gunn, in his introduction to *Some Dreams are
Nightmares* (New York, Scribner's, 1974), p. xiii.

MORE WOMEN OF WONDER

JIREL
MEETS
MAGIC

C. L. MOORE

Larger-than-life heroes stand at the center of many adventurous tales. "Jirel Meets Magic" features a strong heroine. Jirel of Joiry, the superstitious inhabitant of a medieval world, courageously battles with those who command powers beyond her understanding. C. L. Moore has written vividly of a character who is both larger than life and recognizably human.

Over Guischard's fallen drawbridge thundered Joiry's warrior lady, sword swinging, voice shouting hoarsely inside her helmet. The scarlet plume of her crest rippled in the wind. Straight into the massed defenders at the gate she plunged, careering through them by the very impetuosity of the charge, the weight of her mighty warhorse opening up a gap for the men at her heels to widen. For a while there was tumult unspeakable there under the archway, the yells of fighters and the clang of mail on mail and the screams of stricken men. Jirel of Joiry was a shouting battle-machine from which Guischard's men reeled in bloody confusion as she

whirled and slashed and slew in the narrow confines
of the gateway, her great stallion's iron hoofs weapons as potent as her own whistling blade.

In her full armor she was impregnable to the men
on foot, and the horse's armor protected him from
their vengeful blades, so that alone, almost, she
might have won the gateway. By sheer weight and
impetuosity she carried the battle through the defenders under the arch. They gave way before the
mighty warhorse and his screaming rider. Jirel's
swinging sword and the stallion's trampling feet
cleared a path for Joiry's men to follow, and at last
into Guischard's court poured the steel-clad hordes
of Guischard's conquerors.

Jirel's eyes were yellow with blood-lust behind
the helmet bars, and her voice echoed savagely
from the steel cage that confined it, "Giraud! Bring
me Giraud! A gold piece to the man who brings me
the wizard Giraud!"

She waited impatiently in the courtyard, reining
her excited charger in mincing circles over the flags,
unable to dismount alone in her heavy armor and
disdainful of the threats of possible arbalesters in
the arrow-slits that looked down upon her from
Guischard's frowning gray walls. A crossbow shaft
was the only thing she had to fear in her impregnable mail.

She waited in mounting impatience, a formidable
figure in her bloody armor, the great sword lying
across her saddlebow and her eager, angry voice
echoing hoarsely from the helmet, "Giraud! Make
haste, you varlets! Bring me Giraud!"

There was such blood thirsty impatience in that
hollowly booming voice that the men who were re-

turning from searching the castle hung back as they crossed the court toward their lady in reluctant twos and threes, failure eloquent upon their faces.

"What!" screamed Jirel furiously. "You, Giles! Have you brought me Giraud? Watkin! Where is that wizard Giraud? Answer me, I say!"

"We've secured the castle, my lady," said one of the men fearfully as the angry voice paused. "The wizard is gone."

"Now God defend me!" groaned Joiry's lady. "God help a poor woman served by fools! Did you search among the slain?"

"We searched everywhere, Lady Jirel. Giraud has escaped us."

Jirel called again upon her Maker in a voice that was blasphemy in itself.

"Help me down, then, you hell-spawned knaves," she grated. "I'll find him myself. He must be here!"

With difficulty they got her off the sidling horse. It took two men to handle her, and a third to steady the charger. All the while they struggled with straps and buckles she cursed them hollowly, emerging limb by limb from the casing of steel and swearing with a soldier's fluency as the armor came away. Presently she stood free on the bloody flagstones, a slim, straight lady, keen as a blade, her red hair a flame to match the flame of her yellow eyes. Under the armor she wore a tunic of link-mail from the Holy Land, supple as silk and almost as light, and a doeskin shirt to protect the milky whiteness of her skin.

She was a creature of the wildest paradox, this warrior lady of Joiry, hot as a red coal, chill as steel, satiny of body and iron of soul. The set of her chin was firm, but her mouth betrayed a tenderness she would have died before admitting. But she was raging now.

"Follow me, then, fools!" she shouted. "I'll find that God-cursed wizard and split his head with this sword if it takes me until the day I die. I swear it. I'll teach him what it costs to ambush Joiry men. By heaven, he'll pay with his life for my ten who fell at Massy Ford last week. The foul spell-brewer! He'll learn what it means to defy Joiry!"

Breathing threats and curses, she strode across the court, her men following reluctantly at her heels and casting nervous glances upward at the gray towers of Guischard. It had always borne a bad name, this ominous castle of the wizard Giraud, a place where queer things happened, which no man entered uninvited and whence no prisoner had ever escaped, though the screams of torture echoed often from its walls. Jirel's men would have followed her straight through the gates of hell, but they stormed Guischard at her heels with terror in their hearts and no hope of conquest.

She alone seemed not to know fear of the dark sorcerer. Perhaps it was because she had known things so dreadful that mortal perils held no terror for her—there were whispers at Joiry of their lady, and of things that had happened there which no man dared think on. But when Guischard fell, and the wizard's defenders fled before Jirel's mighty steed and the onrush of Joiry's men, they had plucked up heart, thinking that perhaps the ominous tales of Giraud had been gossip only, since the castle fell as any ordinary lord's castle might fall. But now—there were whispers again, and nervous glances over the shoulder, and men huddled together as they re-entered Guischard at their lady's hurrying heels. A castle from which a wizard might vanish into thin air, with all the exits watched, must be a haunted place, better burned and forgotten. They followed Jirel reluctantly, half ashamed but fearful.

∞

In Jirel's stormy heart there was no room for terror as she plunged into the gloom of the archway that opened upon Guischard's great central hall. Anger that the man might have escaped her was a torch to light the way, and she paused in the door with eager anticipation, sweeping the corpse-strewn hall at a glance, searching for some clue to explain how her quarry had disappeared.

"He can't have escaped," she told herself confidently. "There's no way out. He *must* be here somewhere." And she stepped into the hall, turning over the bodies she passed with a careless foot to make sure that death had not robbed her of vengeance.

An hour later, as they searched the last tower, she was still telling herself that the wizard could not have gone without her knowledge. She had taken special pains about that. There was a secret passage to the river, but she had had that watched. And an underwater door opened into the moat, but he could not have gone that way without meeting her men. Secret paths and open, she had found them all and posted a guard at each, and Giraud had not left the castle by any door that led out. She climbed the stairs of the last tower wearily, her confidence shaken.

An iron-barred oaken door closed the top of the

steps, and Jirel drew back as her men lifted the
heavy crosspieces and opened it for her. It had not
been barred from within. She stepped into the little
round room inside, hope fading completely as she
saw that it too was empty, save for the body of a
page-boy lying on the uncarpeted floor. Blood had
made a congealing pool about him, and as Jirel
looked she saw something which roused her flag-
ging hopes. Feet had trodden in that blood, not the
mailed feet of armed men, but the tread of shapeless cloth shoes such as surely none but Giraud
would have worn when the castle was beseiged and
falling, and every man's help needed. Those bloody
tracks led straight across the room toward the wall,
and in that wall—a window.

Jirel stared. To her a window was a narrow slit
deep in stone, made for the shooting of arrows, and
never covered save in the coldest weather. But this
window was broad and low, and instead of the
usual animal pelt for hangings a curtain of purple
velvet had been drawn back to disclose shutters
carved out of something that might have been ivory
had any beast alive been huge enough to yield such
great unbroken sheets of whiteness. The shutters
were unlatched, swinging slightly ajar, and upon
them Jirel saw the smear of bloody fingers.

With a little triumphant cry she sprang forward.
Here, then, was the secret way Giraud had gone.
What lay beyond the window she could not guess.
Perhaps an unsuspected passage, or a hidden room.
Laughing exultantly, she swung open the ivory
shutters.

There was a gasp from the men behind her. She
did not hear it. She stood quite still, staring with

incredulous eyes. For those ivory gates had opened
upon no dark stone hiding-place or secret tunnel.
They did not even reveal the afternoon sky outside,
nor did they admit the shouts of her men still sub-
duing the last of the defenders in the court below.
Instead she was looking out upon a green woodland
over which brooded a violet day like no day she
had ever seen before. In paralyzed amazement she
looked down, seeing not the bloody flags of the
courtyard far below, but a mossy carpet at a level
with the floor. And on that moss she saw the mark
of blood-stained feet. This window might be a
magic one, opening into strange lands, but through
it had gone the man she swore to kill, and where
he fled she must follow.

She lifted her eyes from the tracked moss and
stared out again through the dimness under the
trees. It was a lovelier land than anything seen even
in dreams; so lovely that it made her heart ache
with its strange, unearthly enchantment—green
woodland hushed and brooding in the hushed violet
day. There was a promise of peace there, and for-
getfulness and rest. Suddenly the harsh, shouting,
noisy world behind her seemed very far away and
chill. She moved forward and laid her hand upon
the ivory shutters, staring out.

∞

The shuffle of the scared men behind her awakened Jirel from the enchantment that had gripped
her. She turned. The dreamy magic of the woodland
loosed its hold as she faced the men again, but its
memory lingered. She shook her red head a little,
meeting their fearful eyes. She nodded toward the
open window.

"Giraud has gone out there," she said. "Give me
your dagger, Giles. This sword is too heavy to carry
far."

"But lady—Lady Jirel—dear lady—you can't go out
there—Saint Guilda save us! Lady Jirel!"

Jirel's crisp voice cut short the babble of protest.
"Your dagger, Giles. I've sworn to slay Giraud,
and slay him I shall, in whatever land he hides.
Giles!"

A man-at-arms shuffled forward with averted face,
handing her his dagger. She gave him the sword she
carried and thrust the long-bladed knife into her
belt. She turned again to the window. Green and
cool and lovely, the woodland lay waiting. She
thought as she set her knee upon the sill that she
must have explored this violet calm even had her
oath not driven her; for there was an enchantment
about the place that drew her irresistibly. She
pulled up her other knee and jumped lightly. The
mossy ground received her without a jar.

For a few moments Jirel stood very still, watching, listening. Bird songs trilled intermittently about
her, and breezes stirred the leaves. From very far
away she thought she caught the echoes of a song
when the wind blew, and there was something
subtly irritating about its simple melody that
seemed to seesaw endlessly up and down on two
notes. She was glad when the wind died and the
song no longer shrilled in her ears.

It occurred to her that before she ventured far
she must mark the window she had entered by, and
she turned curiously, wondering how it looked from
this side. What she saw sent an inexplicable little
chill down her back. Behind her lay a heap of mold-

ering ruins, moss-grown, crumbling into decay. Fire had blackened the stones in ages past. She could see that it must have been a castle, for the original lines of it were not yet quite lost. Only one low wall remained standing now, and in it opened the window through which she had come. There was something hauntingly familiar about the lines of those moldering stones, and she turned away with a vague unease, not quite understanding why. A little path wound away under the low-hanging trees, and she followed it slowly, eyes alert for signs that Giraud had passed this way. Birds trilled drowsily in the leaves overhead, queer, unrecognizable songs like the music of no birds she knew. The violet light was calm and sweet about her.

She had gone on in the bird-haunted quiet for many minutes before she caught the first hint of anything at odds with the perfect peace about her. A whiff of wood-smoke drifted to her nostrils on a vagrant breeze. When she rounded the next bend of the path she saw what had caused it. A tree lay across the way in a smother of shaking leaves and branches. She knew that she must skirt it, for the branches were too tangled to penetrate, and she turned out of the path, following the trunk toward its broken base.

She had gone only a few steps before the sound of a curious sobbing came to her ears. It was the gasp of choked breathing, and she had heard sounds like that too often before not to know that she approached death in some form or another. She laid her hand on her knife-hilt and crept forward softly.

The tree trunk had been severed as if by a blast

of heat, for the stump was charred black and still smoking. Beyond the stump a queer tableau was being enacted, and she stopped quite still, staring through the leaves.

∞

Upon the moss a naked girl was lying, gasping her life out behind the hands in which her face was buried. There was no mistaking the death-sound in that failing breath, although her body was unmarked. Hair of a strange green-gold pallor streamed over her bare white body, and by the fragility and tenuosity of that body Jirel knew that she could not be wholly human.

Above the dying girl a tall woman stood. And that woman was a magnet for Jirel's fascinated eyes. She was generously curved, sleepy-eyed. Black hair bound her head sleekly, and her skin was like rich, dark, creamy velvet. A violet robe wrapped her carelessly, leaving arms and one curved shoulder bare, and her girdle was a snake of something like purple glass. It might have been carved from some vast jewel, save for its size and unbroken clarity. Her feet were thrust bare into silver sandals. But it was her face that held Jirel's yellow gaze.

The sleepy eyes under heavily drooping lids were purple as gems, and the darkly crimson mouth curled in a smile so hateful that fury rushed up in Jirel's heart as she watched. That lazy purple gaze dwelt aloofly upon the gasping girl on the moss. The woman was saying in a voice as rich and deep as thick-piled velvet,

"— nor will any other of the dryad folk presume to work forbidden magic in my woodlands for a long, long while to come. Your fate shall be a deadly example to them, Irsla. You dared too greatly. None who defy Jarisme live. Hear me, Irsla!"

The sobbing breath had slowed as the woman spoke, as if life were slipping fast from the dryad-girl on the moss; and as she realized it the speaker's arm lifted and a finger of white fire leaped from her outstretched hand, stabbing the white body at her feet. And the girl Irsla started like one shocked back into life.

"Hear me out, dryad! Let your end be a warning to—"

The girl's quickened breath slowed again as the white brilliance left her, and again the woman's hand rose, again the light-blade stabbed. From behind her shielding hands the dryad gasped.

"Oh, mercy, mercy, Jarisme! Let me die!"

"When I have finished. Not before. Life and death are mine to command here, and I am not yet done with you. Your stolen magic—"

She paused, for Irsla had slumped once more upon the moss, breath scarcely stirring her. As Jarisme's light-dealing hand rose for the third time Jirel leapt forward. Partly it was intuitive hatred of the lazy-eyed woman, partly revolt at this cat-and-mouse play with a dying girl for victim. She swung her arm in an arc that cleared the branches from her path, and called out in her clear, strong voice.

"Have done, woman! Let her die in peace."

Slowly Jarisme's purple eyes rose. They met Jirel's hot yellow glare. Almost physical impact was in that first meeting of their eyes, and hatred flashed between them instantly, like the flash of blades— the instinctive hatred of total opposites, born enemies. Each stiffened subtly, as cats do in the instant before combat. But Jirel thought she saw in the purple gaze, behind all its kindling anger, a faint disquiet, a nameless uncertainty.

"Who are you?" asked Jarisme, very softly, very dangerously.

Something in that unsureness behind her angry eyes prompted Jirel to answer boldly.

"Jirel of Joiry. I seek the wizard Giraud, who fled me here. Stop tormenting that wretched girl and tell me where to find him. I can make it worth your while."

Her tone was imperiously mandatory, and behind Jarisme's drooping lips an answering flare of anger lighted, almost drowning out that faint unease.

"You do not know me," she observed, her voice very gentle. "I am the sorceress Jarisme, and high ruler over all this land. Did you think to buy me, then, earth-woman?"

Jirel smiled her sweetest, most poisonous smile.

"You will forgive me," she purred. "At the first glance at you I did not think your price could be high. . . ."

A petty malice had inspired the speech, and Jirel was sorry as it left her lips, for she knew that the scorn which blazed up in Jarisme's eyes was justified. The sorceress made a contemptuous gesture of dismissal.

"I shall waste no more of my time here," she said. "Get back to your little lands, Jirel of Joiry, and tempt me no further."

The purple gaze rested briefly on the motionless dryad at her feet, flicked Jirel's hot eyes with a glance of scorn which yet did not wholly hide that curious uncertainty in its depths. One hand slid behind her, oddly as if she were seeking a door-latch in empty air. Then like a heat-shimmer the air danced about her, and in an instant she was gone.

Jirel blinked. Her ears had deceived her as well as her eyes, she thought, for as the sorceress vanished a door closed softly somewhere. Yet look though she would, the green glade was empty, the violet air untroubled. No Jarisme anywhere—no door. Jirel shrugged after a moment's bewilderment. She had met magic before.

∞

A sound from the scarcely breathing girl upon the moss distracted her, and she dropped to her knees beside the dying dryad. There was no mark or wound upon her, yet Jirel knew that death could be only a matter of moments. And dimly she recalled that, so legend said, a tree-sprite never survived the death of its tree. Gently she turned the girl over, wondering if she were beyond help.

At the feel of those gentle hands the dryad's lids quivered and rose. Brook-brown eyes looked up at Jirel, with green swimming in their deeps like leaf-reflections in a woodland pool.

"My thanks to you," faltered the girl in a ghostly murmur. "But get you back to your home now—before Jarisme's anger slays you."

Jirel shook her head stubbornly.

"I must find Giraud first, and kill him, as I have sworn to do. But I will wait. Is there anything I can do?"

The green-reflecting eyes searched hers for a moment. The dryad must have read resolution there, for she shook her head a little.

"I must die—with my tree. But if you are determined—hear me. I owe you—a debt. There is a talisman—braided in my hair. When I—am dead— take it. It is Jarisme's sign. All her subjects wear them. It will guide you to her—and to Giraud. He is ever beside her. I know. I think it was her anger at you—that made her forget to take it from me, after she had dealt me my death. But why she did not slay you—I do not know. Jarisme is quick—to kill. No matter—listen now. If you must have Giraud —you must take a risk that no one here—has ever taken—before. Break this talisman—at Jarisme's feet. I do not know—what will happen then. Something —very terrible. It releases powers—even she can not control. It may—destroy you too. But—it is— a chance. May you—have—all good—"

The faltering voice failed. Jirel, bending her head, caught only meaningless murmurs that trailed away to nothing. The green-gold head dropped suddenly forward on her sustaining arm. Through the forest all about her went one long, quivering sigh, as if an intangible breeze ruffled the trees. Yet no leaves stirred.

Jirel bent and kissed the dryad's forehead, then laid her very gently back on the moss. And as she did so her hand in the masses of strangely colored hair came upon something sharp and hard. She remembered the talisman. It tingled in her fingers as she drew it out—an odd little jagged crystal sparkling with curious aliveness from the fire burning in its heart.

When she had risen to her feet, leaving the dead dryad lying upon the moss which seemed so perfectly her couch, she saw that the inner brilliance streaming in its wedge-shaped pattern through the crystal was pointing a quivering apex forward and to the right. Irsla had said it would guide her. Experimentally she twisted her hand to the left. Yes, the shaking light shifted within the crystal, pointing always toward the right, and Jarisme.

One last long glance she gave to the dryad on the moss. Then she set off again down the path, the little magical thing stinging her hand as she walked. And as she went she wondered. This strong hatred which had flared so instinctively between her and the sorceress was hot enough to burn any trace of fear from her mind, and she remembered that look of uncertainty in the purple gaze that had shot such hatred at her. Why? Why had she not been slain as Irsla was slain, for defiance of this queer land's ruler?

For a while she paced unheedingly along under the trees. Then abruptly the foliage ceased and a broad meadow lay before her, green in the clear, violet day. Beyond the meadow the slim shaft of a tower rose dazzlingly white, and toward it in steady radiance that magical talisman pointed.

From very far away she thought she still caught the echoes of that song when the wind blew, an irritating monotony that made her ears ache. She was glad when the wind died and the song no longer shrilled in her ears.

Out across the meadow she went. Far ahead she could make out purple mountains like low clouds on the horizon, and here and there in the distances clumps of woodland dotted the meadows. She walked on more rapidly now, for she was sure that the white tower housed Jarisme, and with her

Giraud. And she must have gone more swiftly than she knew, for with almost magical speed the shining shaft drew nearer.

She could see the arch of its doorway, bluely violet within. The top of the shaft was battlemented, and she caught splashes of color between the teeth of the stone scarps, as if flowers were massed there and spilling blossoms against the whiteness of the tower. The singsong music was louder than ever, and much nearer. Jirel's heart beat a bit heavily as she advanced, wondering what sort of a sorceress this Jarisme might be, what dangers lay before her in the path of her vow's fulfillment. Now the white tower rose up over her, and she was crossing the little space before the door, peering in dubiously. All she could see was dimness and violet mist.

She laid her hand upon the dagger, took a deep breath and stepped boldly in under the arch. In the instant her feet left the solid earth she saw that this violet mist filled the whole shaft of the tower, that there was no floor. Emptiness engulfed her, and all reality ceased.

She was falling through clouds of violet blankness, but in no recognizable direction. It might have been up, down, or sidewise through space. Everything had vanished in the violet nothing. She knew an endless moment of vertigo and rushing motion; then the dizzy emptiness vanished in a breath and she was standing in a gasping surprise upon the roof of Jarisme's tower.

∞

She knew where she was by the white battlements ringing her round, banked with strange blossoms in muted colors. In the center of the circular, marble-paved place a low couch, cushioned in glowing yellow, stood in the midst of a heap of furs. Two people sat side by side on the couch. One was Giraud. Black-robed, dark-visaged, he stared at Jirel with a flicker of disquiet in his small, dull eyes. He said nothing.

Jirel dismissed him with a glance, scarcely realizing his presence. For Jarisme had lowered from her lips a long, silver flute. Jirel realized that the queer, maddening music must have come from that gleaming length, for it no longer echoed in her ears. Jarisme was holding the instrument now in midair, regarding Jirel over it with a purple-eyed gaze that was somehow thoughtful and a little apprehensive, though anger glowed in it, too.

"So," she said richly, in her slow, deep voice. "For the second time you defy me."

At these words Giraud turned his head sharply and stared at the sorceress's impassive profile. She did not return his gaze, but after a moment he looked quickly back at Jirel, and in his eyes too she saw that flicker of alarm, and with it a sort of scared respect. It puzzled her, and she did not like being puzzled. She said a little breathlessly,

"If you like, yes. Give me that skulking potion-brewer beside you and set me down again outside this damned tower of trickery. I came to kill your pet spellmonger here for treachery done me in my own world by this creature who dared not stay to face me."

Her peremptory words hung in the air like the echoes of a gong. For a while no one spoke. Jarisme smiled more subtly than before, an insolent, slow smile that made Jirel's pulses hammer with the desire to smash it down the woman's lush, creamy throat. At last Jarisme said, in a voice as rich and deep as thick-piled velvet,

"Hot words, hot words, soldier-woman! Do you really imagine that your earthly squabbles matter to Jarisme?"

"What matters to Jarisme is of little moment to me," Jirel said contemptuously. "All I want is this skulker here, whom I have sworn to kill."

Jarisme's slow smile was maddening. "You demand it of me—Jarisme?" she asked with soft incredulity. "Only fools offend me, woman, and they but once. None commands me. You will have to learn that."

Jirel smiled thinly. "At what price, then, do you value your pet cur?"

Giraud half rose from the couch at that last insult, his dark face darker with a surge of anger. Jarisme pushed him back with a lazy hand.

"This is between your—friend—and me," she said. "I do not think, soldier"—the appellation was the deadliest of insults in the tone she used—"that any price you could offer would interest me."

"And yet your interest is very easily caught." Jirel flashed a contemptuous glance at Giraud, restive under the woman's restraining hand.

Jarisme's rich pallor flushed a little. Her voice was sharper as she said,

"Do not tempt me too far, earthling."

Jirel's yellow eyes defied her. "I am not afraid."

The sorceress's purple gaze surveyed her slowly. When Jarisme spoke again a tinge of reluctant admiration lightened the slow scorn of her voice.

"No—you are not afraid. And a fool not to be. Fools annoy me, Jirel of Joiry."

She laid the flute down on her knee and lazily lifted a ringless hand. Anger was glowing in her eyes now, blotting out all trace of that little haunting fear. But Giraud caught the rising hand, bending, whispering urgently in her ear. Jirel caught a part of what he said, "—what happens to those who tamper with their own destiny—" And she saw the anger fade from the sorceress's face as apprehension brightened there again. Jarisme looked at Jirel with a long, hard look and shrugged her ample shoulders.

"Yes," she murmured. "Yes, Giraud. It is wisest so." And to Jirel, "Live, then, earthling. Find your way back to your own land if you can, but I warn you, do not trouble me again. I shall not stay my hand if our paths ever cross in the future."

She struck her soft, white palms together sharply. And at the sound the roof-top and the violet sky and the banked flowers at the parapets whirled around Jirel in dizzy confusion. From very far away she heard that clap of peremptory hands still echoing, but it seemed to her that the great, smokily colored blossoms were undergoing an inexplicable transformation. They quivered and spread and thrust upward from the edges of the tower to arch over her head. Her feet were pressing a mossy ground, and the sweet, earthy odors of a garden rose about her. Blinking, she stared around as the world slowly steadied.

∞

She was no longer on the roof-top. As far as she could see through the tangled stems, great flowering

plants sprang up in the gloaming of a strange, enchanted forest. She was completely submerged in
greenery, and the illusion of under-water filled her
eyes, for the violet light that filtered through the
leaves was diffused and broken into a submarine
dimness. Uncertainly she began to grope her way
forward, staring about to see what sort of a miracle
had enfolded her.

It was a bower in fairyland. She had come into a
tropical garden of great, muted blooms and jungle
silences. In the diffused light the flowers nodded
sleepily among the leaves, hypnotically lovely, hypnotically soporific with their soft colors and drowsy,
never-ending motion. The fragrance was overpow-
ering. She went on slowly, treading moss that gave
back no sound. Here under the canopy of leaves
was a little separate world of color and silence and
perfume. Dreamily she made her way among the
flowers.

Their fragrance was so strongly sweet that it
went to her head, and she walked in a waking
dream. Because of this curious, scented trance in
which she went she was never quite sure if she had
actually seen that motion among the leaves, and
looked closer, and made out a huge, incredible serpent of violet transparency, a giant replica of the
snake that girdled Jarisme's waist, but miraculously
alive, miraculously supple and gliding, miraculously
twisting its soundless way among the blossoms and
staring at her with impassive, purple eyes.

While it glided along beside her she had other
strange visions too, and could never remember just
what they were, or why she caught familiar traces

in the tiny, laughing faces that peered at her from among the flowers, or half believed the wild, impossible things they whispered to her, their laughing mouths brushing her ears as they leaned down among the blossoms.

The branches began to thin at last, as she neared the edge of the enchanted place. She walked slowly, half conscious of the great transparent snake like a living jewel writhing along soundlessly at her side, her mind vaguely troubled in its dream by the fading remembrance of what those little, merry voices had told her. When she came to the very edge of the bowery jungle and broke out into clear daylight again she stopped in a daze, staring round in the brightening light as the perfumes slowly cleared from her head.

Sanity and realization returned to her at last. She shook her red head dizzily and looked round, half expecting, despite her returning clarity, to see the great serpent gliding across the grass. But there was nothing. Of course she had dreamed. Of course those little laughing voices had not told her that— that—she clutched after the vanishing tags of remembrance, and caught nothing. Ruefully she laughed and brushed away the clinging memories, looking round to see where she was.

She stood at the crest of a little hill. Below her the flower-fragrant jungle nodded, a little patch of enchanted greenery clothing the slopes of the hill. Beyond and below green meadows stretched away to a far-off line of forest which she thought she recognized as that in which she had first met Jarisme. But the white tower which had risen in the midst of the meadows was magically gone. Where it had stood, unbroken greenery lay under the violet clarity of the sky.

As she stared round in bewilderment a faint prickling stung her palm, and she glanced down, remembering the talisman clutched in her hand. The quivering light was streaming in a long wedge toward some point behind her. She turned. She was in the foothills of those purple mountains she had glimpsed from the edge of the woods. High and shimmering, they rose above her. And, hazily in the heat-waves that danced among their heights, she saw the tower.

Jirel groaned to herself. Those peaks were steep and rocky. Well, no help for it. She must climb. She growled a soldier's oath in her throat and turned wearily toward the rising slopes. They were rough and deeply slashed with ravines. Violet heat beat up from the reflecting rocks, and tiny, brilliantly colored things scuttled from her path—orange lizards and coral red scorpions and little snakes like bright blue jewels.

∞

It seemed to her as she stumbled upward among the broken stones that the tower was climbing too. Time after time she gained upon it, and time after time when she lifted her eyes after a grueling struggle up steep ravines, that mocking flicker of whiteness shimmered still high and unattainable on some distant peak. It had the mistiness of unreality, and if her talisman's guide had not pointed steadily upward she would have thought it an illusion to lead her astray.

But after what seemed hours of struggle, there

came the time when, glancing up, she saw the shaft rising on the topmost peak of all, white as snow against the clear violet sky. And after that it shifted no more. She took heart now, for at last she seemed to be gaining. Every laborious step carried her nearer that lofty shining upon the mountain's highest peak.

She paused after a while, looking up and wiping the moisture from her forehead where the red curls clung. As she stood there something among the rocks moved, and out from behind a boulder a long, slinking feline creature came. It was not like any beast she had ever seen before. Its shining pelt was fabulously golden, brocaded with queer patterns of darker gold, and down against its heavy jaws curved two fangs whiter than ivory. With a grace as gliding as water it paced down the ravine toward her.

Jirel's heart contracted. Somehow she found the knife-hilt in her hand, though she had no recollection of having drawn it. She was staring hard at the lovely and terrible cat, trying to understand the haunting familiarity about its eyes. They were purple, like jewels. Slowly recognition dawned. She had met that purple gaze before, insolent under sleepy lids. Jarisme's eyes. Yes, and the snake in her dream had watched her with a purple stare too. Jarisme?

She closed her hand tightly about the crystal, knowing that she must conceal from the sorceress her one potent weapon, waiting until the time came to turn it against its maker. She shifted her knife so that light glinted down the blade. They stood quite still for a moment, yellow-eyed woman and fabulous, purple-eyed cat, staring at each other with hostility eloquent in every line of each. Jirel clenched her knife tight, warily eyeing the steel-clawed paws on which the golden beast went so softly. They could have ripped her to ribbons before the blade struck home.

She saw a queer expression flicker across the somber purple gaze that met hers, and the beautiful cat crouched a little, tail jerking, lip twitched back to expose shining fangs. It was about to spring. For an interminable moment she waited for that hurtling golden death to launch itself upon her, tense, rigid, knife steady in her hand. . . .

It sprang. She dropped to one knee in the split second of its leaping, instinctively hiding the crystal, but thrusting up her dagger in defense. The great beast sailed easily over her head. As it hurtled past, a peal of derisive laughter rang in her ears, and she heard quite clearly the sound of a slamming door. She scrambled up and whirled in one motion, knife ready. The defile was quite empty in the violet day. There was no door anywhere. Jarisme had vanished.

A little shaken, Jirel sheathed her blade. She was not afraid. Anger turned out all trace of fear as she remembered the scorn in that ringing laugh. She took up her course again toward the tower, white and resolute, not looking back.

The tower was drawing near again. She toiled upward. Jarisme showed no further sign of her presence, but Jirel felt eyes upon her, purple eyes, scornful and sleepy. She could see the tower clearly, just above her at the crest of the highest peak, up to which a long arc of steps curved steeply. They were very old, these steps, so worn that many were little more than irregularities on the stone. Jirel wondered what feet had worn them so, to what door they had originally led.

She was panting when she reached the top and peered in under the arch of the door. To her surprise she found herself staring into a broad, semicircular hallway, whose walls were lined with innumerable doors. She remembered the violet nothingness into which she had stepped the last time she crossed the sill, and wondered as she thrust a tentative foot over it if the hall were an illusion and she were really about to plunge once more into that cloudy abyss of falling. But the floor was firm.

She stepped inside and paused, looking round in some bewilderment and wondering where to turn now. She could smell peril in the air. Almost she could taste the magic that hovered like a mist over the whole enchanted place. Little warning prickles ran down her back as she went forward very softly and pushed open one of those innumerable doors. Behind it a gallery stretched down miles of haze-shrouded extent. Arrow-straight it ran, the arches of the ceiling making an endless parade that melted into violet distance. And as she stood looking down the cloudy vista, something like a puff of smoke obscured her vision for an instant—smoke that eddied and billowed and rolled away from the shape of that golden cat which had vanished in the mountain ravine.

It paced slowly down the hall toward her, graceful and lovely, muscles rippling under the brocaded golden coat and purple eyes fixed upon her in a scornful stare. Jirel's hand went to the knife in her belt, hatred choking up in her throat as she met

the purple eyes. But in the corridor a voice was
echoing softly, Jarisme's voice, saying,

"Then it is war between us, Jirel of Joiry. For you
have defied my mercy, and you must be punished.
Your punishment I have chosen—the simplest, and
the subtlest, and the most terrible of all punishments, the worse that could befall a human creature. Can you guess it? No? Then wonder for a
while, for I am not prepared yet to administer it
fully . . . or shall I kill you now? Eh-h-h? . . ."

The curious, long-drawn query melted into a
purring snarl, and the great cat's lip lifted, a flare of
murderous light flaming up in the purple eyes. It
had been pacing nearer all the while that light voice
had echoed in the air. Now its roar crescendoed into
a crashing thunder that rang from the walls, and
the steel springs of its golden body tightened for a
leap straight at Jirel's throat. Scarcely a dozen paces
away, she saw the brocaded beauty of it crouching,
taut and poised, saw the powerful body quiver and
tighten—and spring. In instinctive panic she leaped
back and slammed the door in its face.

Derisive laughter belled through the air. A cloud
of thin smoke eddied through the crack around the
door and puffed in her face with all the insolence of
a blow. Then the air was clear again. The red mist
of murder swam before Jirel's eyes. Blind with anger, breath beating thickly in her throat, she
snatched at the door again, ripping the dagger from
her belt. Through that furious haze she glared down
the corridor. It was empty. She closed the door a
second time and leaned against it, trembling with
anger, until the mist had cleared from her head and

she could control her shaking hand well enough to
replace the dagger.

When she had calmed a little she turned to scan
the hall, wondering what to do next. And she saw
that there was no escape now, even had she wished,
for the door she had entered by was gone. All
about her now closed the door-studded walls, enigmatic, imprisoning. And the very fact of their presence was an insult, suggesting that Jarisme had
feared she would flee if the entrance were left open.
Jirel forced herself into calmness again. She was not
afraid, but she knew herself in deadly peril.

She was revolving the sorceress's threat as she
cast about for some indication to guide her next step.
The simplest and subtlest and most terrible of punishments—what could it be? Jirel knew much of the
ways of torture—her dungeons were as blood-stained
as any of her neighbors'—but she knew too that
Jarisme had not meant only the pain of the flesh.
There was a subtler menace in her words. It would
be a feminine vengeance, and more terrible than
anything iron and fire could inflict. She knew that.
She knew also that no door she could open now
would lead to freedom, but she could not stay quiet,
waiting. She glanced along the rows of dark, identical panels. Anything that magic could contrive
might lie behind them. In the face of peril more
deadly than death she could not resist the temptation to pull open the nearest one and peer within.

∞

A gust of wind blew in her face and rattled the
door. Dust was in that wind, and bitter cold.
Through an inner grille of iron, locked across the

opening, she saw a dazzle of whiteness like sun on snow in the instant before she slammed the door shut on the piercing gust. But the incident had whetted her curiosity. She moved along the wall and opened another.

This time she was looking through another locked grille into a dimness of gray smoke shot through with flame. The smell of burning rose in her nostrils, and she could hear faintly, as from vast distances, the sound of groans and the shivering echo of screams. Shuddering, she closed the door.

When she opened the next one she caught her breath and stared. Before her a thick crystal door separated her from bottomless space. She pressed her face to the cold glass and stared out and down. Nothingness met her gaze. Dark and silence and the blaze of unwinking stars. It was day outside the tower, but she looked into fathomless night. And as she stared, a long streak of light flashed across the blackness and faded. It was not a shooting star. By straining her eyes she could make out something like a thin sliver of silver flashing across the dark, its flaming tail fading behind it in the sky. And the sight made her ill with sudden vertigo. Bottomless void reeled around her, and she fell back into the hallway, slamming the door upon that terrifying glimpse of starry nothingness.

It was several minutes before she could bring herself to try the next door. When she did, swinging it open timorously, a familiar sweetness of flower perfume floated out and she found herself gazing through a grille of iron bars deep into that drowsy jungle of blossoms and scent and silence which she had crossed at the mountain's foot. A wave of remembrance washed over her. For an instant she could hear those tiny, laughing voices again, and she felt the presence of the great snake at her side, and the wild, mirth-ridden secrets of the little gray voices rang in her ears. Then she was awake again, and the memory vanished as dreams do, leaving nothing but tantalizing fragments of forgotten secrets drifting through her mind. She knew as she stared that she could step straight into that flowery fairyland again if the bars would open. But there was no escape from this magical place, though she might look through any number of opening doors into far lands and near.

She was beginning to understand the significance of the hall. It must be from here that Jarisme by her magical knowledge journeyed into other lands and times and worlds through the doors that opened between her domain and those strange, outland places. Perhaps she had sorcerer friends there, and paid them visits and brought back greater knowledge, stepping from world to world, from century to century, through her enchanted doorways. Jirel felt certain that one of these enigmatic openings would give upon that mountain pass where the golden cat with its scornful purple eyes had sprung at her, and vanished, and laughed backward as the door slammed upon it, and upon the woodland glade where the dryad died. But she knew that bars would close these places away even if she could find them.

She went on with her explorations. One door opened upon a steamy fern-forest of gigantic growths, out of whose deeps floated musky, reptilian

odors, and the distant sound of beasts bellowing
hollowly. And another upon a gray desert stretching flat and lifeless to the horizon, wan under the
light of a dim red sun.

But at last she came to one that opened not into
alien lands but upon a stairway winding down into
solid rock whose walls showed the mark of the tools
that had hollowed them. No sound came up the
shaft of the stairs, and a gray light darkened down
their silent reaches. Jirel peered in vain for some
hint of what lay below. But at last, because inactiv-
ity had palled upon her and she knew that all ways
were hopeless for escape, she entered the doorway
and went slowly down the steps. It occurred to her
that possibly she might find Jarisme below, engaged
in some obscure magic in the lower regions, and she
was eager to come to grips with her enemy.

The light darkened as she descended, until she
was groping her way through obscurity round and
round the curving stairs. When the steps ended at a
depth she could not guess, she could tell that she
had emerged into a low-roofed corridor only by
feeling the walls and ceiling that met her exploring
hands, for the thickest dark hid everything. She
made her slow way along the stone hall, which
wound and twisted and dipped at unexpected angles until she lost all sense of direction. But she
knew she had gone a long way when she began to
see the faint gleam of light ahead.

Presently she began to catch the faraway sound
of a familiar song—Jarisme's monotonous little flute
melody on two notes, and she was sure then that
her intuition had been true, that the sorceress was

down here somewhere. She drew her dagger in the
gloom and went on more warily.

∞

An arched opening ended the passage. Through
the arch poured a blaze of dancing white lumi-
nance. Jirel paused, blinking and trying to make
out what strange place she was entering. The room
before her was filled with the baffling glitter and
shimmer and mirage of reflecting sufaces so bewil-
deringly that she could not tell which was real and
which mirror, and which dancing light. The brilliance dazzled in her face and dimmed into twilight
and blazed again as the mirrors shifted. Little currents of dark shivered through the chaos and brightened into white sparkle once more. That monotonous music came to her through the quivering
lights and reflections, now strongly, now faintly in
the distance.

The whole place was a chaos of blaze and confusion. She could not know if the room were small
or large, a cavern or a palace hall. Queer reflections
danced through the dazzle of it. She could see her
own image looking back at her from a dozen, a
score, a hundred moving planes that grotesquely distorted her and then flickered out again, casting a
blaze of light in her blinded eyes. Dizzily she
blinked into the reeling wilderness of planes.

Then she saw Jarisme in her violet robe watching
her from a hundred identical golden couches reflected upon a hundred surfaces. The figure held a
flute to its lips, and the music pulsed from it in perfect time with the pulsing of the sorceress's swelling
white throat. Jirel stared round in confusion at the
myriad Jarismes all piping the interminable mono-

tones. A hundred sensual, dreamy faces turned to her, a hundred white arms dropped as the flute left a hundred red mouths that Jarisme might smile ironic welcome a hundredfold more scornful for its multiplicity.

When the music ceased, all the flashing dazzle suddenly stilled. Jirel blinked as the chaos resolved itself into shining order, the hundred Jarismes merging into one sleepy-eyed woman lounging upon her golden couch in a vast crystal-walled chamber shaped like the semicircular half of a great, round, domed room. Behind the couch a veil of violet mist hung like a curtain shutting off what would have formed the other half of the circular room.

"Enter," said the sorceress with the graciousness of one who knows herself in full command of the situation. "I thought you might find the way here. I am preparing a ceremony which will concern you intimately. Perhaps you would like to watch? This is to be an experiment, and for that reason a greater honor is to be yours than you can ever have known before; for the company I am assembling to watch your punishment is a more distinguished one than you could understand. Come here, inside the circle."

Jirel advanced, dagger still clenched in one hand, the other closed about her bit of broken crystal. She saw now that the couch stood in the center of a ring engraved in the floor with curious, cabalistic symbols. Beyond it the cloudy violet curtain swayed and eddied within itself, a vast, billowing wall of mist. Dubiously she stepped over the circle and stood eyeing Jarisme, her yellow gaze hot with rigidly curbed emotion. Jarisme smiled and lifted the flute to her lips again.

As the irritating two notes began their seesawing tune Jirel saw something amazing happen. She knew then that the flute was a magic one, and the song magical too. The notes took on a form that overstepped the boundaries of the aural and partook in some inexplicable way of all the other senses too. She could feel them, taste them, smell them, see them. In a queer way they were visible, pouring in twos from the flute and dashing outward like little needles of light. The walls reflected them, and those reflections became swifter and brighter and more numerous until the air was full of flying slivers of silvery brilliance, until shimmers began to dance among them and over them, and that bewildering shift of mirrored planes started up once more. Again reflections crossed and dazzled and multiplied in the shining air as the flute poured out its flashing double notes.

Jirel forgot the sorceress beside her, the music that grated on her ears, even her own peril, in watching the pictures that shimmered and vanished in the mirrored surfaces. She saw flashes of scenes she had glimpsed through the doors of Jarisme's hallway. She saw stranger places than that, passing in instant-brief snatches over the silvery planes. She saw jagged black mountains with purple dawns rising behind them and stars in unknown figures across the dark skies; she saw gray seas flat and motionless beneath gray clouds; she saw smooth meadows rolling horizonward under the glare of double suns. All these and many more awoke to the magic of Jarisme's flute, and melted again to give way to others.

Jirel had the strange fancy, as the music went on,

that it was audible in those lands whose brief pictures were flickering across the background of its visible notes. It seemed to be piercing immeasurable distances, ringing across the cloudy seas, echoing under the double suns, calling insistently in strange lands and far, unknown places, over deserts and mountains that man's feet had never trod, reaching other worlds and other times and crying its two-toned monotony through the darkness of interstellar space. All of this, to Jirel, was no more than a vague realization that it must be so. It meant nothing to her, whose world was a flat plane arched by the heaven-pierced bowl of the sky. Magic, she told herself, and gave up trying to understand.

Presently the tempo of the fluting changed. The same two notes still shrilled endlessly up and down, but it was no longer a clarion call ringing across borderlands into strange worlds. Now it was slower, statelier. And the notes of visible silver that had darted crazily against the crystal walls and reflected back again took on an order that ranked them into one shining plane. Upon that plane Jirel saw the outlines of a familiar scene gradually taking shape. The great door-lined hall above mirrored itself in faithful replica before her eyes. The music went on changelessly.

Then, as she watched, one of those innumerable doors quivered. She held her breath. Slowly it swung open upon that gray desert under the red sun which she had seen before she closed it quickly away behind concealing panels. Again as she looked, that sense of utter desolation and weariness and despair came over her, so uncannily dreary was the scene. Now the door stood wide, its locked grille no longer closing it, and as the music went on she could see a dazzle like a jagged twist of lightning begin to shimmer in its aperture. The gleam strengthened. She saw it quiver once, twice, then sweep forward with blinding speed through the open doorway. And as she tried to follow it with her eyes another moving door distracted her.

This time the steamy fern-forest was revealed as the panels swung back. But upon the threshold sprawled something so frightful that Jirel's free hand flew to her lips and a scream beat up in her throat. It was black—shapeless and black and slimy. And it was alive. Like a heap of putrescently shining jelly it heaved itself over the door-sill and began to flow across the floor, inching its way along like a vast blind ameba. But she knew without being told that it was horribly wise, horribly old. Behind it a black trial of slime smeared the floor.

∞

Jirel shuddered and turned her eyes away. Another door was swinging open. Through it she saw a place she had not chanced upon before, a country of bare red rock strewn jaggedly under a sky so darkly blue that it might have been black, with stars glimmering in it more clearly than stars of earth. Across this red, broken desert a figure came striding that she knew could be only a figment of magic, so tall it was, so spidery-thin, so grotesquely human despite its bulbous head and vast chest. She could not see it clearly, for about it like a robe it clutched a veil of blinding light. On those incredibly long, thin legs it stepped across the door-sill, drew its dazzling garment closer about it, and strode forward. As it neared, the light was so blinding that

she could not look upon it. Her averted eyes caught
the motion of a fourth door.

This time she saw that flowery ravine again, dim
in its underwater illusion of diffused light. And out
from among the flowers writhed a great serpent-
creature, not of the transparent crystal she had seen
in her dream, but iridescently scaled. Nor was it entirely serpent, for from the thickened neck sprang a
head which could not be called wholly unhuman.
The thing carried itself as proudly as a cobra, and
as it glided across the threshold its single, many-
faceted eye caught Jirel's in the reflection. The eye
flashed once, dizzyingly, and she reeled back in sick
shock, the violence of that glance burning through
her veins like fire. When she regained control of
herself many other doors were standing open upon
scenes both familiar and strange. During her daze
other denizens of those strange worlds must have
entered at the call of the magic flute.

She was just in time to see an utterly indescribable thing flutter into the hall from a world which
so violated her eyes that she got no more than a
glimpse of it as she flung up outraged hands to
shut it out. She did not lower that shield until Jarisme's amused voice said in an undertone, "Behold
your audience, Jirel of Joiry," and she realized that
the music had ceased and a vast silence was pressing against her ears. Then she looked out, and drew
a long breath. She was beyond surprise and shock
now, and she stared with the dazed incredulity of
one who knows herself in a nightmare.

Ranged outside the circle that enclosed the two
women sat what was surely the strangest company
ever assembled. They were grouped with a queer

irregularity which, though meaningless to Jirel, yet gave the impression of definite purpose and design. It had a symmetry so strongly marked that even though it fell outside her range of comprehension she could not but feel the rightness of it.

The light-robed dweller in the red barrens sat there, and the great black blob of shapeless jelly heaved gently on the crystal floor. She saw others she had watched enter, and many more. One was a female creature whose robe of peacock iridescence sprang from her shoulders in great drooping wings and folded round her like a bat's leathery cloak. And her neighbor was a fat gray slug of monster size, palpitating endlessly. One of the crowd looked exactly like a tall white lily swaying on a stalk of silver pallor, but from its chalice poured a light so ominously tinted that she shuddered and turned her eyes away.

Jarisme had risen from her couch. Very tall and regal in her violet robe, she rose against the backdrop of mist which veiled the other half of the room. As she lifted her arms, the incredible company turned to her with an eager expectancy. Jirel shuddered. Then Jarisme's flute spoke softly. It was a different sort of music from the clarion that called them together, from the stately melody which welcomed them through the opening doors. But it harped still on the two seesawing notes, with low, rippling sounds so different from the other two that Jirel marveled at the range of the sorceress's ability on the two notes.

For a few moments as the song went on, nothing happened. Then a motion behind Jarisme caught Jirel's eye. The curtain of violet mist was swaying.

The music beat to it and it quivered to the tune. It shook within itself, and paled and thinned, and from behind it a light began to glow. Then on a last low monotone it dissipated wholly and Jirel was staring at a vast globe of quivering light which loomed up under the stupendous arch that soared outward to form the second half of the chamber.

As the last clouds faded she saw that the thing was a huge crystal sphere, rising from the coils of a translucent purple base in the shape of a serpent. And in the heart of the globe burned a still flame, living, animate, instinct with a life so alien that Jirel stared in utter bewilderment. It was a thing she knew to be alive—yet she knew it could *not* be alive. But she recognized even in her daze of incomprehension its relation to the tiny fragment of crystal she clutched in her hand. In that too the still flame burned. It stung her hand faintly in reminder that she possessed a weapon which could destroy Jarisme, though it might destroy its wielder in the process. The thought gave her a sort of desperate courage.

Jarisme was ignoring her now. She had turned to face the great globe with lifted arms and shining head thrown back. And from her lips a piercingly sweet sound fluted, midway between hum and whistle. Jirel had the wild fancy that she could see that sound arrowing straight into the heart of the vast sphere bulking so high over them all. And in the heart of that still, living flame a little glow of red began to quiver.

Through the trembling air shrilled a second sound. From the corner of her eye Jirel could see that a dark figure had moved forward into the circle and fallen to its knees at the sorceress's side. She knew it for Giraud. Like two blades the notes quivered in the utter hush that lay upon the assembly, and in the globe that red glow deepened.

One by one, other voices joined the chorus, queer, uncanny sounds some of them, from throats not shaped for speech. No two voices blended. The chorus was one of single, unrelated notes. And as each voice struck the globe, the fire burned more crimson, until its pallor had flushed wholly into red. High above the rest soared Jarisme's knife-keen fluting. She lifted her arms higher, and the voices rose in answer. She lowered them, and the blade-like music swooped down an almost visible arc to a lower key. Jirel felt that she could all but see the notes spearing straight from each singer into the vast sphere that dwarfed them all. There was no melody in it, but a sharply definite pattern as alien and unmistakable as the symmetry of their grouping in the room. And as Jarisme's arms rose, lifting the voices higher, the flame burned more deeply red, and paled again as the voices fell.

Three times that stately, violet-robed figure gestured with lifted arms, and three times the living flame deepened and paled. Then Jarisme's voice soared in a high, triumphant cry and she whirled with spread arms, facing the company. In one caught breath, all voices ceased. Silence fell upon them like a blow. Jarisme was no longer priestess, but goddess, as she fronted them in that dead stillness with exultant face and blazing eyes. And in one motion they bowed before her as corn bows under wind. Alien things, shapeless monsters, faceless, eyeless, unrecognizable creatures from unknowable dimensions, abased themselves to the crystal floor before the splendor of light in Jarisme's eyes. For a moment of utter silence the tableau held. Then the sorceress's arms fell.

∞

Ripplingly the company rose. Beyond Jarisme the vast globe had paled again into that living, quiet flame of golden pallor. Immense, brooding, alive, it loomed up above them. Into the strained stillness Jarisme's low voice broke. She was speaking in Jirel's native tongue, but the air, as she went on, quivered thickly with something like waves of sound that were pitched for other organs than human ears. Every word that left her lips made another wave through the thickened air. The assembly shimmered before Jirel's eyes in that broken clarity as a meadow quivers under heat waves.

"Worshippers of the Light," said Jarisme sweetly, "be welcomed from your far dwellings into the presence of the Flame. We who serve it have called you to the worship, but before you return, another sort of ceremony is to be held, which we have felt will interest you all. For we have called it truly the simplest and subtlest and most terrible of all punishments for a human creature.

"It is our purpose to attempt a reversal of this woman's physical and mental self in such a way as to cause her body to become rigidly motionless while her mind—her soul—looks eternally backward along the path it has traveled. You who are human, or have known humanity, will understand what deadly torture that can be. For no human creature, by the laws that govern it, can have led a life whose intimate review is anything but pain. To be frozen

into eternal reflections, reviewing all the futility and
pain of life, all the pain that thoughtless or inten-
tional acts have caused others, all the spreading
consequences of every act—that, to a human being,
would be the most dreadful of all torments."

In the silence that fell as her voice ceased, Giraud
laid a hand on Jarisme's arm. Jirel saw terror in his
eyes.

"Remember," he uttered, "remember, for those
who tamper with their known destiny a more fearful thing may come than—"

Jarisme shrugged off the restraining hand impatiently. She turned to Jirel.

"Know, earthling," she said in a queerly strained
voice, "that in the books of the future it is written
that Jarisme the Sorceress must die at the hands of
the one human creature who defies her thrice—and
that human creature a woman. Twice I have been
weak, and spared you. Once in the forest, once on
the roof-top, you cast your puny defiance in my
face, and I stayed my hand for fear of what is written. But the third time shall not come. Though you
are my appointed slayer, you shall not slay. With
my own magic I break Fate's sequence, now, and
we shall see!"

In the blaze of her purple eyes Jirel saw that the
moment had come. She braced herself, fingers closing about the fragment of crystal in her hand uncertainly as she hesitated, wondering if the time had
come for the breaking of her talisman at the sorceress's feet. She hesitated too long, though her waiting was only a split-second in duration. For Jarisme's magic was more supremely simple than Jirel
could have guessed. The sorceress turned a blazing

purple gaze upon her and sharply snapped her plump fingers in the earthwoman's face.

At the sound Jirel's whole world turned inside out about her. It was the sheerest physical agony. Everything vanished as that terrible shift took place. She felt her own body being jerked inexplicably around in a reversal like nothing that any living creature could ever have experienced before. It was a backward-facing in a direction which could have had no existence until that instant. She felt the newness in the second before sight came to her—a breathless, soundless, new-born *now* in which she was the first dweller, created simultaneously with the new plane of being. Then sight broke upon her consciousness.

∞

The thing spread out before her was so stupendous that she would have screamed if she had possessed an animate body. All life was open to her gaze. The sight was too immeasurable for her to grasp it fully—too vast for her human consciousness to look upon at all save in flashing shutter-glimpses without relation or significance. Motion and immobility existed simultaneously in the thing before her. Endless activity shuttling to and fro—yet the whole vast panorama was frozen in a timeless calm through which a mighty pattern ran whose very immensity was enough to strike terror into her soul. Threaded through it the backward trail of her own life stretched. As she gazed upon it such floods of conflicting emotion washed over her that she could not see anything clearly, but she was fiercely insisting to her inner consciousness that she would not —*would not*—look back, dared not, could not—and all the while her sight was running past days and weeks along the path which led inexorably toward the one scene she could not bear to think of.

Very remotely, as her conscious sight retraced the backward way, she was aware of overlapping planes of existence in the stretch of limitless activity before her. Shapes other than human, scenes that had no meaning to her, quivered and shifted and boiled with changing lives—yet lay motionless in the mighty pattern. She scarcely heeded them. For her, of all that panoramic impossibility one scene alone had meaning—the one scene toward which her sight was racing now, do what she would to stop it—the one scene that she knew she could never bear to see again.

Yet when her sight reached that place the pain did not begin at once. She gazed almost calmly upon that little interval of darkness and flaring light, the glare of torches shining upon a girl's bent red head and on a man's long body sprawled motionless upon flagstones. In the deepest stillness she stared. She felt no urge to look farther, on beyond the scene into the past. This was the climax, the center of all her life—this torch-lit moment on the flagstones. Vividly she was back again in the past, felt the hardness of the cold flags against her knees, and the numbness of her heart as she stared down into a dead man's face. Timelessly she dwelt upon that long-ago heartbreak, and within her something swelled unbearably.

That something was a mounting emotion too great to have name, too complexly blending agony and grief and hatred and love—and rebellion; so strong that all the rest of the stupendous thing before her was blotted out in the gathering storm of what seethed in her innermost consciousness. She was aware of nothing but that overwhelming emotion. And it was boiling into one great unbearable explosion of violence in which rage took precedence over all. Rage at life for permitting such pain to be. Rage at Jarisme for forcing her into memory. Such rage that everything shook before it, and melted and ran together in a heat of rebellion, and—something snapped. The panorama reeled and shivered and collapsed into the dark of semi-oblivion.

Through the clouds of her half-consciousness the agony of change stabbed at her. Half understanding, she welcomed it, though the piercing anguish of that reversal was so strong it dragged her out of her daze again and wrung her anew in the grinding pain of that change which defied all natural laws. In heedless impatience she waited for the torture to pass. Exultation was welling up in her, for she knew that her own violence had melted the spell by which Jarisme held her. She knew what she must do when she stood free again, and conscious power flowed intoxicatingly through her.

She opened her eyes. She was standing rigidly before the great fire-quickened globe. The amazing company was grouped around her intently, and Jarisme, facing her, had taken one angry, incredulous step forward as she saw her own spell break. Upon that tableau Jirel's hot yellow eyes opened, and she laughed in grim exultation and swung up her arm. Violet light glinted upon crystal.

In the instant Jarisme saw what she intended, convulsive terror wiped all other expression from her face. A cry of mingled inarticulateness thundered up from the transfixed crowd. Giraud started forward from among them, frantic hands clawing out toward her.

"No, no!" shrieked Jarisme. "Wait!"

It was too late. The crystal dashed itself from Jirel's down-swinging arm, the light in it blazing. With a splintering crash it struck the floor at the sorceress's sandaled feet and flew into shining fragments.

For an instant nothing happened. Jirel held her breath, waiting. Giraud had flung himself flat on the shining floor, reaching out for her in a last desperate effort. His hands had flown out to seize her, and found only her ankles. He clung to them now with a paralyzed grip, his face hidden between his arms. Jarisme cowered motionless, arms clasped about her head as if she were trying to hide. The motley throng of watchers was rigid in fatalistic quiet. In tense silence they waited.

Then in the great globe above them the pale flame flickered. Jarisme's gaspingly caught breath sounded loud in the utter quiet. Again the flame shook. And again. Then abruptly it went out. Darkness stunned them for a moment; then a low muttering roar rumbled up out of the stillness, louder and deeper and stronger until it pressed unbearably upon Jirel's ears and her head was one great aching surge of sound. Above that roar a sharply crackling noise broke, and the crystal walls of the room trembled, reeled dizzily—split open in long jagged rents through which the violet day poured in thin fingers of light. Overhead the shattering sound of falling walls roared loud. Jarisme's magic tower was crumbling all around them. Through the long, shivering cracks in the walls the pale violet day poured more strongly, serene in the chaos.

In that clear light Jirel saw a motion among the throng. Jarisme had risen to her full height. She saw the sleek black head go up in an odd, defiant, desperate poise, and above the soul-shaking tumult she heard the sorceress's voice scream,

"Urda! Urda-sla!"

In the midst of the roar of the falling walls for the briefest instant a deathly silence dropped. And out of that silence, like an answer to the sorceress's cry, came a Noise, an indescribable, intolerable loudness like the crack of cyclopean thunder. And suddenly in the sky above them, visible through the crumbling crystal walls, a long black wedge opened. It was like a strip of darkest midnight splitting the violet day, a midnight through which stars shone unbearably near, unbearably bright.

Jirel stared up in dumb surprise at that streak of starry night cleaving the daylit sky. Jarisme stood rigid, arms outstretched, defiantly fronting the thunderous dark whose apex was drawing nearer and nearer, driving downward like a vast celestial spear. She did not flinch as it reached toward the tower. Jirel saw the darkness sweep forward like a racing shadow. Then it was upon them, and the earth shuddered under her feet, and from very far away she heard Jarisme scream.

∞

When consciousness returned to her, she sat up painfully and stared around. She lay upon green grass, bruised and aching, but unharmed. The violet day was serene and unbroken once more. The purple peaks had vanished. No longer was she high among mountains. Instead, the green meadow where she had first seen Jarisme's tower stretched about her. In its dissolution it must have returned to its original sight, flashing back along the magical ways it had traveled as the sorceress's magic was broken. For the tower too was gone. A little distance away, she saw a heap of marble blocks outlining a rough circle, where that white shaft had risen. But the stones were weathered and cracked like the old, old stones of an ancient ruin.

She had been staring at this for many minutes, trying to focus her bewildered mind upon its significance, before the sound of groaning which had been going on for some time impressed itself on her brain. She turned. A little way off, Giraud lay in a tangle of torn black robes. Of Jarisme and the rest she saw no sign. Painfully she got to her feet and staggered to the wizard, turning him over with a disdainful toe. He opened his eyes and stared at her with a cloudy gaze into which recognition and realization slowly crept.

"Are you hurt?" she demanded.

He pulled himself to a sitting position and flexed his limbs experimentally. Finally he shook his head, more in answer to his own investigation than to her query, and got slowly to his feet. Jirel's eyes sought the weapon at his hip.

"I am going to kill you now," she said calmly. "Draw your sword, wizard."

The little dull eyes flashed up to her face. He stared. Whatever he saw in the yellow gaze must have satisfied him that she meant what she said, but he did not draw, nor did he fall back. A tight little smile drew his mouth askew, and he lifted his black-

robed arms. Jirel saw them rise, and her gaze followed the gesture automatically. Up they went, up.
And then in the queerest fashion she lost all control of her own eyes, so that they followed some invisible upward line which drew her on and on sky-
ward until she was rigidly staring at a fixed point of
invisibility at the spot where the lines of Giraud's
arms would have crossed, where they extended to a
measureless distance. Somehow she actually saw
that point, and could not look away. Gripped in the
magic of those lifted arms, she stood rigid, not even
realizing what had happened, unable even to think
in the moveless magic of Giraud.

His little mocking chuckle reached her from im-
measurably far away.

"Kill me?" he was laughing thickly. "Kill me, Giraud? Why, it was you who saved me, Joiry! Why
else should I have clung to your ankles so tightly?
For I knew that when the Light died, the only one
who could hope to live would be the one who slew
it—nor was that a certainty, either. But I took the
risk, and well I did, or I would be with Jarisme now
in the outer dark whence she called up her no-god
of the void to save her from oblivion. I warned her
what would happen if she tampered with Fate. And
I would rather—yes, much rather—be here, in this
pleasant violet land which I shall rule alone now.
Thanks to you, Joiry! Kill me, eh? I think not!"

That thick, mocking chuckle reached her remotely, penetrated her magic-stilled mind. It echoed
round and round there, for a long while, before she
realized what it meant. But at last she remembered,
and her mind woke a little from its inertia, and such

anger swept over her that its heat was an actual pain. Giraud, the runaway sorcerer, laughing at Joiry! Holding Jirel of Joiry in his spell! Mocking her! Blindly she wrenched at the bonds of magic, blindly urged her body forward. She could see nothing but that non-existent point where the lifted arms would have crossed, in measureless distances, but she felt the dagger-hilt in her hand, and she lunged forward through invisibility, and did not even know when the blade sank home.

Sight returned to her then in a stunning flood. She rubbed dazed eyes and shook herself and stared round the green meadow in the violet day uncomprehendingly, for her mind was not yet fully awake. Not until she looked down did she remember.

Giraud lay there. The black robes were furled like wings over his quiet body, but red in a thick flood was spreading on the grass, and from the tangled garments her dagger-hilt stood up. Jirel stared down at him, emotionless, her whole body still almost asleep from the power of the dead man's magic. She could not even feel triumph. She pulled the blade free automatically and wiped it on his robes. Then she sat down beside the body and rested her head in her hands, forcing herself to awaken.

After a long while she looked up again, the old hot light rising in her eyes, life flushing back into her face once more. Shaking off the last shreds of the spell, she got to her feet, sheathing the dagger. About her the violet-misted meadows were very still. No living creature moved anywhere in sight. The trees were motionless in the unstirring air. And

beyond the ruins of the marble tower she saw the
opening in the woods out of which her path had
come, very long ago.

Jirel squared her shoulders and turned her back
upon her vow fulfilled, and without a backward
glance set off across the grass toward the tree-hid
ruins which held the gate to home.

THE LAKE OF THE GONE FOREVER

LEIGH BRACKETT

In "The Lake of the Gone Forever," Leigh Brackett writes of a man searching for wealth and power. He is aided in his quest by a woman seeking to assert her own worth. In this colorful story by one of science fiction's most popular authors, the protagonist makes an unexpected discovery about his father, and about himself as well.

I LANDING ON ISKAR

In his cabin aboard the spaceship *Rohan,* Rand Conway slept—and dreamed.

He stood in a narrow valley. On both sides the cliffs of ice rose up, sheer and high and infinitely beautiful out of the powdery snow. The darkling air was full of whirling motes of frost, like the dust of diamonds, and overhead the shining pinnacles stood clear against a sky of deepest indigo, spangled with great stars.

As always, the place was utterly strange to Conway and yet, somehow, not strange at all. He began to walk forward through the drifting snow and he seemed almost to know what he was seeking around the bend of the valley.

Fear came upon him then but he could not stop.

And as always in that icy place his dead father stood waiting. He stood just as he had years ago, on the night he died, and he spoke slowly and sadly the words he had spoken then to his uncomprehending small son.

"I can never go back to Iskar, to the Lake of the Gone Forever."

Tears dropped slowly from under the closed lids of his eyes and the echo went to and fro between the cliffs, saying, ". . . Lake of the Gone Forever . . . Gone Forever . . ."

Conway crept on, trembling. Above him the golden stars wheeled in the dark blue sky and the beauty of them was evil and the shimmering turrets of the ice were full of lurking laughter.

He passed into the shadows under the sheathed rocks that hid the end of the valley and as he did so the dead man cried out in a voice of agony, "I can never go back to Iskar!"

And the cliffs caught up the name and shouted it thunderously through the dream.

Iskar! Iskar!

Rand Conway started up in his bunk, wide awake, shaken and sweating as always by the strangeness of that vision. Then his hands closed hard on the edge of the bunk and he laughed.

"*You* couldn't go back," he whispered to the man dead twenty years. "But *I'm* going. By heaven, I'm going, at last!"

It seemed to him that the very fabric of the ship

murmured the name as it rushed on into deep space, that the humming machines purred it, that the thundering jets bellowed it.

Iskar! Iskar!

A savage triumph rose in Conway. So many times he had awakened from that dream to hopelessness —the hopelessness of ever reaching his goal. So many times, in these years of hard dangerous spaceman's toil, the lost little world that meant power and riches had seemed remote beyond attainment.

But he had hung on, too stubborn ever quite to give up. He had waited and planned and hoped until finally he had made his chance. And he was on his way now to the place that his father had lost and never regained.

"Iskar!"

∞

Conway started up, his face swiftly losing its brooding look. That wasn't just an echo of his dream. Someone was shouting the name outside his cabin door.

"Conway! Rand Conway! We've sighted *Iskar!*"

Of course! Why else would the jets be thundering? He had been half asleep still, not to know it at once. He sprang up and crossed the dimly-lighted cabin, a tall man, very lean and hard, yet with a certain odd grace about him, a certain beauty in the modeling of his bones. His eyes, of a color somewhere between grey and blue, were brilliant with excitement and full of a wolfish hunger.

He flung open the door. The glare from the corridor set him to blinking painfully—an inherited sensitivity to light was his one weakness and he had often cursed his father for passing it on to him. Through a dancing haze he saw Peter Esmond's mild good-looking face, as excited as his own.

Esmond said something, but Conway neither heard it nor cared what it was. He pushed past him and went with long strides down the passage and up the ladder to the observation bridge.

It was dark up there under the huge port. Immediately everything came clear to his vision—the blue-black sky of the Asteroid Belt, full of flashing golden stars where the little worlds caught the light of the distant Sun.

And ahead, dead ahead, he saw the tiny misty globe that was Iskar.

He stood for a long time, staring at it, and he neither moved nor spoke except that a deep trembling ran through him.

Close beside him he heard Charles Rohan's deep voice. "Well, there's the new world. Quite a thrill, eh?"

Instantly Conway was on his guard. Rohan was no fool. A man does not make forty million dollars by being a fool and it was going to be hard enough to get away with this without tipping his hand to Rohan now.

Inwardly he cursed, not Rohan, but his daughter Marcia.

It was she who had talked her father into going along to see about opening up trade with Iskar. Rohan controlled the lion's share of trade with the Jovian Moons and the idea was logical enough. Marcia's interest, naturally, was not financial. It was simply that she could not bear to be parted from

Esmond and there was no other way for her to go
with him.

Conway glanced at Marcia, who was standing
with her arm around her fiancé. A nice girl. A pretty
girl. Ordinarily he would have liked her. But she
didn't belong here and neither did Rohan—not for
Conway's purposes.

Esmond alone he could have handled easily. Esmond was the Compleat Ethnologist to his fingertips. As long as he had a brand-new race to study
and catalogue he would neither know nor care what
other treasures a world might hold.

Now that he looked back on it the whole chain of
circumstances seemed flimsy and unsure to Conway
—his meeting with Esmond on a deep-space flight
from Jupiter, the sudden inspiration when he
learned of Esmond's connection with the Rohans,
the carefully casual campaign to get the ethnologist
interested in the unknown people of Iskar, the final
business of producing his father's fragmentary notes
to drive Esmond quite mad with longing to see this
inhabited world that only one other Earthman had
ever seen.

Esmond to Marcia Rohan, Marcia to her father—
and now here they were. Esmond was going to get
a Fellowship in the Interplanetary Society of Eth-
nologists and Rand Conway was going to get what
he had lusted for ever since he had stumbled upon
his father's notes and read in them the story of what
lay in the Lake of the Gone Forever, waiting to be
picked up by the first strong pair of hands.

That portion of the notes he had never shown to
anyone.

Here they were, plunging out of the sky toward Iskar, and it had all been so easy—too easy. Conway was a spaceman and therefore superstitious, whether he liked it or not. He had a sudden feeling that he was going to have to pay for that easiness before he got through.

∞

Esmond had pressed forward in the cramped space, staring raptly out at the distant glittering of silver light that was Iskar.

"I wonder what they're like?" he said as he had said a million times before. Marcia smiled.

"You'll soon know," she answered.

"It *is* odd," said Rohan, "that your father didn't tell more about the people of Iskar, Conway. His notes were strangely fragmentary—almost as though he had written much more and then destroyed it."

Conway tried to detect an edge of suspicion in Rohan's voice, but could not.

"Perhaps he did," said Conway. "I never could find any more."

With that one exception it was the truth.

Marcia's face was thoughtful and a little sad, in the dim glow of that outer sky.

"I've read those notes over and over again," she said. "I think you're right, Dad. I think Mr. Conway wrote his whole heart into those notes and then destroyed them because he couldn't bear to have them read, even by his son."

She put a sympathetic hand on Conway's arm.

"I can understand your wanting to know, Rand. I hope you'll find your answer."

"Thanks," said Conway gravely.

He had had to account for his own interest in

Iskar and he had been able to do that too without lying except by omission. The story of his father was true enough—the dark brooding man, broken in health and spirit, living alone with a child and a dream. He had died before Rand was ten, by his own hand and with the name of Iskar on his lips. *I can never go back, to the Lake of the Gone Forever!*

Conway himself had never doubted what his father's secret tragedy was. He had found a fortune on Iskar and had not been able to go back to claim it. That was enough to drive any man mad.

But it was easy, out of his childhood memories and those strangely incoherent notes, to build a romantic mystery around the lonely prospector's discovery of an unknown world and his subsequent haunted death. Marcia had found it all fascinating and did not doubt for a moment Conway's statement that he was seeking to solve that mystery which, he said, had overshadowed his whole life.

And it had. Waking or sleeping, Rand Conway could not forget Iskar and the Lake of the Gone Forever.

He watched the misty globe grow larger in the sky ahead, and the beating of his heart was a painful thing. Already his hands ached with longing to close around Iskar and wring from it the power and the wealth that would repay him for all the bitter years of waiting.

He thought of his dream. It was always unpleasantly vivid, and remained with him for hours after he woke. But this time it was different. He thought of the vision of his father, standing in the crystal valley, alone with his dark sorrow, and he said to the vision, *You should have waited. You should have had the courage to wait, like me.*

For the first time he was not sorry for his father.

Then he forgot his father. He forgot time and Esmond and the Rohans. He forgot everything but Iskar.

The *Rohan* shuddered rhythmically to the brake-blasts. Iskar filled the port, producing a skyline of shimmering pinnacles so like his dream that Conway shuddered too in spite of himself.

The pinnacles shot up swiftly into a wall of ice and the *Rohan* swept in to a landing.

II THE WHITE CITY

The spaceship lay like a vast black whale, stranded on a spotless floe. Behind it the ice-wall rose, its upper spires carved by the wind into delicate fantastic shapes. Spreading away from it to the short curve of the horizon was a sloping plain of snow, broken here and there by gleaming tors. In the distance other ranges lifted sharply against the deep dark blue of the sky.

Rand Conway stood apart from the others. His face had a strange look. He slipped the warm hood back, lifting his head in the icy wind.

Great golden stars wheeled overhead and the air was full of dancing motes of frost. The wind played with the powdery snow, whirling it up into shining veils, smoothing it again into curious patterns of ripples.

The pain, the sky, the frozen spires, had a wondrous beauty of color, infinitely soft and subtle.

There was no glare here to plague Conway's eyes. Iskar glimmered in a sort of misty twilight, like the twilight of a dream.

Iskar—the bulk of it solid under his feet at last after all these years. Conway trembled and found it difficult to breathe. His eyes, black and luminous as a cat's now with the expansion of the pupils, glistened with a hard light. Iskar!

Quite suddenly he was afraid.

Fear rushed at him out of the narrow valleys, down from the singing peaks. It came in the wind and rose up from the snow under his feet. It wrapped him in a freezing shroud and for a moment reality slipped away from him and he was lost.

The shadows were deep under the icy cliffs and the mouths of the valleys were black and full of whispers. It seemed to him that the lurking terror of his dream was very close, close and waiting.

He must have made some sound or sign, for Marcia Rohan came to him and took him by the arm.

"Rand," she said. "Rand, what is it?"

He caught hold of her. In a moment everything was normal again and he was able to force what might pass for a laugh.

"I don't know," he said. "Something came to me just then." He could not tell her about the dream. He told her instead what he knew must be the cause of it.

"My father must have told me something about this place when I was a child, something I can't remember. Something ugly. I—" He paused and then plunged on. "I thought for a moment that I had been here before, that I knew . . ."

He stopped. The shadow was gone now. To the devil with dreams and subconscious memories. The reality was all that mattered—the reality that was going to make Rand Conway richer than the Rohans. He stared away across the plain. For a moment his face was unguarded and Marcia was startled by the brief cruel look of triumph that crossed it.

The others came up, Rohan and young Esmond and Captain Frazer, the well-fed but very competent skipper of the *Rohan*. They were all shivering slightly in spite of their warm coveralls. Esmond looked at Conway, who was still bare-headed.

"You'll freeze your ears off," he said.

Conway laughed, not without a faint edge of contempt. "If you had kicked around in deep space as many years as I have you wouldn't be bothered by a little cold."

He pointed off to where the distant ranges were, across the plain.

"According to my father's maps, the village, or what have you, lies between those ranges."

"I think," said Marcia, "that we had better break out the sledges and go before Peter bursts something."

Esmond laughed. He was obviously trembling with eagerness.

"I hope nothing's happened to them," he said. "I mean, since your father was here. You know—famine, plague or anything."

"I imagine they're a pretty hardy lot," said Rohan, "or they couldn't have survived at all in this godforsaken place." He turned to Frazer, laughing. "For heaven's sake, get the sledges."

∞

Frazer nodded. The crew had come tumbling out and were rollicking like schoolboys in the snow, glad to be released from the long confinement of the voyage. The Second Officer and the engineer were coming up and Frazer went to meet them. The Second turned back to round up his men.

The sledges came presently out of the cargo hatch. There were three of the light plastic hulls—two to carry the exploring party, one to be left with the ship in case of emergency. They were fully equipped, including radio and the efficient Samson riot guns, firing shells of anaesthetic gas.

Rohan looked at his daughter. "I want you to stay here, Marcia."

The girl must have been expecting that, Conway thought, because her only reaction was to set her jaw so that she looked ridiculously like her father—smaller and prettier but even more stubborn.

"No," said Marcia.

Esmond said, "Please, darling. These people may not be friendly at first. You can go next time."

"No," said Marcia.

"Marcia," said Rohan pleasantly. "I don't want any foolishness about this. Go with Frazer, back to the ship."

Marcia studied him. Then she turned and kissed Esmond lightly on the cheek and said, "Good luck, darling." She went off with Frazer. Conway saw that there were tears in her eyes. He warmed to Marcia. She hadn't been trying to show off. She just wanted to be with Esmond in case anything happened.

Rohan said, "I guess we might as well go."

They climbed in, six men to a sledge, all burly spacehands with the exception of Rohan and the ethnologist and Conway, who had sweated his way up from the ranks to Master Pilot.

The small jets hissed, roared and settled down to a steady thrumming. The sledges shot out across the trackless plain like two small boats on a white sea, throwing up waves of snowy spray.

Conway was in the leading sledge. He leaned forward like a leashed hound, impatient to be slipped. Part of him was mad with excitement and another part, completely cool and detached, was making plans.

The spaceship began to grow smaller. Almost imperceptibly the gleaming pinnacles of ice lengthened into the sky.

Presently the pace of the sledges grew slower and slower still. Tors, half rock, half ice, rose up out of the snow and here and there a reef, mailed and capped with the shining armor, was scoured clear by the wind. The man at the controls thrust his head forward, squinting.

"What's the matter?" asked Conway. "Why the delay?"

The man said irritably, "I'm afraid of ramming into something, sir. It's so bloody dark and shadowy, I can't see."

"Is that all!" Conway laughed and shoved him aside. "Here—let an owl do it."

He took the controls and sent the sledge spinning ahead. Every reef and tor, every ripple in the snow, was as clear to him as it would have been to most men in broad daylight. He laughed again.

"I'm beginning to like Iskar," he said to Rohan. "I think I'll start a colony for people with hemeralopia, and we can all be as happy as bats in the dark. My father must have loved it here."

Rohan glanced up at him. Conway had forgotten to put his hood back up. The wind was whipping an icy gale through his hair and there was rime on his lashes. He seemed to be enjoying it. Rohan shivered.

"I'm nyctalopic myself," he said. "I'll stick to plenty of sunlight—*and* heat!"

Esmond did not bother to listen to either one of them. His dream was as strong as Conway's and at this moment he had room for nothing else.

The sledges rushed on across the plain, the one following the tiny jet-flares of the other. The spaceship was lost in the white distance behind them. Ahead the twin ranges grew against the stars. Nothing stirred but the wind. It was very lovely, very peaceful, Conway thought. A cold, sweet jewel of a world.

The words sang in his ears, the words that had themed his father's death and run through his own life as a promise and a challenge. "The Lake of the Gone Forever—Gone Forever . . ."

He had long ago ceased to wonder what that name meant. Only in his nightmare dream did it have the power to frighten him. He wanted what was there and nothing else mattered.

The Lake of the Gone Forever. Soon—soon—soon!

Yet it seemed a very long time to Conway before they entered the broad defile between the twin ranges.

He was forced to slow his breakneck pace because here the ground was broken and treacherous. Finally he stopped altogether.

"We'll have to go on foot from here," he said.

∞

In a fever of impatience he waited while the men climbed out, shouldering the Samson guns. They left two to guard the sledges and went on, scrambling in single file over the tumbled rocks. The wind howled between the mountain walls so that the air was blind with snow. There was no sight of the city.

Conway was in the lead. He was like a man driven by fiends. Where the others slipped and stumbled he went over the rough ground like a cat, swift and sure-footed even among the deceptive drifts. Several times he was forced to stop and wait lest he leave the party too far behind.

Suddenly, above the organ notes of the wind, there was another sound.

Conway lifted his head to listen. Clear and sweet and strong he heard the winding of horns from the upper slopes. They echoed away down the valley, calling one to the other with ringing voices that stirred Conway's blood to a wild excitement. He shook the snow out of his hair and plunged on, leaving the rest to follow as best they could.

A jutting shoulder of the mountains loomed before him. The wind blew and the deep-throated horns called and called again across the valley. The blown drifts leaped at him and the icy screes were a challenge to his strength but they could not slow him down. He laughed and went on around the shoulder and saw the white city glittering under the stars.

It spread across the valley floor and up the slopes

as though it grew from the frozen earth, a part of it, as enduring as the mountains. At Conway's first glance, it seemed to be built all of ice, its turrets and crenellations glowing with a subtle luminescence in the dusky twilight, fantastically shaped, dusted here and there with snow. From the window openings came a glow of pearly light.

Beyond the city the twin ranges drew in and in until their flanks were parted only by a thin line of shadow, a narrow valley with walls of ice reaching up to the sky.

Conway's heart contracted with a fiery pang.

A narrow valley—*The* valley.

For a moment everything vanished in a roaring darkness. Dream and reality rushed together—his father's notes, his father's dying cry, his own waking visions and fearful wanderings beyond the wall of sleep.

It lies beyond the city, in a narrow place between the mountains—the Lake of the Gone Forever. And I can never go back!

Conway said aloud to the wind and the snow and the crying horns, "But *I* have come back. I have come!"

Exulting, triumphant, he looked again at the city, the white beauty of it, the wind-carved towers bright beneath the golden stars.

It was a strong place, walled and fortified against whatever enemies there might be on this world of Iskar. Conway ran toward it and as he did so the braying of horns rose louder and then was joined by the shrill war-cry of pipes.

They went skirling along the wall and through the snow-mist he saw that men were there above him looking down. The glitter of their spears ran like a broken line of silver from both sides of the great stone gate.

III THE FEAR

Conway's blood leaped hot within him. The pipes set him mad and he flung up his arm and shouted at the men, a long hail. He could see them clearly now. They were tall lean men with bodies tough as rawhide and strong bone in their faces and eyes like the eyes of eagles. They wore the white fur of beasts kilted about them, thrown loosely over their naked shoulders, and they were bareheaded and careless of the cold.

Their spears rose up and menaced him.

He stopped. Once again he cried out, a cry as wild and shrill as the martial pipes. Then he stood still, waiting.

Slowly behind him came Rohan and the others. They formed into a sort of knot around him. Some of the men reached nervously for their riot guns and Rohan spoke sharply. The pipes fell silent and the sounding horns. They waited, all of them.

There was movement on the wall and an old man came forward among the warriors, a cragged gnarled old man with a proud face and fierce eyes, standing strong as a granite rock.

He looked down at the alien men below him. His hair and his long beard blew in the bitter wind, and the white furs whipped around him, and for a long time he did not speak. His eyes met Conway's and there was hatred in them and deep pain.

Finally he said, very slowly, as though the words

came haltingly from some long-locked vault of memory, "Men of Earth!"

Conway started. It had not occurred to him that his father might have left some knowledge of English behind him.

"Yes," he answered, holding out his empty hands. "Friends."

The old man shook his head. "No. Go, or we kill."

He looked again at Conway, very strangely, and a little chill ran through the Earthman. Was it possible that the old man saw in him some resemblance to the Conway he had known before? He and his father had not looked alike.

Esmond stepped forward. "Please," he said. "We mean you no harm. We only want to talk to you. We will obey you, we will bring no weapons—only let us in!"

He was very like a child pleading, almost on the verge of tears. It was unthinkable that he should be denied now.

The old man said again, "Go."

Rohan spoke. "We have gifts, many things for your people. We want nothing. We come as friends."

The old man flung up his head and laughed, and his mirth was like vitriol poured on the wind.

"*Friend!* Conna was my friend. In my house, as my own son, lived Conna, my friend!"

He cried out something in his own harsh tongue and Conway knew that it was a curse and he knew that Conna was his own name. They had not forgotten his father on Iskar, it seemed.

He was suddenly angry, more terribly angry than he had ever been in his life. Beyond the city, almost within reach, lay the valley of the Lake and nothing, not all their spears, not death itself, was going to stop him now.

He strode up under the wall and looked at the old man with eyes as black and baleful as his own.

"We know nothing of this Conna," he said. "We come in peace. But if you want war we will make war. If you kill us others will come—many others. Our ship is huge and very terrible. Its fire alone can destroy your city. Will you let us in, old man, or must we . . ."

After a long time the other said slowly, "What is your name?"

"Rand," said Conway.

"Rand," repeated the old man softly. "Rand." He was silent for a time, brooding, his chin sunk on his breast. His eyes were hooded and he did not look again at Conway.

Abruptly he turned and issued orders in his own tongue. Then, to the Earthmen, he shouted, "*Enter!*"

The great stone was rolled away.

Conway went back to the others. Both Esmond and Rohan were furious.

"Who gave you the right—" Rohan began, and Esmond broke in passionately,

"You shouldn't have threatened them! A little more talk would have convinced them."

Conway looked at them contemptuously.

"You wanted in, didn't you?" he demanded. "All right, the gate's open and they'll think twice about getting tough with us after we're through it."

He unbuckled his gun belt and tossed it, holster and all, to a man on the wall. It was a gesture and no more because he had hidden a small anaesthetic needle-gun under his coverall in case of need—but it would look good to the Iskarians.

"I'd do the same if I were you," he said to the others. "Also, I would send the men back. They're not going to do us any good inside the wall and they might do us harm. Tell them to bring the trade goods and one of the radios from the sledges and then return to the ship—and stand by."

Rohan scowled. He did not like having the command taken from him. But Conway's orders made sense and he relayed them. Then he tossed his own gun to one of the warriors. Esmond did not carry one. The men went away, back to the sledges.

"Remember," said Conway, "you never heard of 'Conna', or his son."

The others nodded. They turned then and went into the city and the stone gate was closed behind them.

The old man was waiting for them, and with him a sort of honor guard of fifteen tall fighting men.

"I am Krah," said the old patriarch. He waited politely until Esmond and Rohan had said their names and then he said, "Come."

The guard formed up. The Earthmen went—half guest, half captive—into the streets of the city.

They were narrow winding streets, rambling up and down over the broken ground. In some places they were scoured clean to the ice by the whistling wind, in others they were choked by drifts. Conway could see now that the buildings were all of solid stone, over which the cold shining mail had formed for centuries, except where the openings were kept clear.

The people of the city were gathered to watch as the strangers went by.

It was a strangely silent crowd. Men, women and children, old and young, all of them as stalwart and handsome as mountain trees, with their wide black pupils and pale hair, the men clad in skins, the women in kirtles of rough woolen cloth. Conway noticed that the women and children did not mingle with the men.

Silent, all of them, and watching. There was something disquieting in their stillness. Then, somewhere, an old woman sent up a keening cry of lament, and another took it up, and another, until the eerie *ochone* echoed through the twisting streets as though the city itself wept in pain.

The men began to close in. Slowly at first, now one stepping forward, now another, like the first pebbles rolling before the rush of the avalanche. Conway's heart began to pound and there was a bitter taste in his mouth.

Esmond cried out to the old man, "Tell them not to fear us! Tell them we are friends!"

Krah looked at him and smiled. His eyes went then to Conway and he smiled again.

"I will tell them," he said.

"Remember," said Conway harshly. "Remember the great ship and its fires."

Krah nodded. "I will not forget."

He spoke to the people, shouting aloud, and reluctantly the men drew back and rested the butts of their spears on the ground. The women did not cease to wail.

Conway cursed his father for the things he had not written in his notes.

Quite suddenly, out of a steep side lane, a herd boy drove his flock with a scramble and a clatter. The queer white-furred beasts milled in the narrow space, squealing, filling the air with their sharp, not unpleasant odor.

As though that pungency were a trigger, a shutter clicked open somewhere in Conway's mind and he knew that he had seen these streets before, known the sounds and smells of the city, listened to the harsh staccato speech. The golden wheeling of the stars overhead hurt him with a poignant familiarity.

Conway plunged again into that limbo between fact and dream. It was far worse this time. He wanted to sink down and cling to something until his mind steadied again but he did not dare do anything but walk behind the old man as though nothing on Iskar could frighten him.

Yet he was afraid—afraid with the fear of madness, where the dream becomes the reality.

Beads of sweat came out on his face and froze there. He dug his nails into his palms and forced himself to remember his whole life, back to his earliest memory and beyond, when his father must have talked and talked of Iskar, obsessed with the thought of what he had found there and lost again.

He had not spoken so much of Iskar when his son was old enough to understand. But it seemed that the damage was already done. The formative years, the psychologists call them, when the things learned and forgotten will come back to haunt one later on.

Conway was a haunted man, walking through that strange city. And old Krah watched him sidelong and smiled and would not be done with smiling.

The women wailed, howling like shewolves to the dark heavens.

IV "GO ASK OF HER . . ."

It seemed like centuries to Conway, but it could not have been so long in actual time before Krah stopped beside a doorway and pulled aside the curtain of skins that covered it.

"Enter," he said and the Earthmen filed through, leaving the guard outside, except for five who followed the old man.

"My sons," said Krah.

All grown men, far older than Conway, and scarred, tough-handed warriors. Yet they behaved toward Krah with the deference of children.

The ground floor of the house was used for storage. Frozen sides of meat and bundles of a dried moss-like stuff occupied one side. On the other was a pen and a block for butchering. Apparently there was no wood on Iskar, for the pen was built of stone and there were no doors, only the heavy curtains.

Krah lifted another one of these, leading the way up a closed stair that served as a sort of airlock to keep out the draughts and the extreme cold of the lower floor. The upper chamber was freezing by any Earthly standards but a small, almost smokeless fire of moss burned on the round hearth and the enormously thick walls were perfect insulation against the wind. Immediately Conway began to sweat, probably from sheer nervousness.

A girl sat by the hearth, tending the spit and the

cooking pot. Obviously she had only just run back
in from the street, for there was still snow in her
silvery hair and her sandals were wet with it.

She did not lift her head when the men came in,
as though such happenings were not for her to notice. Yet Conway caught a sidelong glance of her
eyes. In the soft light of the stone lamps her pupils
had contracted to show the clear blue iris, and for
all her apparent meekness, he saw that her eyes
were bright and rebellious and full of spirit. Conway smiled.

She met his gaze fairly for a moment with a curious intensity, as though she would tear away his
outer substance and see everything that lay beneath
it—his heart, his soul, his innermost thoughts, greed-
ily, all in a minute. Then the old man spoke and she
was instantly absorbed in the turning of the spit.

"Sit," said Krah, and the Earthmen sat on heaps
of furs spread over cushions of moss.

The five tall sons sat also but Krah remained
standing.

"So you know nothing of Conna," he said and
Conna's son answered blandly,

"No."

"Then how came you to Iskar?"

Conway shrugged. "How did Conna come? The
men of Earth go everywhere." Unconsciously he
had slipped into Krah's ceremonial style of phras-
ing. He leaned forward, smiling.

"My words were harsh when I stood outside your
gate. Let them be forgotten, for they were only the
words of anger. Forget Conna also. He has nothing
to do with us."

"Ah," said the old man softly. "Forget. That is a

word I do not know. Anger, yes—and vengeance also. But not forget."

He turned to Rohan and Esmond and spoke to them and answered them courteously while they explained their wishes. But his gaze, frosty blue now in the light, rested broodingly on Conway's face and did not waver. Conway's nerves tightened and tightened and a great unease grew within him.

He could have sworn that Krah knew who he was and why he had come to Iskar.

Reason told him that this was ridiculous. It had been many years since Krah had seen his father and in any case they were physically dissimilar. Nor did it seem likely that he should have preserved intact any of his father's mannerisms.

Yet he could not be sure and the uncertainty preyed upon him. The old man's bitter gaze was hard to bear.

The five sons neither moved nor spoke. Conway was sure that they understood the conversation perfectly and he reflected that, according to Krah, they had lived with Conna as his brothers. They seemed to be waiting, quite patiently, as though they had waited a long time and could afford to wait a little longer.

From time to time the girl stole a secret smouldering look at Conway and in spite of his uneasiness he grew very curious about her, wondering what devil of unrest lurked in her mind. She had a fascinating little face, full of odd lights and shadows where the glow of the fire touched it.

"Trade," said Krah at last. "Friendship. Study. They are good words. Let us eat now, and then rest, and I will think of these good words, which I have heard before from Conna."

"Look here," said Rohan rather testily, "I don't know what Conna did here but I see no reason to condemn us for his sins."

"We speak the truth," said Esmond gently. He glanced at Conway, waiting for him to ask the question that was his to ask. But Conway could not trust himself and finally Esmond's curiosity drove him to blurt out,

"What was Conna's crime?"

The old man turned upon him a slow and heavy look.

"Do not ask of me," he said. "Ask of her who waits, by the Lake of the Gone Forever."

∞

That name stung Conway's nerves like a whip-lash. He was afraid he had betrayed himself but if he started no one seemed to notice. The faces of Esmond and Rohan were honestly blank.

"The Lake of the Gone Forever," Esmond repeated. "What is that?"

"Let there be an end to talk," said Krah.

He turned and spoke to the girl in his own tongue and Conway caught the name Ciel. She rose obediently and began to serve the men, bringing the food on platters of thin carved stone. When she was done she sat down again by the fire and ate her own dinner from what was left, a slim, humble shadow whose eyes were no more humble than the eyes of a young panther. Conway stole her a smile and was rewarded by a brief curving of her red mouth.

When the meal was finished Krah rose and led

the Earthmen down a corridor. There were two cur-
tained doorways on each side and beyond them
were small windowless cells, with moss and furs
heaped soft to make a sleeping place.

Ciel came quietly to light the stone lamps and it
seemed to Conway that she took special note of the
cubicle he chose for his own.

"Sleep," said Krah, and left them. Ciel vanished
down a narrow back stair at the end of the hall.

The Earthmen stood for a moment, looking at
each other, and then Conway said sullenly, "Don't
ask me any questions because I don't know the
answers."

He turned and went into his chamber, dropping
the curtain behind him. In a vile mood he sat down
on the furs and lighted a cigarette, listening to Rohan's low half-angry voice telling Esmond that he
thought Rand was acting very strangely. Esmond
answered soothingly that the situation would be a
strain on anyone. Presently Conway heard them go
to bed. He blew out his lamp.

He sat for quite a while, in a terrible sweat of
nerves, thinking of Krah, thinking of the narrow valley that lay so nearly within his reach, thinking of
his father, hating him because of the black memories he had left behind on Iskar, so that now the
way was made very hard for his son.

Heaven help him if old Krah ever found out!

He waited for some time after everything was
still. Then, very carefully, he lifted the curtain and
stepped out into the hall.

He could see into the big main room. Four of
Krah's brawny sons slept on the furs by the embers.

The fifth sat crosslegged, his spear across his knees, and he did not sleep.

Conway glanced at the back stair. He was perfectly sure that it led to the women's quarters and that any venturing that way would bring the whole house around his ears. He shrugged and returned to his cell.

Stretched out on the furs he lay frowning into the dark, trying to think. He had not counted on the hatred of the Iskarians for Earthmen. He wondered for the hundredth time what his father had done to make all the women of Iskar wail a dirge when they were reminded of him. *Ask of her who waits, by the Lake of the Gone Forever . . .*

It didn't really matter. All that mattered was that they were under close watch and that it was a long way through the city for an Earthman to go and stay alive, even if he could get away from Krah.

Quite suddenly, he became aware that someone had crept down the hall outside and stopped at his door.

Without making a sound, Conway reached into the breast of his coverall and took hold of the gun that was hidden there. Then he waited.

The curtain moved a little, then a little more, and Conway lay still and breathed like a sleeping man. Faint light seeped in, outlining the widening gap of the curtain, showing clearly to Conway's eyes the figure that stood there, looking in.

Ciel, a little grey mouse in her hodden kirtle, her hair down around her shoulders like a cape of moonbeams. Ciel, the mouse with the wildcat's eyes.

Partly curious to see what she would do, partly

afraid that a whisper might attract attention from the other room, Conway lay still, feigning sleep.

For a long moment the girl stood without moving, watching him. He could hear the sound of her breathing, quick and soft. At last she took one swift step forward, then paused, as though her courage had failed her. That was her undoing.

The big man with the spear must have caught some flicker of movement, the swirl of her skirt, perhaps, for she had made no noise. Conway heard a short exclamation from the main room, and Ciel dropped the curtain and ran. A man's heavier footfalls pelted after her.

There was a scuffling at the other end of the hall and some low intense whispering. Conway crept over and pulled the curtain open a crack.

∞

Krah's son held the girl fast. He seemed to be lecturing her, more in sorrow than in anger, and then, deliberately and without heat, he began to beat her. Ciel bore it without a whimper but her eyes glazed and her face was furious.

Conway stepped silently out into the hall. The man's back was turned, but Ciel saw him. He indicated in pantomime what she should do and she caught the idea at once—or perhaps only the courage to do it.

Twisting like a cat, she set her teeth hard in the arm that held her.

The man let her go from sheer astonishment rather than pain. She fled down the woman-stair and he stood staring after her, his mouth wide open, as dumbfounded as though the innocent stones he walked on had risen suddenly and attacked him.

Conway got the feeling that such a thing had never happened before in the history of Iskar.

He leaned lazily against the wall and said aloud, "What's going on?"

Krah's son turned swiftly and the look of astonishment was replaced instantly by anger.

Conway made a show of yawning, as though he had just waked up. "Was that Ciel you were thrashing? She's a pretty big girl to be spanked." He grinned at the marks on the man's arm. "By the way, who is she—Krah's granddaughter?"

The answer came slowly in stumbling but understandable English.

"Krah's fosterling, daughter of my sister's friend. Ciel drank wickedness with mother's milk—wickedness she learn from my sister, who learn from Conna."

Quite suddenly the big man reached out and took Conway's jacket-collar in a throttling grip. Amazingly there were tears in his eyes and a deep, bitter rage.

"I will warn you, man of Earth," he said softly. "Go—go swiftly while you still live."

He flung Conway from him and turned away, back to the big room to brood again by the fire. And the Earthman was left to wonder whether the warning was for them all or for himself alone.

Hours later he managed to fall into an uneasy sleep, during which he dreamed again of the icy valley and the hidden terror that waited for him beyond the wall of rock. It seemed closer to him than ever before, so close that he awoke with a strangled cry. The stone cell was like a burial vault, and he left it, in a mood of desperation such as he

had never known before. Outside, the wind was
rising.

He came into the big room just as Krah entered
from the outer stair. Behind him, very white-faced
and proud, came Marcia Rohan. Her cheek was
bleeding and her lovely dark hair was wet and
draggled and her eyes hurt Conway to look at them.

"Marcia!" he cried and she ran to him, clinging
with tight hands like a frightened child. He held
her, answering her question before she could gasp it
out.

"Peter's safe," he said. "So is your father. They're
quite safe."

Old Krah spoke. There was a strange stony quality about him now, as though he had come to some
decision from which nothing could shake him. He
looked at Conway.

"Go," he said. "Call your—friends."

V WARRIOR OF ISKAR

Conway went, taking Marcia with him. Rohan
came out at once but Esmond was sleeping like
the dead. Apparently he had worked for hours by
the light of the stone lamp, making notes on the
people of Iskar.

Conway wondered, as he shook him awake,
whether any of that data was going to get safely
back to Earth. He knew, as certainly as he knew his
own name, that their stay here was ended and he
did not like the look in Krah's eyes.

"It's nobody's fault," Marcia was saying, over and

over. "I couldn't stand it. I didn't know whether you were alive or dead. Your radio didn't answer. I stole a sledge."

"Did you come alone?" asked Rohan.

"Yes."

"My God!" said Esmond softly, and picked her up in his arms. She laid her bleeding cheek against his and sobbed out. "They stoned me, Peter, the women did. The men brought me through the streets and the women stoned me."

Esmond's mild face became perfectly white. His eyes turned cold as the snow outside. He strode down the hall bearing Marcia in his arms, and his very step was stiff with fury. Rohan followed, crowding on his heels.

Old Krah never gave them a chance to speak. His five sons were ranged behind him and there was something very formidable about them, the five tall fair men and the tall old one who was like an ancient dog-wolf, white with years but still leader of the pack.

Krah held up his hand, and the Earthmen stopped. From her place by the fire Conway saw that Ciel was watching, staring with fascinated eyes at the alien woman who had come alone across the snow-fields to stand beside her men. The wind piped loud in the window embrasures, coming down from the high peaks with a rush and a snarl that set Conway's nerves to quivering with a queer excitement.

Krah spoke, looking at Marcia.

"For this I am sorry," he said. "But the woman should not have come." His frosty gaze rose then to take in all of them. "I offer you your lives. Go now —leave the city, leave Iskar and never return. If you do not I cannot save you."

"Why did they stone her?" demanded Esmond. He had one thing on his mind, no room for any other thought.

"Because she is different," said Krah simply, "and they fear her. She wears the garments of a man and she walks among men and these things are against their beliefs. Now, will you go?"

Esmond set the girl on her feet beside him, leaving his arm around her shoulders.

"*We* will go," he said. "And I will kill the first one who touches her."

Krah was gentleman enough to ignore the emptiness of that very sincere threat. He bowed his head.

"That," he said, "is as it should be."

He looked at Rohan.

"Don't worry," Robin snapped. "We'll leave and may you all go to the devil. This is a fit world for wolves and only wolves live in it!"

He started toward the door with Esmond and his daughter and Krah's eyes turned now to Conway. He asked softly, "And you, man who is called Rand?"

Conway shrugged, as though the whole thing were a matter of no importance to him. "Why should I want to stay?" His hands were shaking so that he thrust them into his pockets to conceal it and little trickles of sweat ran down his back. He nodded toward the window opening.

"There's a white wind blowing, Krah," he said. He drew himself erect, and his voice rose and rang. "It will catch us on the open plain. The woman will

surely die and perhaps the rest of us also. Neverthe-
less we will go. But let it be told through the city
that Krah has laid aside his manhood and put on a
woman's kirtle, for he has slain by stealth and not by
an honest spear!"

There was silence. Esmond stopped and turned in
the doorway, the girl held close in the circle of his
arm. Rohan stopped also, and their faces showed
the shock of this new thought.

Conway's heart beat like a trip-hammer. He was
bluffing—with all the resources of the sledge, he
thought, their chances of perishing were fairly
small, but there was just that germ of truth to pitch
it on. He was in agony while he waited to see if the
bluff had worked. Once outside the city walls he
knew that the Lake was lost to him as it had been
to his father.

After what seemed a very long time, Krah sighed
and said quietly, "The white wind. Yes. I had forgotten that the Earth stock is so weak."

A subtle change had come over the old man. It
was almost as though he too had been waiting
tensely for some answer and now it had come. A
deep, cold light crept into his eyes and burned
there, something almost joyous.

"You may stay," he said, "until the wind drops."

Then he turned sharply and went away down the
stair and his sons went with him.

Esmond stared after them and Conway was
amused to see the wolfish fury in his round, mild
face.

"He would have sent us out to die," said Esmond,
as though he wished he could kill Krah on the spot.
Danger to Marcia had transformed him from a sci-

entist into a rather primitive man. He turned to Conway.

"Thanks. You were right when you threatened them on the wall. And if anything happens to us I hope Frazer will make them pay for it!"

"Nothing's going to happen," said Conway. "Take Marcia back to the sleeping rooms—it's warmer there and she can lie down." He looked at Ciel and said sharply, "Can you understand me?"

She nodded, rather sullenly.

Conway pointed to Marcia. "Go with her. Bring water, something to put on that cut."

Ciel rose obediently but her eyes watched him slyly as she followed the Earth-folk out and down the hall.

Conway was left quite alone.

∞

He forced himself to stand still for a moment and think. He forced his heart to stop pounding and his hands to stop shaking. He could not force either his elation or his fear to leave him.

His way was clear now, at least for the moment. Why was it clear? Why had Krah gone away and taken his sons with him?

The wind swooped and screamed, lifting the curtains of hide, scattering snow on the floor. The white wind. Conway smiled. He had this chance. He would never have another.

He turned and went swiftly into the second corridor that opened opposite the one where the others had gone. It too contained four small sleeping rooms. One, however, was twice as large as the others and Conway was sure it belonged to Krah.

He slipped into it, closing the curtain carefully behind him.

All that he needed was there. All that he needed to make possible this one attempt that he could ever make upon the hidden valley of his dream.

He began to strip. The coverall, the thin jersey he wore underneath, the boots—everything that was of Earth. He must go through the city and he could not go as an Earthman. He had realized that there was only one way. He was glad of the white wind, for that would make his deception easier.

It would be cold and dangerous. But he was contemptuous of cold and beyond caring about danger. He was not going to eat his heart out and die, as his father had, because his one chance was lost forever.

In a few minutes Rand Conway was gone and in the stone chamber stood a nameless warrior of Iskar, a tall fair man wrapped in white furs, shod in rough hide boots and carrying a spear.

He retained two things, hidden carefully beneath his girdle—the little gun and a small vial, sheathed and stoppered with lead.

He turned, and Ciel was standing there, staring at him with wide astonished eyes.

She had slipped in so quietly that he had not heard her. And he knew that with one loud cry she could destroy all his plans.

In two swift angry strides he had caught her and put one hand hard over her mouth.

"Why did you come here?" he snarled. "What do you want?"

Her eyes looked up at him, steady and fierce as his own. He said, "Don't cry out or I'll kill you."

She shook her head and he took his hand away a little, not trusting her.

In slow painful English she said, "Take me with you."

"Where?"

"To Earth!"

It was Conway's turn to be astonished.

"But why?"

She said vehemently, "Earth-woman proud like man. Free."

So that was the smouldering anger she had in her. She was not patient like the other women of Iskar, for she had had a glimpse of something else. He remembered what Krah's son had said.

"Did Conna teach this?"

She nodded. "You take me?" she demanded. "You take me? I run away from Krah. Hide. You take me?"

Conway smiled. He liked her. They were the same kind, he and she—nursing a hopeless dream and risking everything to make it come true.

"Why not?" he said. "Sure, I'll take you."

Her joy was a savage thing. "If you lie," she whispered, "I kill you!" Then she kissed him.

He could tell it was the first time she had ever kissed a man. He could also tell that it was not going to be the last.

He thrust her away. "You must help me then. Take these." He handed her the bundle of his discarded clothing. "Hide them. Is there a back way from the house?"

"Yes."

"Show it to me. Then wait for me—and talk to no one. *No one*. Understand?"

"Where you go?" she asked him. The look of wonder came back into her eyes, and something of fear. "What you do, man of Iskar?"

He shook his head. "If you don't help me, if I die —you'll never see Earth."

"Come," she said, and turned.

Esmond and Rohan were still with Marcia, still full of their fears and angers—too full to worry about Conway, the outsider. The house of Krah was empty and silent except for the wind that swept through the embrasures with a shriek of laughter, like the laughter of wolves before the kill. Conway shivered, an animal twitching of the skin.

Ciel led him down a little stair and showed him a narrow passage built for the taking of offal from the slaughtering pen—woman's work, unfit for warriors.

"I wait," she said. Her fingers closed hard on the muscles of his arm. "Come back. Come soon!"

Her fear was not for him but for herself, lest now in this last hour her hope of freedom should be snatched away. Conway knew how she felt.

He bent and gave her a quick rough kiss. "I'll come back." Then he lifted the curtain of hide and slipped out into the darkness.

VI ECHOES OF A DREAM

The city was alive and vocal with the storm. The narrow streets shouted with it, the icy turrets of the houses quivered and rang. No snow was falling but the thick brown whiteness drove and leaped and whirled, carried across half of Iskar in the rush of the wind. Above the tumult the stars burned clear and steady in the sky.

The cold bit deep into Conway's flesh, iron barbs reaching for his heart. He drew the warm furs closer. His heartbeat quickened. His blood raced, fighting back the cold, and a strange exaltation came over him, something born out of the wild challenge of the wind. His pupils dilated, black and feral as a cat's. He began to walk, moving at a swift pace, setting his feet down surely on the glare of ice and the frozen stones.

He knew the direction he must take. He had determined that the first time he saw the city and it was burned into his memory for all time.

The way to the Lake, the Lake of the Gone Forever.

There were not many in the streets and those he passed gave him no second look. The white wind laid a blurring veil over everything and there was nothing about Conway to draw attention, a lean proud-faced man bent against the wind, a solitary warrior on an errand of his own.

Several times he tried to see if he were being followed. He could not forget Krah's face with its look of secret joy, nor cease to wonder uneasily why the old man had so suddenly left the Earthfolk unwatched. But he could see nothing in that howling smother.

He made sure of the little gun and smiled.

He found his way by instinct through the twisting streets, heading always in the same direction. The houses began to thin out. Quite suddenly they were gone and Conway stood in the open valley beyond. High above he could distinguish the shining peaks of the mountains lifting against the stars.

The full sweep of the wind met him here. He faced it squarely, laughing, and went on over the tumbled rocks. The touch of madness that had been in him ever since he reached Iskar grew into an overwhelming thing.

Part of his identity slipped away. The wind and the snow and the bitter rocks were part of him. He knew them and they knew him. They could not harm him. Only the high peaks looked down on him with threatening faces and it seemed to him that they were angry.

He was beginning to hear the echoes of his dream but they were still faint. He was not yet afraid. He was, in some strange way, happy. He had never been more alone and yet he did not feel lonely. Something wild and rough woke within him to meet the wild roughness of the storm and he felt a heady pride, a certainty that he could stand against any man of Iskar on his own ground.

The city was lost behind him. The valley had him between its white walls, vague and formless now, closing in upon him imperceptibly beyond the curtain of the storm. There was a curious timelessness about his journey, almost a spacelessness, as though he existed in a dimension of his own.

∞

And in that private world of his it did not seem strange nor unfitting that Ciel's voice should cry out thinly against the wind, that he should turn to see her clambering after him, nimble-footed, reckless with haste.

She reached him, spent with running. "Krah," she gasped. "He go ahead with four. One follow. I see.

I follow too." She made a quick, sharp gesture that took in the whole valley. "Trap. They catch. They kill. Go back."

Conway did not stir. She shook him, in a passion of urgency. "Go back! Go back now!"

He stood immovable, his head raised, his eyes questing into the storm, seeking the enemies he only half believed were there. And then, deep and strong across the wind, came the baying of a hunter's horn. It was answered from the other side of the valley. Another spoke, and another, and Conway counted them. Six—Krah and his five sons around and behind him, so that the way back to the city was closed.

Conway began to see the measure of the old man's cunning and he smiled, an animal baring of the teeth.

"You go," he said to Ciel. "They will not harm you."

"What I do they punish," she answered grimly. "No. You must live. They hunt you but I know trails, ways. Go many times to Lake of the Gone Forever. They not kill there. Come."

She turned but he caught her and would not let her go, full of a quick suspicion.

"Why do you care so much about me?" he demanded. "Esmond or Rohan could take you to Earth as well."

"Against Krah's will?" She laughed. "They are soft men, not like you." Her eyes met his fairly in the gloom, the black pupils wide and lustrous, looking deep into him so that he was strangely stirred. "But there is more," she said. "I never love before. Now I do. And—you are Conna's son."

Conway said, very slowly, "How did you know that?"

"Krah know. I hear him talk."

Then it had been a trap all along, from the beginning. Krah had known. The old man had given him one chance to go from Iskar and he had not taken it —and Krah had been glad. After that he had withdrawn and waited for Conway to come to him.

The girl said, "But I know without hearing. Now come, son of Conna."

She led off, swift as a deer, her skirts kilted above her knees. Conway followed and behind and around them the horns bayed and answered with the eager voices of hounds that have found the scent and will never let it go.

All down the long valley the hunters drove them and the mountain walls narrowed in and in, and the ringing call of the horns came closer. There was a sound of joy in them, and they were without haste. Never once, beyond the white spume of the blowing snow, did Conway catch a glimpse of his pursuers. But he knew without seeing that old Krah's face bore a bleak and bitter smile, the terrible smile of a vengeance long delayed.

Conway knew well where the hunt would end. The horns would cry him into the throat of the cleft, and then they would be silent. He would not be permitted to reach the Lake.

Again he touched the little gun and his face could not have been less savage than Krah's. He was not afraid of spears.

The girl led him swiftly, surely, among the tangled rocks and the spurs of ice, her skirt whipping

like a grey flag in the wind. High overhead the cold
peaks filled the sky, leaving only a thin rift of stars.
And suddenly, as though they were living things,
the walls of the valley rushed together upon him,
and the shouting of the horns rose to an exultant
clamor in his ears, racing, leaping toward him.

He flung up his head and yelled, an angry, defiant cry. Then there was silence, and through the
driven veils of snow he saw the shapes of men and
the dim glittering of spears.

He would have drawn the gun and loosed its
bright spray of instant sleep into the warriors. The
drug would keep them quiet long enough for him
to do what he had to do. But Ciel gave him no time.
She wrenched at him suddenly, pulling him almost
bodily into a crack between the rocks.

"Hurry!" she panted. *"Hurry!"*

The rough rock scraped him as he jammed his
way through. He could hear voices behind him,
loud and angry. It was pitch dark, even to his eyes,
but Ciel caught his furs and pulled him along—a
twist, a turn, a sharp corner that almost trapped him
where her smallness slipped past easily. Then they
were free again and he was running beside her, following her urgent breathless voice.

For a few paces he ran and then his steps slowed
and dragged at last to a halt. There was no wind
here in this sheltered place. There were no clouds
of blowing snow to blur his vision.

He stood in a narrow cleft between the mountains. On both sides the cliffs of ice rose up, sheer
and high and infinitely beautiful out of the powdery
drifts. The darkling air was full of whirling motes

of frost, like the dust of diamonds, and overhead the shining pinnacles stood clear against a sky of deepest indigo, spangled with great stars.

He stood in the narrow valley of his dream. And now at last he was afraid.

Truth and nightmare had come together like the indrawn flanks of the mountains and he was caught between them. Awake, aware of the biting cold and the personal sensation of his flesh, still the nameless terror of the dream beset him.

He could almost see the remembered shadow of his father weeping by the sheathed rocks that hid the end of the cleft, almost hear that cry of loss—*I can never go back to the Lake of the Gone Forever!*

He knew that now he was going to see the end of the dream. He would not wake this time before he passed the barrier rocks. The agonizing fear that had no basis in his own life stood naked in his heart and would not go.

He had known, somehow, all his life that this time must come. Now that it was here he found that he could not face it. The formless baseless terror took his strength away and not all his reasoning could help him. He could not go on.

And yet he went, as always, slowly forward through the drifting snow.

He had forgotten Ciel. He was surprised when she caught at him, urging him to run. He had forgotten Krah.

He remembered only the despairing words whispered back and forth by the cold lips of the ice. *Gone Forever . . . Gone Forever . . . !* He looked up and the golden stars wheeled above him in the dark blue sky. The beauty of them was evil and the shimmering turrets of the ice were full of lurking laughter.

Nightmare—and he walked in it broad awake.

It was not far. The girl dragged him on, drove him, and he obeyed automatically, quickening his slow pace. He did not fight. He knew that it was no use. He went on as a man walks patiently to the gallows.

He passed the barrier rocks. He was not conscious now of movement. In a sort of stasis, cold as the ice, he entered the cave that opened beyond them and looked at last upon the Lake of the Gone Forever.

VII BLACK LAKE

It was black, that Lake. Utterly black and very still, lying in its ragged cradle of rock under the arching roof where, finally, the mountains met.

A strange quality of blackness, Conway thought, and shuddered deeply with the hand of nightmare still upon him. He stared into it, and suddenly, as though he had always known, he realized that the lake was like the pupil of a living eye, having no light of its own but receiving into itself all light, all impression.

He saw himself reflected in that great unstirring eye and Ciel beside him. Where the images fell there were faint lines of frosty radiance, as though the substance of the Lake were graving upon itself in glowing acid the memory of what it saw.

Soft-footed from behind him came six other shadows—Krah and his five sons—and Conway could see that a great anger was upon them. But they had left their spears outside.

"We may not kill in this place," said Krah slowly, "but we can keep you from the thing you would do."

"How do you know what I mean to do?" asked Conway and his face was strange as though he listened to distant voices speaking in an unknown tongue.

Krah answered, "As your father came before you, so you have come—to steal from us the secret of the Lake."

"Yes," said Conway absently. "Yes, that is so."

The old man and his tall sons closed in around Conway and Ciel came and stood between them.

"Wait!" she said.

For the first time they acknowledged the presence of the girl.

"For your part in this," said Krah grimly, "you will answer later."

"No!" she cried defiantly. "I answer no! Listen. Once you love Conna. You learn from him good things. His mate happy, not slave. He bring wisdom to Iskar—but now you hate Conna, you forget.

"I go to Earth with Conna's son. But first he must come here. It is right he come. But you kill, you full of hate for Rand—so I come to save him."

She stood up to Krah, the little grey mouse transfigured into a bright creature of anger, blazing with it, alive with it—

"All my life—hate! Because of Rand you try to kill memory of Conna, you teach people hate and fear. But my mother learn from Conna. I learn from her —and I no forget! Rand happy, free. My mother know—and I no forget."

It came to Conway with a queer shock that she was not speaking of him but of another Rand. He listened to the girl and there was a stillness in him as deep and lightless as the stillness of the lake.

"You not kill, old man," Ciel whispered. "Not yet. Let him see, let him know. Then kill if he is evil."

She swung around.

"Son of Conna! Look into the Lake. All the dead of Iskar buried here. They gone forever but memory lives. All come here in life, so that the Lake remember. Look, son of Conna, and think of your father!"

Still with that strange quiet heavy on his heart Rand Conway looked into the Lake and did as Ciel told him to do. Krah and his sons looked also and did not move.

At first there was nothing but the black infinite depth of the Lake. *It is semi-liquid,* said his father's notes, the notes he had kept secret from everyone— *and in this heavy medium are suspended particles of some transuranic element—perhaps an isotope of uranium itself that is unknown to us. Incalculable wealth—incalculable pain! My soul is there, lost in the Lake of the Gone Forever.*

Rand Conway stood waiting and the thought of his father was very strong in him. His father, who had died mourning that he could never come back.

Slowly, slowly, the image of his father took shape in the substance of the lake, a ghostly picture painted with a brush of cold firs against the utter dark.

It was no projection of Rand Conway's own memory mirrored there, for this was not the man he had known, old before his time and broken with longing. This man was young, and his face was happy.

He turned and beckoned to someone behind him, and the shadowy figure of a girl came into the circle of his outstretched arm. They stood together, and a harsh sob broke from old Krah's throat. Conway knew that his father and the pale-haired lovely girl had stood where he stood now on the brink of the Lake and looked down as he was looking, that their images might be forever graven into the heart of the strange darkness below.

They kissed. And Ciel whispered, "See her face, how it shines with joy."

The figures moved away and were gone. Conway watched, beyond emotion, beyond fear. Some odd portion of his brain even found time to theorize on the electrical impulses of thought and how they could shape the free energy in the unknown substance of the Lake, so that it became almost a second subconscious mind for everyone on Iskar, storehouse from which the memories of a race could be called at will.

The eye of the Lake had seen and now, at the urging of those intense minds, it produced the pictures it had recorded like the relentless unreeling of

∞

some cosmic film.

Rand Conway watched, step by step, the disintegration of a man's soul. And it was easy for him to understand, since his own life had been ruled by that same consuming greed.

Conna came again and again to the Lake, alone. It seemed to hold a terrible fascination for him. After all he was a prospector, with no goal before him for many years but the making of a big strike. Finally he brought instruments and made tests and after that the fascination turned to greed and the greed in time to a sort of madness.

It was a madness that Conna fought against and he had reason. The girl came again. With her this time were Krah and his sons, all younger and less bitter than now, and others whom Conway did not know. It was obviously a ritual visit and it had to do with the new-born child the girl held in her arms.

Rand Conway's heart tightened until it was hardly beating. And through the frozen numbness that held him the old fear began to creep back, the nightmare fear of the dream, where something was hidden from him that he could not endure to see.

Conna, the girl, and a new-born child.

I cannot escape. I cannot awake from this.

Conna's inward struggle went on. He must have suffered the tortures of hell, for it was plain that what he meant to do would cut him off from all he loved. But he was no longer quite sane. The Lake mocked him, taunted him with its unbelievable wealth, and he could not forget it.

The last time that Conna came to the Lake of the Gone Forever, he had laid aside the furs and the spear of Iskar, and put on again his spaceman's leather and the holstered gun. He brought with him a leaden container, to take back proof of the Lake and what it held.

But while he worked to take his sample—the sample that would, in the end, mean the destruction of the Lake and all it meant to Iskar—the pale-haired girl came, her eyes full of pain and pleading, and the child was with her, a well-grown boy now, nearly two years old.

And Conna's son cried out suddenly and swayed

so that Ciel put out her hand to him, and he clung to it, with the universe dark and reeling about him.

I know now! I know the fear behind the dream!

Within the Lake the shadowy child watched with uncomprehending horror how his mother snatched the little heavy box from his father's hands—his father who had grown so strange and violent and was dressed so queerly in black.

He watched how his mother wept and cried out to his father, pleading with him, begging him to stop and think and not destroy them all.

But Conna would not stop. He had fought his fight and lost and he would not stop.

He tried to take the box again. There was a brief moment when he and the girl swayed together on the brink of the Lake. And then—quickly, so very quickly that she had only time for one look at Conna as she fell—the girl fell over the edge. The disturbed cold fires of the Lake boiled up and overwhelmed her and there was no sight of her ever again.

The child screamed and ran to the edge of the rock. He too would have fallen if his father had not held him back.

For a long while Conna stood there, holding the whimpering child in his arms. The girl had taken the leaden box with her but Conna had forgotten that. He had forgotten everything except that his mate was dead, that he had killed her. And it was as though Conna too had died.

Then he turned and fled, taking the boy with him.

∞

The surface of the Lake was as it had been, dark and still.

Rand Conway went slowly to his knees. He felt dully as though he had been ill for a long time. All the strength was gone out of him. He stayed there on the icy rock, motionless and silent, beyond feeling, beyond thought. He was only dimly aware that Ciel knelt beside him, that he was still clinging to her hand.

Presently he looked up at Krah.

"That was why you gave me my chance to leave Iskar. I was Conna's son—but I was the son of your daughter, too."

"For her sake," said Krah slowly, "I would have let you go."

Conway nodded. He was very tired. So many things were clear to him now. Everything had changed, even the meaning of the name he bore. Rand. It was all very strange, very strange indeed.

Ciel's hand was warm and comforting in his.

Slowly he took from his girdle the little gun and the leaden vial, and let them drop and slide away.

"Father of my mother," he said to Krah, "let me live." He bowed his head and waited.

But Krah did not answer. He only said, "Does Conna live?"

"No. He paid for her life, Krah, with his own."

"That is well," whispered the old man. And his sons echoed, "That is well."

Conway stood up. His mood of weary submission had left him.

"Krah," he said, "I had no part in Conna's crime and for my own—you know. I am of your blood, old man. I will not beg again. Take your spears and give me mine and we will see who dies!"

A ghost of a grim smile touched Krah's lips. He

looked deeply into his grandson's eyes and presently he nodded.

"You are of my blood. And I think you will not forget. There will be no taking of spears."

He stepped back and Conway said, "Let the others go. They know nothing of the Lake and will not know. I will stay on Iskar."

He caught Ciel to him. "One thing, Krah. Ciel must not be punished."

Again the grim smile. Some of the frosty cold had gone from Krah's eyes. In time, Conway thought, the old bitterness might vanish altogether.

"You have stood together by the Lake," said Krah. "It is our record of marriage. So if Ciel is beaten that is up to you."

He turned abruptly and left the cavern and his sons went with him. Slowly, having yet no words to say, Rand Conway and Ciel followed them—into the narrow valley that held no further terrors for the man who had at last found his own world.

Behind them, the Lake of the Gone Forever lay still and black, as though it pondered over its memories, the loves and hatreds and sorrows of a world gathered from the beginning of time, safe there now until the end of it.

THE
SECOND
INQUISITION
JOANNA RUSS

"The Second Inquisition" tells of a young girl, troubled by the problems of adolescence, and a mysterious visitor who will have a lasting effect on her life. Joanna Russ has written a moving story about a girl chafing against the bonds of her culture and her time.

If a man can resist the influences of his townsfolk, if he can cut free from the tyranny of neighborhood gossip, the world has no terrors for him; there is no second inquisition.

—John Jay Chapman

I often watched our visitor reading in the living room, sitting under the floor lamp near the new, standing Philco radio, with her long, long legs stretched out in front of her and the pool of light on her book revealing so little of her face: brownish, coppery features so marked that she seemed to be a kind of freak and hair that was reddish black but so rough that it looked like the things my mother used for scouring pots and pans. She read a great deal, that summer. If I ventured out of the archway,

where I was not exactly hiding but only keeping in
the shadow to watch her read, she would often raise
her face and smile silently at me before beginning to
read again, and her skin would take on an abrupt,
surprising pallor as it moved into the light. When
she got up and went into the kitchen with the gracefulness of a stork, for something to eat, she was almost too tall for the doorways; she went on legs like
a spider's, with long swinging arms and a little body
in the middle, the strange proportions of the very
tall. She looked down at my mother's plates and
dishes from a great, gentle height, remarkably absorbed; and asking me a few odd questions, she
would bend over whatever she was going to eat,
meditate on it for a few moments like a giraffe, and
then straightening up back into the stratosphere, she
would pick up the plate in one thin hand, curling
around it fingers like legs, and go back gracefully
into the living room. She would lower herself into
the chair that was always too small, curl her legs
around it, become dissatisfied, settle herself, stretch
them out again—I remember so well those long,
hard, unladylike legs—and begin again to read.

She used to ask, "What is that? What is that? And
what is this?" but that was only at first.

My mother, who disliked her, said she was from
the circus and we ought to try to understand and be
kind. My father made jokes. He did not like big
women or short hair—which was still new in places
like ours—or women who read, although she was interested in his carpentry and he liked that.

But she was six feet four inches tall; this was in
1925.

My father was an accountant who built furniture

as a hobby; we had a gas stove which he actually fixed once when it broke down and some outdoor tables and chairs he had built in the back yard. Before our visitor came on the train for her vacation with us, I used to spend all my time in the back yard, being underfoot, but once we had met her at the station and she shook hands with my father—I think she hurt him when she shook hands—I would watch her read and wish that she might talk to me.

. She said: "You are finishing high school?"

I was in the archway, as usual; I answered yes.

She looked up at me again, then down at her book. She said, "This is a very bad book." I said nothing. Without looking up, she tapped one finger on the shabby hassock on which she had put her feet. Then she looked up and smiled at me. I stepped tentatively from the floor to the rug, as reluctantly as if I were crossing the Sahara; she swung her feet away and I sat down. At close view her face looked as if every race in the world had been mixed and only the worst of each kept; an American Indian might look like that, or Ikhnaton from the encyclopedia, or a Swedish African, a Maori princess with the jaw of a Slav. It occurred to me suddenly that she might be a Negro, but no one else had ever seemed to think so, possibly because nobody in our town had ever seen a Negro. We had none. They were "colored people."

She said, "You are not pretty, yes?"

I got up. I said, "My father thinks you're a freak."

"You are sixteen," she said, "sit down," and I sat down. I crossed my arms over my breasts because they were too big, like balloons. Then she said, "I am reading a very stupid book. You will take it away from me, yes?"

"No," I said.

"You must," she said, "or it will poison me, sure as God," and from her lap she plucked up *The Green Hat: A Romance*, gold letters on green binding, last year's best-seller which I had had to swear never to read, and she held it out to me, leaning back in her chair with that long arm doing all the work, the book enclosed in a cage of fingers wrapped completely around it. I think she could have put those fingers around a basketball. I did not take it.

"Go on," she said, "read it, go on, go away," and I found myself back at the archway, by the foot of the stairs with *The Green Hat: A Romance* in my hand. I turned it so the title was hidden. She was smiling at me and had her arms folded back under her head. "Don't worry," she said. "Your body will be in fashion by the time of the next war." I met my mother at the top of the stairs and had to hide the book from her; my mother said, "Oh, the poor woman!" She was carrying some sheets. I went to my room and read through almost the whole night, hiding the book in the bedclothes when I was through. When I slept, I dreamt of Hispano-Suizas, of shingled hair and tragic eyes; of women with painted lips who had Affairs, who went night after night with Jews to low dives, who lived as they pleased, who had miscarriages in expensive Swiss clinics; of midnight swims, of desperation, of money, of illicit love, of a beautiful Englishman and getting into a taxi with him while wearing a cloth-of-silver cloak and a silver turban like the ones shown in the society pages of the New York City newspapers.

Unfortunately our guest's face kept recurring in my dream, and because I could not make out whether she was amused or bitter or very much of both, it really spoiled everything.

∞

My mother discovered the book the next morning. I found it next to my plate at breakfast. Neither my mother nor my father made any remark about it; only my mother kept putting out the breakfast things with a kind of tender, reluctant smile. We all sat down, finally, when she had put out everything, and my father helped me to rolls and eggs and jam. Then he took off his glasses and folded them next to his plate. He leaned back in his chair and crossed his legs. Then he looked at the book and said in a tone of mock surprise, "Well! What's this?"

I didn't say anything. I only looked at my plate.

"I believe I've seen this before," he said. "Yes, I believe I have." Then he asked my mother, "Have you seen this before?" My mother made a kind of vague movement with her head. She had begun to butter some toast and was putting it on my plate. I knew she was not supposed to discipline me; only my father was. "Eat your egg," she said. My father, who had continued to look at *The Green Hat: A Romance* with the same expression of unvarying surprise, finally said:

"Well! This isn't a very pleasant thing to find on a Saturday morning, is it?"

I still didn't say anything, only looked at my food. I heard my mother say worriedly, "She's not eating, Ben," and my father put his hand on the back of my chair so I couldn't push it away from the table, as I was trying to do.

"Of course you have an explanation for this," he said. "Don't you?"

I said nothing.

"Of course she does," he said, "doesn't she, Bess? You wouldn't hurt your mother like this. You wouldn't hurt your mother by stealing a book that you knew you weren't supposed to read and for very good reason, too. You know we don't punish you. We talk things over with you. We try to explain. Don't we?"

I nodded.

"Good," he said. "Then where did this book come from?"

I muttered something; I don't know what.

"Is my daughter angry?" said my father. "Is my daughter *being rebellious?*"

"She told you all about it!" I blurted out. My father's face turned red.

"Don't you dare talk about your mother that way!" he shouted, standing up. "Don't you *dare* refer to your mother in that way!'"

"Now, Ben—" said my mother.

"Your mother is the soul of unselfishness," said my father, "and don't you forget it, missy; your mother has worried about you since the day you were born and if you don't appreciate that, you can damn well—"

"Ben!" said my mother, shocked.

"I'm sorry," I said, and then I said, "I'm very sorry, Mother." My father sat down. My father had a mustache and his hair was parted in the middle and slicked down; now one lock fell over the part in front and his whole face was gray and quivering. He was staring fixedly at his coffee cup. My mother came over and poured coffee for him; then she took the coffeepot into the kitchen and when she came back she had milk for me. She put the glass of milk on the table near my plate. Then she sat down again. She smiled tremblingly at my father; then she put her hand over mine on the table and said:

"Darling, why did you read that book?"

"Well?" said my father from across the table.

There was a moment's silence. Then:

"Good morning!"

and

"Good morning!"

and

"Good morning!"

said our guest cheerfully, crossing the dining room in two strides, and folding herself carefully down into her breakfast chair, from where her knees stuck out, she reached across the table, picked up *The Green Hat*, propped it up next to her plate and began to read it with great absorption. Then she looked up. "You have a very progressive library," she said. "I took the liberty of recommending this exciting book to your daughter. You told me it was your favorite. You sent all the way to New York City on purpose for it, yes?"

"I don't—I quite—" said my mother, pushing back her chair from the table. My mother was trembling from head to foot and her face was set in an expression of fixed distaste. Our visitor regarded first my mother and then my father, bending over them tenderly and with exquisite interest. She said:

"I hope you do not mind my using your library."

"No no no," muttered my father.

"I eat almost for two," said our visitor modestly, "because of my height. I hope you do not mind that?"

"No, of course not," said my father, regaining control of himself.

"Good. It is all considered in the bill," said the visitor, and looking about at my shrunken parents, each hurried, each spooning in the food and avoiding her gaze, she added deliberately:

"I took also another liberty. I removed from the endpapers certain—ah—drawings that I did not think bore any relation to the text. You do not mind?"

And as my father and mother looked in shocked surprise and utter consternation—at each other—she said to me in a low voice, "Don't eat. You'll make yourself sick," and then smiled warmly at the two of them when my mother went off into the kitchen and my father remembered he was late for work. She waved at them. I jumped up as soon as they were out of the room.

"There were no drawings in that book!" I whispered.

"Then we must make some," said she, and taking a pencil off the whatnot, she drew in the endpapers of the book a series of sketches: the heroine sipping a soda in an ice-cream parlor, showing her legs and very chic; in a sloppy bathing suit and big grin, holding up a large fish; driving her Hispano-Suiza into a tree only to be catapulted straight up into the air; and in the last sketch landing demure and coy in the arms of the hero, who looked violently surprised. Then she drew a white mouse putting on lipstick, getting married to another white mouse in a church, the two entangled in some manner I thought I should not look at, the lady mouse with a big belly and two little mice inside (who were playing chess), then the little mice coming out in separate envelopes and finally the whole family having a picnic, with some things around the picnic basket that I did not recognize and underneath in capital letters "I did not bring up my children to test cigarettes." This left me blank. She laughed and rubbed it out, saying that it was out of date. Then she drew a white mouse with a rolled-up umbrella chasing my mother. I picked that up and looked at it for a while; then I tore it into pieces, and tore the others into pieces as well. I said, "I don't think you have the slightest right to—" and stopped. She was looking at me with—not anger exactly—not warning exactly—I found I had to sit down. I began to cry.

"Ah! The results of practical psychology," she said dryly, gathering up the pieces of her sketches. She took matches off the whatnot and set fire to the pieces in a saucer. She held up the smoking match between her thumb and forefinger, saying, "You see? The finger is—shall we say, perception?—but the thumb is money. The thumb is hard."

"You oughtn't to treat my parents that way!" I said, crying.

"You ought not to tear up my sketches," she said calmly.

"Why not! Why not!" I shouted.

"Because they are worth money," she said, "in some quarters. I won't draw you any more," and indifferently taking the saucer with the ashes in it in one palm, she went into the kitchen. I heard her voice and then my mother's, and then my mother's again, and then our visitor's in a tone that would've made a rock weep, but I never found out what they said.

∞

I passed our guest's room many times at night that summer, going in by the hall past her rented room where the second-floor windows gave out onto the dark garden. The electric lights were always on brilliantly. My mother had sewn the white curtains because she did everything like that and had bought the furniture at a sale: a marble-topped bureau, the wardrobe, the iron bedstead, an old Victrola against the wall. There was usually an open book on the bed. I would stand in the shadow of the open doorway and look across the bare wood floor, too much of it and all as slippery as the sea, bare wood waxed and shining in the electric light. A black dress hung on the front of the wardrobe and a pair of shoes like my mother's, T-strap shoes with thick heels. I used to wonder if she had silver evening slippers inside the wardrobe. Sometimes the open book on the bed was Wells's *The Time Machine* and then I would talk to the black glass of the window, I would say to the transparent reflections and the black branches of trees that moved beyond it:

"I'm only sixteen."

"You look eighteen," she would say.

"I know," I would say. "I'd like to be eighteen. I'd like to go away to college. To Radcliffe, I think."

She would say nothing, out of surprise.

"Are you reading Wells?" I would say then, leaning against the door jamb. "I think that's funny. No-

body in this town reads anything; they just think
about social life. I read a lot, however. I would like
to learn a great deal."

She would smile then, across the room.

"I did something funny once," I would go on. "I
mean funny ha-ha, not funny peculiar." It was a real
line, very popular. "I read *The Time Machine* and
then I went around asking people were they Eloi
or were they Morlocks; everyone liked it. The point
is which you would be if you could, like being an
optimist or a pessimist or do you liked bobbed hair."
Then I would add, "Which are you?" and she would
only shrug and smile a little more. She would prop
her chin on one long, long hand and look into my
eyes with her black Egyptian eyes and then she
would say in her curious hoarse voice:

"It is you who must say it first."

"I think," I would say, "that you are a Morlock,"
and sitting on the bed in my mother's rented room
with *The Time Machine* open beside her, she would
say:

"You are exactly right. I am a Morlock. I am a
Morlock on vacation. I have come from the last
Morlock meeting, which is held out between the
stars in a big goldfish bowl, so all the Morlocks have
to cling to the inside walls like a flock of black bats,
some right side up, some upside down, for there is
no up and down there, clinging like a flock of black
crows, like a chestnut burr turned inside out. There
are half a thousand Morlocks and we rule the
worlds. My black uniform is in the wardrobe."

"I knew I was right," I would say.

"You are always right," she would say, "and you
know the rest of it, too. You know what murderers

we are and how terribly we live. We are waiting for the big bang when everything falls over and even the Morlocks will be destroyed; meanwhile I stay here waiting for the signal and I leave messages clipped to the frame of your mother's amateur oil painting of Main Street because it will be in a museum some day and my friends can find it; meanwhile I read *The Time Machine*."

Then I would say, "Can I come with you?" leaning against the door.

"Without you," she would say gravely, "all is lost," and taking out from the wardrobe a black dress glittering with stars and a pair of silver sandals with high heels, she would say, "These are yours. They were my great-grandmother's, who founded the Order. In the name of Trans-Temporal Military Authority." And I would put them on.

It was almost a pity she was not really there.

∞

Every year in the middle of August the Country Club gave a dance, not just for the rich families who were members but also for the "nice" people who lived in frame houses in town and even for some of the smart, economical young couples who lived in apartments, just as if they had been in the city. There was one new, red-brick apartment building downtown, four stories high, with a courtyard. We were supposed to go, because I was old enough that year, but the day before the dance my father became ill with pains in his left side and my mother had to stay home to take care of him. He was propped up on pillows on the living-room daybed, which we had pulled out into the room so he could watch what my mother was doing with the garden

out back and call to her once in a while through
the windows. He could also see the walk leading up
to the front door. He kept insisting that she was doing things all wrong. I did not even ask if I could
go to the dance alone. My father said:

"Why don't you go out and help your mother?"

"She doesn't want me to," I said. "I'm supposed to
stay here," and then he shouted angrily, "Bess!
Bess!" and began to give her instructions through
the window. I saw another pair of hands appear in
the window next to my mother's and then our guest
—squatting back on her heels and smoking a cigarette—pulling up weeds. She was working quickly
and efficiently, the cigarette between her teeth. "No,
not that way!" shouted my father, pulling on the
blanket that my mother had put over him. "Don't
you know what you're doing! Bess, you're ruining
everything! Stop it! Do it right!" My mother looked
bewildered and upset; she passed out of the window
and our visitor took her place; she waved to my
father and he subsided, pulling the blanket up
around his neck. "I don't like women who smoke,"
he muttered irritably. I slipped out through the
kitchen.

My father's toolshed and working space took up
the farther half of the back yard; the garden was
spread over the nearer half, part kitchen garden,
part flowers, and then extended down either side
of the house where we had fifteen feet or so of space
before a white slat fence and the next people's side
yard. It was an on-and-offish garden, and the house
was beginning to need paint. My mother was working in the kitchen garden, kneeling. Our guest was

standing, pruning the lilac trees, still smoking. I said:

"Mother, can't I go, can't I *go!*" in a low voice.

My mother passed her hand over her forehead and called "Yes, Ben!" to my father.

"Why *can't* I go!" I whispered. "Ruth's mother and Betty's mother will be there. Why couldn't you call Ruth's mother and Betty's mother?"

"*Not that way!*" came a blast from the living-room window. My mother sighed briefly and then smiled a cheerful smile. "Yes, Ben!" she called brightly. "I'm listening." My father began to give some more instructions.

"Mother," I said desperately, "why couldn't you—"

"Your father wouldn't approve," she said, and again she produced a bright smile and called encouragingly to my father. I wandered over to the lilac trees where our visitor, in her usual nondescript black dress, was piling the dead wood under the tree. She took a last puff on her cigarette, holding it between thumb and forefinger, then ground it out in the grass and picked up in both arms the entire lot of dead wood. She carried it over to the fence and dumped it.

"My father says you shouldn't prune trees in August," I blurted suddenly.

"Oh?" she said.

"It hurts them," I whispered.

"Oh," she said. She had on gardening gloves, though much too small; she picked up the pruning shears and began snipping again through inch-thick trunks and dead branches that snapped explosively when they broke and whipped out at your face. She was efficient and very quick.

I said nothing at all, only watched her face.

She shook her head decisively.

"But Ruth's mother and Betty's mother—" I began, faltering.

"I never go out," she said.

"You needn't stay," I said, placating.

"Never," she said. "Never at all," and snapping free a particularly large, dead, silvery branch from the lilac tree, she put it in my arms. She stood there looking at me and her look was suddenly very severe, very unpleasant, something foreign, like the look of somebody who had seen people go off to battle to die, the "movies" look but hard, hard as nails. I knew I wouldn't get to go anywhere. I thought she might have seen battles in the Great War, maybe even been in some of it. I said, although I could barely speak:

"Were you in the Great War?"

"Which great war?" said our visitor. Then she said, "No, I never go out," and returned to scissoring the trees.

∞

On the night of the dance my mother told me to get dressed, and I did. There was a mirror on the back of my door, but the window was better; it softened everything; it hung me out in the middle of a black space and made my eyes into mysterious shadows. I was wearing pink organdy and a bunch of daisies from the garden, not the wild kind. I came downstairs and found our visitor waiting for me at the bottom: tall, bare-armed, almost beautiful, for she'd done something to her impossible hair and the rusty reddish black curled slickly like the best photographs. Then she moved and I thought she was altogether beautiful, all black and rippling silver like a Paris dress or better still a New York dress, with a silver band around her forehead like an Indian princess's and silver shoes with the chunky heels and the one strap over the instep.

She said, "Ah! don't you look nice," and then in a whisper, taking my arm and looking down at me with curious gentleness, "I'm going to be a bad chaperone. I'm going to disappear."

"Well!" said I, inwardly shaking, "I hope I can take care of myself, I should think." But I hoped she wouldn't leave me alone and I hoped that no one would laugh at her. She was really incredibly tall.

"Your father's going to sleep at ten," said my mother. "Be back by eleven. Be happy." And she kissed me.

But Ruth's father, who drove Ruth and I and Ruth's mother and our guest to the Country Club, did not laugh. And neither did anyone else. Our visitor seemed to have put on a strange gracefulness with her dress, and a strange sort of kindliness, too, so that Ruth, who had never seen her but had only heard rumors about her, cried out, "Your friend's lovely!" and Ruth's father, who taught mathematics at high school, said (clearing his throat), "It must be lonely staying in," and our visitor said only, "Yes. Oh yes. It is," resting one immensely long, thin, elegant hand on his shoulder like some kind of unwinking spider, while his words and hers went echoing out into the night, back and forth, back and forth, losing themselves in the trees that rushed past the headlights and massed blackly to each side.

"Ruth wants to join a circus!" cried Ruth's mother, laughing.

"I do *not!*" said Ruth.

"You *will* not," said her father.

"I'll do exactly as I please," said Ruth with her nose in the air, and she took a chocolate cream out of her handbag and put it in her mouth.

"You will *not!*" said Ruth's father, scandalized.

"Daddy, you know I will too," said Ruth, serenely though somewhat muffled, and under cover of the dark she wormed over to me in the back seat and passed, from her hot hand to mine, another chocolate cream. I ate it; it was unpleasantly and piercingly sweet.

"Isn't it *glorious?*" said Ruth.

The Country Club was much more bare than I had expected, really only a big frame building with a veranda three-quarters of the way around it and not much lawn, but there was a path down front to two stone pillars that made a kind of gate and somebody had strung the gate and the whole path with colored Chinese lanterns. That part was lovely. Inside, the whole first story was one room, with a varnished floor like the high school gym, and a punch table at one end and ribbons and Chinese lanterns hung all over the ceiling. It did not look quite like the movies but everything was beautifully painted. I had noticed that there were wicker armchairs scattered on the veranda. I decided it was "nice." Behind the punch table was a flight of stairs that led to a gallery full of tables where the grown-ups could go and drink (Ruth insisted they would be bringing real liquor for "mixes," although of course

the Country Club had to pretend not to know about
that) and on both sides of the big room French
windows that opened onto the veranda and the
Chinese lanterns, swinging a little in the breeze.
Ruth was wearing a better dress than mine. We
went over to the punch table and drank punch
while she asked me about our visitor and I made up
a lot of lies. "You don't know anything," said Ruth.
She waved across the room to some friends of hers;
then I could see her start dancing with a boy in
front of the band, which was at the other end of
the room. Older people were dancing and people's
parents, some older boys and girls. I stayed by the
punch table. People who knew my parents came
over and talked to me; they asked me how I was
and I said I was fine; then they asked me how my
father was and I said he was fine. Someone offered
to introduce me to someone but I said I knew him.
I hoped somebody would come over. I thought I
would skirt around the dance floor and try to talk
to some of the girls I knew, but then I thought I
wouldn't; I imagined myself going up the stairs
with Iris March's lover from *The Green Hat* to sit
at a table and smoke a cigarette or drink something.
I stepped behind the punch table and went out
through the French windows. Our guest was a few
chairs away with her feet stretched out, resting on
the lowest rung of the veranda. She was reading a
magazine with the aid of a small flashlight. The
flowers planted around the veranda showed up a
little in the light from the Chinese lanterns: shadowy clumps and masses of petunias, a few of the
white ones springing into life as she turned the page
of her book and the beam of the flashlight moved

in her hand. I decided I would have my cigarette in a long holder. The moon was coming up over the woods past the Country Club lawns, but it was a cloudy night and all I could see was a vague lightening of the sky in that direction. It was rather warm. I remembered something about *an ivory cigarette holder flaunting at the moon.* Our visitor turned another page. I thought that she must have been aware of me. I thought again of Iris March's lover, coming out to get me on the "terrace'" when somebody tapped me on the shoulder; it was Ruth's father. He took me by the wrist and led me to our visitor, who looked up and smiled vaguely, dreamily, in the dark under the colored lanterns. Then Ruth's father said:

"What do you know? There's a relative of yours inside!" She continued to smile but her face stopped moving; she smiled gently and with tenderness at the space next to his head for the barely perceptible part of a moment. Then she completed the swing of her head and looked at him, still smiling, but everything had gone out of it.

"How lovely," she said. Then she said, "Who is it?"

"I don't know," said Ruth's father, "but he's tall, looks just like you—beg pardon. He says he's your cousin."

"*Por nada,*" said our guest absently, and getting up, she shook hands with Ruth's father. The three of us went back inside. She left the magazine and flashlight on the chair; they seemed to belong to the Club. Inside, Ruth's father took us up the steps to the gallery and there, at the end of it, sitting at one of the tables, was a man even taller than our visi-

tor, tall even sitting down. He was in evening dress
while half the men at the dance were in business
suits. He did not really look like her in the face; he
was a little darker and a little flatter of feature; but
as we approached him, he stood up. He almost
reached the ceiling. He was a giant. He and our visitor did not shake hands. The both of them looked at
Ruth's father, smiling formally, and Ruth's father
left us; then the stranger looked quizzically at me
but our guest had already sunk into a nearby seat,
all willowiness, all grace. They made a handsome
couple. The stranger brought a silver-inlaid flask
out of his hip pocket; he took the pitcher of water
that stood on the table and poured some into a clean
glass. Then he added whisky from the flask, but our
visitor did not take it. She only turned it aside,
amused, with one finger, and said to me, "Sit down,
child," which I did. Then she said:

"Cousin, how did you find me?"

"*Par chance*, cousin," said the stranger. "By luck."
He screwed the top back on the flask very deliberately and put the whole thing back in his pocket. He
began to stir the drink he had made with a wooden
muddler provided by the Country Club.

"I have endured much annoyance," he said,
"from that man to whom you spoke. There is not a
single specialized here; they are all half-brained:
scattered and stupid."

"He is a kind and clever man," said she. "He
teaches mathematics."

"The more fool he," said the stranger, "for the
mathematics he thinks he teaches!" and he drank
his own drink. Then he said, "I think we will go
home now."

"Eh! This person?" said my friend, drawing up the ends of her lips half scornfully, half amused. "Not this person!"

"Why not this person, who knows me?" said the strange man.

"Because," said our visitor, and turning deliberately away from me, she put her face next to his and began to whisper mischievously in his ear. She was watching the dancers on the floor below, half the men in business suits, half the couples middle-aged, Ruth and Betty and some of their friends, and some vacationing college boys. The band was playing the fox-trot. The strange man's face altered just a little; it darkened; he finished his drink, put it down, and then swung massively in his seat to face me.

"Does she go out?" he said sharply.

"Well?" said our visitor idly.

"Yes," I said. "Yes, she goes out. Every day."

"By car or on foot?" I looked at her but she was doing nothing. Her thumb and finger formed a circle on the table.

"I don't know," I said.

"Does she go on foot?" he said.

"No," I blurted suddenly, "no, by car. Always by car!" He sat back in his seat.

"You would do anything," he said conversationally. "The lot of you."

"I?" she said. "I'm not dedicated. I can be reasoned with."

After a moment of silence he said, "We'll talk."

She shrugged. "Why not?"

"This girl's home," he said. "I'll leave fifteen minutes after you. Give me your hand."

"Why?" she said. "You know where I live. I am not going to hide in the woods like an animal."

"Give me your hand," he repeated. "For old time's sake." She reached across the table. They clasped hands and she winced momentarily. Then they both rose. She smiled dazzlingly. She took me by the wrist and led me down the stairs while the strange man called after us, as if the phrase pleased him, "For old time's sake!" and then "Good health, cousin! Long life!" while the band struck up a march in ragtime. She stopped to talk to five or six people, including Ruth's father who taught mathematics in the high school, and the band leader, and Betty, who was drinking punch with a boy from our class. Betty said to me under her breath. "Your daisies are coming loose. They're gonna fall off." We walked through the parked cars until we reached one that she seemed to like; they were all open and some owners left the keys in them; she got in behind the wheel and started up.

"But this *isn't your car!*" I said. "You can't just—"

"Get in!" I slid in next to her.

"It's after ten o'clock," I said. "You'll wake up my father. Who—"

"Shut up!"

I did. She drove very fast and very badly. Halfway home she began to slow down. Then suddenly she laughed out loud and said very confidentially, not to me but as if to somebody else:

"I told him I had planted a Neilsen loop around here that would put half of Greene County out of phase. A dead man's control. I had to go out and stop it every week."

"What's a Neilsen loop?" I said.

"Jam yesterday, jam tomorrow, but never jam to-day," she quoted.

"What," said I emphatically, "is a—"

"I've told you, baby," she said, "and you'll never know more, God willing," and pulling into our driveway with a screech that would have wakened the dead, she vaulted out of the car and through the back door into the kitchen, just as if my mother and father had both been asleep or in a cataleptic trance, like those in the works of E. A. Poe. Then she told me to get the iron poker from the garbage burner in the back yard and find out if the end was still hot; when I brought the thing in, she laid the hot end over one of the flames of the gas stove. Then she rummaged around under the sink and came up with a bottle of my mother's Clear House-hold Ammonia.

"That stuff's awful," I said. "If you let that get in your eyes—"

"Pour some in a water glass," she said, handing it to me. "Two-thirds full. Cover it with a saucer. Get another glass and another saucer and put all of them on the kitchen table. Fill your mother's water pitcher, cover that, and put that on the table."

"Are you going to *drink* that?" I cried, horrified, halfway to the table with the covered glass. She merely pushed me. I got everything set up, and also pulled three chairs up to the kitchen table; I then went to turn off the gas flame, but she took me by the hand and placed me so that I hid the stove from the window and the door. She said, "Baby, what is the specific heat of iron?"

"What?" I said.

"You know it, baby," she said. "What is it?"

I only stared at her.

"But you know it, baby," she said. "You know it better than I. You know that your mother was burning garbage today and the poker would still be hot. And you know better than to touch the iron pots when they come fresh from the oven, even though the flame is off, because iron takes a long time to heat up and a long time to cool off, isn't that so?"

I nodded.

"And you don't know," she added, "how long it takes for aluminum pots to become cold because nobody uses aluminum for pots yet. And if I told you how scarce the heavy metals are, and what a radionic oven is, and how the heat can go *through* the glass and the plastic and even the ceramic lattice, you wouldn't know what I was talking about, would you?"

"No," I said, suddenly frightened, "no, no, no."

"Then you know more than some," she said. "You know more than me. Remember how I used to burn myself, fiddling with your mother's things?" She looked at her palm and made a face. "He's coming," she said. "Stand in front of the stove. When he asks you to turn off the gas, turn it off. When I say 'Now,' hit him with the poker."

"I can't," I whispered. "He's too big."

"He can't hurt you," she said. "He doesn't dare; that would be an anachronism. Just do as I say."

"What are you going to *do*?" I cried.

"When I say 'Now,'" she repeated serenely, "hit him with the poker," and sitting down by the kitchen table, she reached into a jam-jar of odds and ends my mother kept on the windowsill and

began to buff her nails with a Lady Marlene emery
stick. Two minutes passed by the kitchen clock.
Nothing happened. I stood there with my hand on
the cold end of the poker, doing nothing until I felt
I had to speak, so I said, "Why are you making a
face? Does something hurt?"

"The splinter in my palm," she said calmly. "The
bastard."

"Why don't you take it out?"

"It will blow up the house."

He stepped in through the open kitchen door.

Without a word she put both arms palm upward
on the kitchen table and without a word he took
off the black cummerbund of his formal dress and
flicked it at her. It settled over both her arms and
then began to draw tight, molding itself over her
arms and the table like a piece of black adhesive,
pulling her almost down onto it and whipping one
end around the table edge until the wood almost
cracked. It seemed to paralyze her arms. He put
his finger to his tongue and then to her palm, where
there was a small black spot. The spot disappeared.
He laughed and told me to turn off the flame, so I
did.

"Take it off," she said then.

He said, "Too bad you are in hiding or you too
could carry weapons," and then, as the edge of the
table let out a startling sound like a pistol shot, he
flicked the black tape off her arms, returning it to
himself, where it disappeared into his evening
clothes.

"Now that I have used this, everyone knows
where we are," he said, and he sat down in a

kitchen chair that was much too small for him and lounged back in it, his knees sticking up into the air.

Then she said something I could not understand. She took the saucer off the empty glass and poured water into it; she said something unintelligible again and held it out to him, but he motioned it away. She shrugged and drank the water herself. "Flies," she said, and put the saucer back on. They sat in silence for several minutes. I did not know what to do; I knew I was supposed to wait for the word "Now" and then hit him with the poker, but no one seemed to be saying or doing anything. The kitchen clock, which I had forgotten to wind that morning, was running down at ten minutes to eleven. There was a cricket making a noise close outside the window and I was afraid the ammonia smell would get out somehow; then, just as I was getting a cramp in my legs from standing still, our visitor nodded. She sighed, too, regretfully. The strange man got to his feet, moved his chair carefully out of the way and pronounced:

"Good. I'll call them."

"Now?" said she.

I couldn't do it. I brought the poker in front of me and stood there with it, holding it in both hands. The stranger—who almost had to stoop to avoid our ceiling—wasted only a glance on me, as if I were hardly worth looking at, and then concentrated his attention on her. She had her chin in her hands. Then she closed her eyes.

"Put that down, please," she said tiredly.

I did not know what to do. She opened her eyes

and took the saucer off the other glass on the table.

"Put that down right now," she said, and raised the glass of ammonia to her lips.

I swung at him clumsily with the poker. I was not sure what happened next, but I think he laughed and seized the end—the hot end—and then threw me off balance just as he screamed, because the next thing I knew I was down on all fours watching her trip him as he threw himself at her, his eyes screwed horribly shut, choking and coughing and just missing her. The ammonia glass was lying empty and broken on the floor; a brown stain showed where it had rolled off the white tablecloth on the kitchen table. When he fell, she kicked him in the side of the head. Then she stepped carefully away from him and held out her hand to me; I gave her the poker, which she took with the folded edge of the tablecloth, and reversing it so that she held the cold end, she brought it down with immense force—not on his head, as I had expected, but on his windpipe. When he was still, she touched the hot end of the poker to several places on his jacket, passed it across where his belt would be, and to two places on both of his shoes. Then she said to me, "Get out."

I did, but not before I saw her finishing the job on his throat, not with the poker but with the thick heel of her silver shoe.

When I came back in, there was nobody there. There was a clean, rinsed glass on the drainboard next to the wooden sink and the poker was propped up in one corner of the sink with cold water running on it. Our visitor was at the stove, brewing tea in my mother's brown teapot. She was standing under the Dutch cloth calendar my mother, who was very modern, kept hanging on the wall. My mother pinned messages on it; one of them read "Be Careful. Except for the Bathroom, More Accidents Occur in the Kitchen Than in Any Other Part of the House."

"Where—" I said, "where is—is—"

"Sit down," she said. "Sit down here," and she put me into *his* seat at the kitchen table. But there was no *he* anywhere. She said, "Don't think too much." Then she went back to the tea and just as it was ready to pour, my mother came in from the living room, with a blanket around her shoulders, smiling foolishly and saying, "Goodness, I've been asleep, haven't I?"

"Tea?" said our visitor.

"I fell asleep just like that," said my mother, sitting down.

"I forgot," said our visitor. "I borrowed a car. I felt ill. I must call them on the telephone," and she went out into the hall, for we had been among the first to have a telephone. She came back a few minutes later. "Is it all right?" said my mother. We drank our tea in silence.

"Tell me," said our visitor at length. "How is your radio reception?"

"It's perfectly fine," said my mother, a bit offended.

"That's fine," said our visitor, and then, as if she couldn't control herself, "because you live in a dead area, you know, thank God, a dead area!"

My mother said, alarmed, "I beg your par—"

"Excuse me," said our visitor, "I'm ill," and she put her cup into her saucer with a clatter, got up and went out of the kitchen. My mother put one hand caressingly over mine.

"Did anyone . . . insult her at the dance?" said my mother, softly.

"Oh no," I said.

"Are you sure?" my mother insisted. "Are you perfectly sure? Did anyone comment? Did anyone say anything about her appearance? About her height? Anything that was not nice?"

"Ruth did," I said. "Ruth said she looked like a giraffe." My mother's hand slid off mine; gratified, she got up and began to gather up the tea things. She put them into the sink. She clucked her tongue over the poker and put it away in the kitchen closet. Then she began to dry the glass that our visitor had previously rinsed and put on the drainboard, the glass that had held ammonia.

"The poor woman," said my mother, drying it. "Oh, the poor woman."

∞

Nothing much happened after that. I began to get my books ready for high school. Blue cornflowers sprang up along the sides of the house and my father, who was better now, cut them down with a scythe. My mother was growing hybrid ones in the back flower garden, twice as tall and twice as big as any of the wild ones; she explained to me about hybrids and why they were bigger, but I forgot it. Our visitor took up with a man, not a nice man, really, because he worked in the town garage and was Polish. She didn't go out but used to see him in the kitchen at night. He was a thickset, stocky man, very blond, with a real Polish name, but everyone called him Bogalusa Joe because he had spent fifteen years in Bogalusa, Louisiana (he called it "Loosiana") and he talked about it all the time. He had a theory, that the colored people were just like us and that in a hundred years everybody would be all mixed up, you couldn't tell them apart. My mother was very advanced in her views but she wouldn't ever let me talk to him. He was very respectful; he called her "Ma'am," and didn't use any bad language, but he never came into the living room. He would always meet our visitor in the kitchen or sometimes on the swing in the back garden. They would drink coffee; they would play cards. Sometimes she would say to him, "Tell me a story, Joe. I love a good story," and he would talk about hiding out in Loosiana; he had had to hide out from somebody or something for three years in the middle of the Negroes and they had let him in and let him work and took care of him. He said, "The coloreds are like anybody." Then he said, "The nigras are smarter. They got to be. They ain't nobody's fool. I had a black girl for two years once was the smartest woman in the world. Beautiful woman. Not beautiful like a white, though, not the same."

"Give us a hundred years," he added, "and it'll all be mixed."

"Two hundred?" said our visitor, pouring coffee. He put a lot of sugar in his; then he remarked that he had learned that in Bogalusa. She sat down. She was leaning her elbows on the table, smiling at him. She was stirring her own coffee with a spoon. He looked at her a moment, and then he said softly:

"A black woman, smartest woman in the world. You're black, woman, ain't you?"

"Part," she said.

"Beautiful woman," he said. "Nobody knows?"

"They know in the circus," she said. "But there they don't care. Shall I tell you what we circus people think of you?"

"Of who?" he said, looking surprised.

"Of all of you," she said. "All who aren't in the circus. All who can't do what we can do, who aren't the biggest or the best, who can't kill a man barehanded or learn a new language in six weeks or slit a man's jugular at fifteen yards with nothing but a pocketknife or climb the Greene County National Bank from the first story to the sixth with no equipment. I can do all that."

"I'll be damned," said Bogalusa Joe softly.

"We despise you," she said. "That's what we do. We think you're slobs. The scum of the earth! The world's fertilizer, Joe, that's what you are."

"Baby, you're blue," he said. "You're blue tonight," and then he took her hand across the table, but not the way they did it in the movies, not the way they did it in the books; there was a look on his face I had never seen on anyone's before, not the high school boys when they put a line over on a girl, not on grown-ups, not even on the brides and grooms because all that was romantic or showing off or "lust" and he only looked infinitely kind, infinitely concerned. She pulled her hand out of his. With the same faint, detached smile she had had all night, she pushed back her chair and stood up. She said flatly:

"All I can do! What good is it?" She shrugged. She added, "I've got to leave tomorrow." He got up and put his arm around her shoulders. I thought

that looked bad because he was actually a couple
of inches shorter than she was.

He said, "Baby, you don't have to go." She was
staring out into the back garden, as if looking miles
away, miles out, far away into our vegetable patch
or our swing or my mother's hybrids, into something
nobody could see. He said urgently, "Honey, look—"
and then, when she continued to stare, pulling her
face around so she had to look at him, both his
broad, mechanic's hands under her chin, "Baby,
you can stay with me." He brought his face closer to
hers. "Marry me," he said suddenly. She began to
laugh. I had never heard her laugh like that before.
Then she began to choke. He put his arms around
her and she leaned against him, choking, making
funny noises like someone with asthma, finally clapping her hands over her face, then biting her palm,
heaving up and down as if she were sick. It took me
several seconds to realize that she was crying. He
looked very troubled. They stood there: she cried,
he, distressed—and I hiding, watching all of it. They
began to walk slowly toward the kitchen door.
When they had gone out and put out the light, I
followed them out into the back garden, to the
swing my father had rigged up under the one big
tree: cushions and springs to the ground like a piece
of porch furniture, big enough to hold four people.
Bushes screened it. There was a kerosene lantern
my father had mounted on a post, but it was out. I
could just about see them. They sat for a few minutes, saying nothing, looking up through the tree
into the darkness. The swing creaked a little as our
visitor crossed and uncrossed her long legs. She
took out a cigarette and lit it, obscuring their faces

with even that little glow: an orange spot that wavered up and down as she smoked, making the darkness more black. Then it disappeared. She had ground it out underfoot in the grass. I could see them again. Bogalusa Joe, the garage mechanic, said:

"Tomorrow?"

"Tomorrow," she said. Then they kissed each other. I liked that; it was all right; I had seen it before. She leaned back against the cushions of the swing and seemed to spread her feet in the invisible grass; she let her head and arms fall back onto the cushion. Without saying a word, he lifted her skirt far above her knees and put his hand between her legs. There was a great deal more of the same business and I watched it all, from the first twistings to the stabbings, the noises, the life-and-death battle in the dark. The word *Epilepsy* kept repeating itself in my head. They got dressed and again began to smoke, talking in tones I could not hear. I crouched in the bushes, my heart beating violently.

I was horribly frightened.

∞

She did not leave the next day, or the next or the next; and she even took a dress to my mother and asked if she could have it altered somewhere in town. My school clothes were out, being aired in the back yard to get the mothball smell out of them. I put covers on all my books. I came down one morning to ask my mother whether I couldn't have a jumper taken up at the hem because the magazines said it was all right for young girls. I expected a fight over it. I couldn't find my mother in the hall or the kitchen so I tried the living room, but before

I had got halfway through the living-room arch,
someone said, "Stop there," and I saw both my parents sitting on two chairs near the front door, both
with their hands in their laps, both staring straight
ahead, motionless as zombies.

I said, "Oh for heaven's sake, what're you—"

"Stop there," said the same voice. My parents did
not move. My mother was smiling her social smile.
There was no one else in the room. I waited for a
little while, my parents continuing to be dead, and
then from some corner on my left, near the new
Philco, our visitor came gliding out, wrapped in my
mother's spring coat, stepping softly across the rug
and looking carefully at all the living-room windows. She grinned when she saw me. She tapped
the top of the Philco radio and motioned me in.
Then she took off the coat and draped it over the
radio.

She was in black from head to foot.

I thought *black*, but black was not the word; the
word was *blackness*, dark beyond dark, dark that
drained the eyesight, something I could never have
imagined even in my dreams, a black in which there
was no detail, no sight, no nothing, only an awful,
desperate dizziness, for her body—the thing was
skin-tight, like a diver's costume or an acrobat's—
had actually disappeared, completely blotted out except for its outline. Her head and bare hands floated
in the air. She said, "Pretty, yes?" Then she sat cross-
legged on our radio. She said, "Please pull the curtains," and I did, going from one to the other and
drawing them shut, circling my frozen parents and
then stopping short in the middle of the quaking
floor. I said, "I'm going to faint." She was off the

radio and into my mother's coat in an instant; holding me by the arm, she got me onto the living-room couch and put her arm around me, massaging my back. She said, "Your parents are asleep." Then she said, "You have known some of this. You are a wonderful little pickup but you get mixed up, yes? All about the Morlocks? The Trans-Temporal Military Authority?"

I began to say "Oh oh oh oh—" and she massaged my back again.

"Nothing will hurt you," she said. "Nothing will hurt your parents. Think how exciting it is! Think! The rebel Morlocks, the revolution in the Trans-Temporal Military Authority."

"But I— I—" I said.

"We are friends," she continued gravely, taking my hands. "We are real friends. You helped me. We will not forget that," and slinging my mother's coat off onto the couch, she went and stood in front of the archway. She put her hands on her hips, then began rubbing the back of her neck nervously and clearing her throat. She turned around to give me one last look.

"Are you calm?" she said. I nodded. She smiled at me. "Be calm," she said softly. "*Sois tranquille.* We're friends," and then she put herself to watching the archway. She said once, almost sadly, "Friends," and then stepped back and smiled again at me.

The archway was turning into a mirror. It got misty, then bright, like a cloud of bright dust, then almost like a curtain; and then it was a mirror, although all I could see in it was our visitor and myself, not my parents, not the furniture, not the living room.

Then the first Morlock stepped through.

And the second.

And the third.

And the others.

Oh, the living room was filled with giants! They were like her, like her in the face, like her in the bodies of the very tall, like her in the black uniforms, men and women of all the races of the earth, everything mixed and huge as my mother's hybrid flowers but a foot taller than our visitor, a flock of black ravens, black bats, black wolves, the professionals of the future world, perched on our furniture, on the Philco radio, some on the very walls and drapes of the windows as if they could fly, hovering in the air as if they were out in space where the Morlocks meet, half a thousand in a bubble between the stars.

Who rule the worlds.

Two came through the mirror who crawled on the rug, both in diving suits and goldfish-bowl helmets, a man and a woman, fat and shaped like seals. They lay on the rug breathing water (for I saw the specks flowing in it, in and out of strange frills around their necks, the way dust moves in air) and looking up at the rest with tallowy faces. Their suits bulged. One of the Morlocks said something to one of the seals and one of the seals answered, fingering a thing attached to the barrels on its back, gurgling.

Then they all began to talk.

Even if I'd know what language it was, I think it would have been too fast for me; it was very fast, very hard-sounding, very urgent, like the numbers pilots call in to the ground or something like that, like a code that everybody knows, to get things done as fast as you can. Only the seal-people talked slowly, and they gurgled and stank like a dirty beach. They did not even move their faces except to make little round mouths, like fish. I think I was put to sleep for a while (or maybe I just fell asleep) and then it was something about the seal-people, with the Morlock who was seated on the radio joining in—and then general enough—and then something going round the whole room—and then that fast, hard urgent talk between one of the Morlocks and my friend. It was still business, but they looked at *me*; it was awful to be looked at and yet I felt numb; I wished I were asleep; I wanted to cry because I could not understand a word they were saying. Then my friend suddenly shouted; she stepped back and threw both arms out, hands extended and fingers spread, shaking violently. She was shouting instead of talking, shouting desperately about something, pounding one fist into her palm, her face contorted, just as if it was not business. The other Morlock was breathing quickly and had gone pale with rage. He whispered something, something very venomous. He took from his black uniform, which could have hidden anything, a silver dime, and holding it up between thumb and forefinger, he said in perfectly clear English, while looking at me:

"In the name of the war against the Trans-Tempor—"

She had jumped him in an instant. I scrambled up; I saw her close his fist about the dime with her own; then it was all a blur on the floor until the two of them stood up again, as far as they could get from each other, because it was perfectly clear that they hated each other. She said very distinctly, "*I do insist.*" He shrugged. He said something short and sharp. She took out of her own darkness a knife—only a knife—and looked slowly about the room at each person in it. Nobody moved. She raised her eyebrows.

"*Tchal grozny?*"

The seal-woman hissed on the floor, like steam coming out of a leaky radiator. She did not get up but lay on her back, eyes blinking, a woman encased in fat.

"You?" said my friend insultingly. "You will stain the carpet."

The seal-woman hissed again. Slowly my friend walked toward her, the others watching. She did not bend down, as I had expected, but dove down abruptly with a kind of sidewise roll, driving herself into the seal-woman's side. She had planted one heel on the stomach of the woman's diving suit; she seemed to be trying to tear it. The seal-woman caught my friend's knife-hand with one glove and was trying to turn it on my friend while she wrapped the other gloved arm around my friend's neck. She was trying to strangle her. My friend's free arm was extended on the rug; it seemed to me that she was either leaning on the floor or trying to pull herself free. Then again everything went into a sudden blur. There was a gasp, a loud, mechanical click; my friend vaulted up and backward, dropping her knife and clapping one hand to her left eye. The seal-woman was turning from side to side on the floor, a kind of shudder running from her feet to her head, an expressionless flexing of her body and face. Bubbles were forming in the goldfish-bowl helmet. The other seal-person did not move. As I watched, the water began falling in the seal-woman's helmet and then it was all air. I supposed she was dead. My friend, our visitor, was standing in the middle of the room, blood welling from under her hand; she was bent over with pain and her face was horribly distorted but not one person in that room moved to touch her.

"Life—" she gasped, "for life. Yours," and then she crashed to the rug. The seal-woman had slashed open her eye. Two of the Morlocks rushed to her then and picked up her and her knife; they were dragging her toward the mirror in the archway when she began muttering something.

"Damn your sketches!" shouted the Morlock she had fought with, completely losing control of himself. "We are at war; Trans-Temp is at our heels; do you think we have time for dilettantism? You presume on being that woman's granddaughter! We are fighting for the freedom of fifty billions of people, not for your scribbles!" and motioning to the others, who immediately dragged the body of the seal-woman through the mirror and began to follow it themselves, he turned to me.

"You!" he snapped. "You will speak to nobody of this. Nobody!"

I put my arms around myself.

"Do not try to impress anyone with stories," he added contemptuously. "You are lucky to live," and without another look he followed the last of the Morlocks through the mirror, which promptly disappeared. There was blood on the rug, a few inches from my feet. I bent down and put my fingertips in

it, and then with no clear reason, I put my fingers
to my face.

"—come back," said my mother. I turned to face
them, the wax manikins who had seen nothing.

"Who the devil drew the curtains!" shouted my
father. "I've told you" (to me) "that I don't like
tricks, young lady, and if it weren't for your
mother's—"

"Oh, Ben, Ben! She's had a nosebleed!" cried my
mother.

They told me later that I fainted.

∞

I was in bed a few days, because of the nosebleed, but then they let me up. My parents said I
probably had had anemia. They also said they had
seen our visitor off at the railroad station that morning, and that she had boarded the train as they
watched her: tall, frizzy-haired, freakish, dressed
in black down to between the knees and ankles,
legged like a stork and carrying all her belongings
in a small valise. "Gone to the circus," said my
mother. There was nothing in the room that had
been hers, nothing in the attic, no reflection in the
window at which she had stood, brilliantly lit
against the black night, nothing in the kitchen and
nothing at the Country Club but tennis courts over-
grown with weeds. Joe never came back to our
house. The week before school I looked through all
my books, starting with *The Time Machine* and
ending with *The Green Hat;* then I went downstairs
and looked through every book in the house. There
was nothing. I was invited to a party; my mother
would not let me go. Cornflowers grew around the

house. Betty came over once and was bored. One afternoon at the end of summer, with the wind blowing through the empty house from top to bottom and everybody away, nobody next door, my parents in the back yard, the people on the other side of us gone swimming, everybody silent or sleeping or off somewhere—except for someone down the block whom I could hear mowing the lawn—I decided to sort and try on all my shoes. I did this in front of a full-length mirror fastened to the inside of my closet door. I had been taking off and putting on various of my winter dresses, too, and I was putting one particular one away in a box on the floor of the closet when I chanced to look up at the inside of the closet door.

She was standing in the mirror. It was all black behind her, like velvet. She was wearing something black and silver, half-draped, half-nude, and there were lines on her face that made it look sectioned off, or like a cobweb; she had one eye. The dead eye radiated spinning white light, like a Catherine wheel. She said:

"Did you ever think to go back and take care of yourself when you are little? Give yourself advice?"

I couldn't say anything.

"I am not you," she said, "but I have had the same thought and now I have come back four hundred and fifty years. Only there is nothing to say. There is never anything to say. It is a pity, but natural, no doubt."

"Oh, please!" I whispered. "Stay!" She put one foot up on the edge of the mirror as if it were the threshold of a door. The silver sandal she had worn at the Country Club dance almost came into my bedroom: thick-heeled, squat, flaking, as ugly as sin; new lines formed on her face and all over her bare skin, ornamenting her all over. Then she stepped back; she shook her head, amused; the dead eye waned, filled again, exploded in sparks and went out, showing the naked socket, ugly, shocking and horrible.

"Tcha!" she said, "my grandma thought she would bring something hard to a world that was soft and silly but nice, and now it's silly and not so nice and the hard has got too hard and the soft too soft and my great-grandma—it is she who founded the order —is dead. Not that it matters. Nothing ends, you see. Just keeps going on and on."

"But you can't *see*!" I managed. She poked herself in the temple and the eye went on again.

"Bizarre," she said. "Interesting. Attractive. Stone blind is twice as good. I'll tell you my sketches."

"But you don't—you can't—" I said.

"The first," she said, lines crawling all over her, "is an Eloi having the Go-Jollies, and that is a bald, fat man in a toga, a frilled bib, a sunbonnet and shoes you would not believe, who has a crystal ball in his lap and from it wires plugged into his eyes and his nose and his ears and his tongue and his head, just like your lamps. That is an Eloi having the Go-Jollies."

I began to cry.

"The second," she went on, "is a Morlock working; and that is myself holding a skull, like *Hamlet*, only if you look closely at the skull you will see it is the world, with funny things sticking out of the seas and the polar ice caps, and that it is full of people. Much too full. There are too many of the worlds, too."

"If you'll *stop*—!" I cried.

"They are all pushing each other off," she continued, "and some are falling into the sea, which is a pity, no doubt, but quite natural, and if you will look closely at all these Eloi you will see that each one is holding his crystal ball, or running after an animated machine which runs faster than he, or watching another Eloi on a screen who is cleverer and looks fascinating, and you will see that under the fat the man or woman is screaming, screaming and dying.

"And my third sketch," she said, "which is a very little one, shows a goldfish bowl full of people in black. Behind that is a smaller goldfish bowl full of people in black, which is going after the first goldfish bowl, and behind the second is a third, which is going after the second, and so on, or perhaps they alternate; that would be more economical. Or perhaps I am only bitter because I lost my eye. It's a personal problem."

I got to my feet. I was so close I could have touched her. She crossed her arms across her breast and looked down at me; she then said softly, "My dear, I wished to take you with me, but that's impossible. I'm very sorry," and looking for the first time both serious and tender, she disappeared behind a swarm of sparks.

I was looking at myself. I had recently made, passionately and in secret, the uniform of the Trans-Temporal Military Authority as I thought it ought to look: a black tunic over black sleeves and black tights. The tights were from a high school play I had been in the year before and the rest was cut out of the lining of an old winter coat. That was what I was wearing that afternoon. I had also fastened a silver curling-iron to my waist with a piece of cord. I put one foot up in the air, as if on the threshold of the mirror, and a girl in ragged black stared back at me. She turned and frantically searched the entire room, looking for sketches, for notes, for specks of silver paint, for anything at all. Then she sat down on my bed. She did not cry. She said to me, "You look idiotic." Someone was still mowing the lawn outside, probably my father. My mother would be clipping, patching, rooting up weeds; she never stopped. Someday I would join a circus, travel to the moon, write a book; after all, I had helped kill a man. I had been somebody. It was all nonsense. I took off the curling-iron and laid it on the bed. Then I undressed and got into my middy-blouse and skirt and I put the costume on the bed in a heap. As I walked toward the door of the room, I turned to take one last look at myself in the mirror and at my strange collection of old clothes. For a moment something else moved in the mirror, or I thought it did, something behind me or to one side, something menacing, something half-blind, something heaving slowly like a shadow, leaving perhaps behind it faint silver flakes like the shadow of a shadow or some carelessly dropped coins, something glittering, something somebody had left on the edge of vision, dropped by accident in the dust and cobwebs of an attic. I wished for it violently; I stood and clenched my fists; I almost cried; I wanted something to come out of the mirror and strike me

dead. If I could not have a protector, I wanted a
monster, a mutation, a horror, a murderous disease,
anything! anything at all to accompany me downstairs so that I would not have to go down alone.

Nothing came. Nothing good, nothing bad. I
heard the lawnmower going on. I would have to
face by myself my father's red face, his heart disease, his temper, his nasty insistencies. I would have
to face my mother's sick smile, looking up from the
flowerbed she was weeding, always on her knees
somehow, saying before she was ever asked, "Oh
the poor woman. Oh the poor woman."

And quite alone.

No more stories.

THE POWER OF TIME

JOSEPHINE SAXTON

Josephine Saxton depicts two women, a twentieth-century English housewife and her eccentric descendant from the future. The interface between their very different lives, and its effects on each of them, are skillfully portrayed by this British author.

"It shouldn't present much difficulty if you approach it in a positive way," I said to the Chief of the Mohawks, Flying Spider. "Your tribe is expert in this kind of thing. All you have to do is number the parts, get it translated in terms of a computer jigsaw multi-dimensional complex, get the land measured out and prepared in advance—new sewage systems and so on, flood the Trent and the Soar to form an island—aw, cummarn Spider, you can do it. . . ."

My power complex that I never thought about, working on his power complex that he nurtured and lived by. He was very powerful and his tribe had worked for five hundred years to make it so, and other tribes too; time was when Flying Spider's ancestors had been a very small minority, working

high above the streets of New York, building on
higher bits, repairing, cleaning. Work other people
would not do, nor could do; the Mohawks took
naturally to heights. Yes, Flying Spider was powerful all right: he owned the whole of Manhattan Island. His ancestors had sold out for twenty-four dollars worth of trinkets, and he had bought it back
for an unimaginable sum. He didn't only own the
land either, but every stone of every building, every
plate of glass, scrap of metal, nut, bolt, electric wire.
He owned all the companies too except for DuPont
on the eleventh floor of the Empire State who had
a special concession in return for making all the
Tribal Costumes free of charge and before any other
order. Like Spider for instance always wore full re-
galia, masses of gorgeous feathers but rain- and
stain-proofed; you could have poured printing ink
all over him and it would have brushed off when
dry. Not that anyone would ever do such a thing,
not to Flying Spider. So Spider was powerful and
rich and so was I. There were only about a hundred
of us as rich as that, all descended from former depressed peoples and groups, like about five genera-
tions back my great-multi-great grandmother was
secretary to the Stir-Crazy Housewives League of
Loughborough Ltd., England. That's what I call
progress, I mean, out of the sixteen million or so
people left on this planet after the Great Emigra-
tions, I should end up being one of the Elite. Everybody else lived well too, but we hundred or so
Top People decided how well. I not only wanted to
get one up on Spider though (that's just a kind of
hobby we had, buying things from each other and
then proving it more valuable than the price paid),

I wanted Manhattan Island for myself. You see, my family have always had a kind of thing about Manhattan, it's been a kind of Mecca for them although I can't say why; it has just been a thing to sit at Mother's knee and listen to tales of Manhattan. Families have things like that. But I had never been there. Yes I know it sounds a bit odd what with travel so easy, anti-grav sledge would have got me there in half an hour but not only had I always been rich and powerful I had always been—well, English Eccentric, which is a type you probably never heard of but in my case it took the form of never leaving the village where I was born. Travel never appealed to me; three-D-TV was as much of the outside world as I wanted to experience. I had everything I wanted right there in East Leake which was Reservation Country for the Ancient Britons, a small village that made two leaps in its development; first in the thirteenth century when it got itself built round the church, and second around the twentieth when they added a few thousand houses, a supermarket, a library and a health-center. And a couple of Boutiques which were places where the women bought clothes. Crazy, and kind of nice.

So I was already thirty-four when I had this whim to see something different. In spite of its niceness it was very very dull around East Leake. Mudflats, forest with sparse red deer, Nottingham City for occasional outings—oh, I think I'd seen Robin Hood's Oak just once too often, and that, in case you were wondering, is an ancient monument to some guy who represented a depressed minority, some very long time back. It was a kind of nostalgia got me I think, those traditional tales of Manhattan;

it was said that my great-multi-great grandmother
had actually been there. I have a pair of her false
eyelashes set in lucite, they look like underwater
caterpillars, and I'd been looking at them . . .

Well I'll explain to you quite straight now just in
case you haven't got it. What I wanted to do was
buy the whole of Manhattan Island and have it re-
erected on the site of East Leake, a village between
Nottingham and Loughborough, in England. It was
only a matter of marking every piece correctly and
sticking piece A onto piece B.

"Okay, okay it's a challenge. I'll transact. Let's
say the entire thing including inhabitants within six
weeks, in working order?"

"That's what I had in mind, Spider. Is that your
earliest delivery date?"

∞

She finished typing the last letter of the day as
Secretary of the Stir-crazy Housewives League of
Loughborough Ltd. and went to look out of the window for a while, through the cotton mandalas of
Nottingham lace. Mailman should be due, more
mail, please let there be more mail. There was, in
lieu of telephone messages. Her husband didn't like
telephones, they made him too accessible from
work at the weekends, and in any case, they were
expensive.

CONGRATULATIONS ON BEING WINNER
OF ONE WEEK IN NEW YORK. YOUR GUESS
NUMBER OF SUGAR TWEETIES IN ONE TON
ACCURATE ABSOLUTELY NOT COUNTING
PLASTIC TURKEYS WHICH WAS THE CATCH.
OUR REP WILL CALL TO ARRANGE TICKETS
RESERVATIONS ESCORTS TO SUIT YOU.

After the initial shock and fuss there were envi-ous good-bys, passionate kisses that were expres-sions of perfect trust in fidelity that betrayed a hor-ror of betrayal, after all, she's a good-looking woman for her age, all those escorts laid on, stand-ing in line to take her out, Manhattan at her feet for a week. Brand new white tweed suit, huge straw hat, export-reject shoes that looked like perfects. Lucky woman zooming up to thirty thousand feet, far above the cat-spit of the rest of the Stir-crazies. Worried about things like her ankles swelling at the altitude, being struck by lightning, being struck dumb with shyness on arrival, her hair and com-plexion reacting badly to the New York air and water, all figment nightmares that began to dissolve even as lunch was served on the plane, and the man in the next seat told her what it was like for a month on a Greek island, what it is like in St. Louis where he owned a chain of supermarkets. Oh, she thought, it must be marvelous to be an American and travel a lot. He was stopping over in New York to take in culture in the form of off-Broadway plays, one must not allow the mind to stagnate. Nope. Nossir. Ac-cent blossoming even before landing.

The JFK Airport, two valises at her feet, hands clutching purse, raincoat, passport, tickets, just standing there wondering what to do. More people in one place than she has ever seen before, and how they rush around, how worried they look. The tem-perature is in the nineties and humid, her face shines, she prickles all over. And with fear too, not just heat, for she can sense something horrible and her stomach contracts around the warmed-up Strog-anoff that the air-hostess gave her. What is it that

is so evil? It vibrates everywhere, it is in the very
breath of the place. The organizers of the competition arrived to whisk her off in a yellow taxi driven
by a big handsome Negro who seemed oblivious of
the fact that there were other cars on the street,
thousands of them. The noise was incredible, car
horns going all the time, tires screeching—a thing
one never heard in England, but in America they
always seemed to corner on brakes and two wheels,
people calling, traffic rumble, subway roar coming
up out of the ground, police sirens. Police sirens,
does that mean someone has been murdered? Could
be. And then it seemed to her that she could smell
and hear the vibrations of Hell, she could see how
it had all come to be, suddenly one day the lid of
the Pit had crumbled up because of the pressure,
and all this had come oozing up out of the earth,
materialized as City. Oh, no, I want to go home, I
wish I had never come, my husband, my children,
take me back. . . .

But she never said it aloud, kept smiling and looking and asking, kept the false eyelashes fluttering.
The hotel room they gave her was clean and comfortable, and she would be fetched next morning to
go on a tour of the Fifth Avenue dress shops followed by lunch at the Russian Tea Room near Car-
negie Hall. No sleep to speak of because it took
several hours to unpack her things, find her soap
and brushes, even though they had been efficiently
packed. She felt kind of not herself at all in some
funny way, was it—disoriented? Dangerous sort of
state to be in, nothing that was back home in England seemed real, her family seemed like dim photographs, East Leake was just a very tiny unim-

portant place. But the next day things improved.
There were pancakes stuffed with goats-milk
creamcheese, caviar and sour cream and vodka for
lunch, the kind of food that one could cook up out
of recipe books at home but by no means obtain
when eating out. She began to feel better, the center of a great deal of unaccustomed attention, and
it was all very pleasant. The escort for that day was
charming and intelligent with golden ginger hair, a
soft, silky-looking beard, and impeccable manners.
They discussed Russian literature as far as she was
able, although she blessed the time she had spent
years before forcing herself to read *Crime and Punishment*, because she could remember details of the
book that he did not, which made her feel very
good indeed. He told her that the trimmings on the
central chandelier of the restaurant were Christmas
witch-balls from six years previous. So they were
fallible and human in America even if it was a Russian place. It certainly was not all noise and machinery and rush and food in cans . . .

A conducted tour of the East Fifty-seventh Street
art galleries in the afternoon, an introduction to
kinetic art. Glass globe on black cube, inside the
globe a long symmetrical loop of neon that moved
backwards and forwards changing from red to blue
in a regular rhythm, caused swelling and receding
patterns on and in the glass globe, gave a hooting
bleep that went into her ears and bounced off the
inside of her skull. Regularly. She stood watching it
entranced, she had never seen the like. . . . It was
hypnotic, compelling, it seemed to catch one up,
one floated one did, who did? Timeless space, bodi-
less, beautiful, and it had a message. Buy me and

take me home. But three thousand dollars was more
than she would ever have all at one time, and the
money she had won was meant to be spent in dress
and cosmetic shops. Her escort dragged her away
from the artwork, allowing her a glimpse of large
steel sequins revolving on black velvet, catching the
pulsing lights from the glass globe, it was sensuous,
like a woman dancing. She felt so very much more
relaxed and at home in the city by the end of the
second day; she had only needed rest after the flight.
What a city it was, a unique creation of Man. Nowhere else exactly like it on Earth; that fact in
itself was exciting.

∞

"Yes, sure, Spider, it's the perfect site for it. A dis-
used gypsum mine right under the hill, stretches
over an area of approximately three hundred square
miles, you can use what you like of it to suspend
the sewers and subways and all of that in, it'll be a
cinch, I mean, East Leake is built over a vast cavern, you won't have any blasting to do at all and it's
like the Rock of Ages for strength, they don't even
get a split in the wallpaper from subsidence, and
you won't need to flood much of Nottingham to get
it all in, I was talking to the surveyors only this
morning, you see, there's no problem at all, don't
make any. Down to the eleventh floor and DuPont
giving trouble? Build them a solid concrete base
with elevator, and when the whole building is transported put DuPont's floor back onto that, they'll
have everything they're legally entitled to but who
else will care? Anybody else grumbles at coming to
England, offer them the same treatment, tell 'em
they can stay behind. They'll come to their senses,

what business are they going to do on Manhattan Desert Island?"

I was really flying with the idea, it was taking shape already only a couple of days after I had signed the deal with Spider. I had had to sell out thousands of square miles of Finland to do it but as I had no intention of going there I did not care. I had never been to Manhattan, it was coming to me! I sorted it out with the town councils and started on the evacuation of all the inhabitants in the area, and when we actually got the measurements it included West Leake, Sutton Bonington, Hoton and Costock, Stanford, and part of Bunny. But as I pointed out to them as I worked it out on my desk IBM—what was their problem? They would benefit. I was having it seen to that everyone got a better house than the one they were leaving, that new factories and shops would be built, that their whole standard of living would improve not to mention the retirement pensions for every head of household inconvenienced. They might have been Ancient Britons on Reservation Country, but they were open to reason if it smelled of comfort. By the time I had finished talking to them they couldn't wait for the subsonic rasers to move in.

Everybody stand back! The alarm hooters making all of Sherwood Forest tremble, all of Charnwood shake. And then, the strange drone that was almost a silence, quite quickly, the whole area I needed to re-erect Manhattan on became dust which was of course siphoned off to my breeze-block factory in Yorkshire. "I may create chaos at times, but I have never liked waste," I said to a Flying Spider stunned with admiration.

"I do believe you have genius," he said to me. That's what I call progress I thought. It had only been a matter of weeks since our first head-on meetings and he had thought me unadventurous and neurotic with my dislike of travel, and hopeless at buying and selling. That compliment from him made me feel fabulous. A powerful fella, Flying Spider.

∞

The escort for the day was a delight to be with: a large young man with long hair and moustaches that would have twirled themselves had he not kept on so doing, smiling the while and occasionally allowing one eye to slide inwards creating an effect that somehow enhanced him. Wild, like a pirate. In smart places he wore a silk tie, polished shoes, and neat socks to his dark suit and light-blue shirt, and in downtown bars he brought out from his briefcase a pair of leather sandals and a scarlet handkerchief. He would swagger in with the scarf around his head, shirt ripped open and sandals on his feet, grinning wildly so that she went along with everything he said instead of pausing to think him slightly nutty. Such a man in East Leake, oh they would think him so strange! They talked about the literary scene, authors like John Barth and Donald Barthelme, the poems of Sonya Dorman and Nabokov's entry into the world of science fiction. The man was only doing escort duty to make money, his true ambition was to be a writer. She made mental notes to read up things all winter and to see if her husband could be persuaded to wear a pirate-style handkerchief around the house and to give a lecture to the Stir-crazies on New Wave writing in America.

She was beginning to feel lightheaded and elated and could logically refer her state of mind to the vodka and camparis he bought her on the strength of the competition expense account, and yet it was not just quite that. It reminded her of the first evenings she had spent out with her husband before they had married. She looked around her and everything seemed so wonderful. It was the authentic feeling: falling in love.

∞

"Well, if DuPont won't come across, and it means that there will only be one hundred and nineteen floors to the Empire State, then I have to have it built right on top of the hill, on the site of Adastral House you know? Appropriate name no? Yes I do insist, I want it to be as tall as it was, higher above actual sea-level than its original site. Think of the view! On a clear day I'll be able to see as far as Northampton or Derby, depending on which way I looked. Right over the new rivers, and by the way, the flooding went well, the new course stood up to the inundating perfectly, there's not a ripple difference in the shape of the water around New Manhattan, the currents run exactly right, you can move the ferry tomorrow, check that the tollgates on the tunnels and bridges are sorted out properly, like the Pennsylvania lane will now be the lane for North Wales. We'll make twopence or so too, people will drive down from Edinburgh to ride on the ferry at night, it's quite spectacular I hear." Spider was delighted with me, I could tell from the way he laughed. He liked women with imagination. He told me that already the city was in pieces and stored on the Palisades and the Poconos in the order of re-

erection and that whole blocks of masonry were
continually on their way across the Atlantic by anti-
grav sledge. They had been obliged to use subsonic rasers on whole tracts of forest, but if I
wanted fast delivery, then they hadn't time to store
out in Arizona. The thing was worked out to split-
second timing, just about. Spider wanted to show
me how efficient he was; I was sorry about the forest but I appreciated his efforts. I gave orders to
have the area replanted at the first opportunity. I
took a two-seater sledge myself to watch the foundations of the Empire State being relaid right on the
site I had specified. I hovered around for hours and
could hardly explain to myself why I felt so scared.
I put it down to excitement. After all, it was no
mean thing I had set in motion. It was a First all
right. I couldn't sleep that night even though the
luxury houseboat I had fixed up on the East River,
formerly the Trent, was as comfortable a place as
any I had ever known. I was not to sleep properly
for many nights although I was not to know it at
the time. And it was soundproofed too against the
twenty-four-hour activity of anti-grav sledges hom-
ing in with the next bit of the jigsaw, armies of
fiberglass and old-time concrete mixers, the clang of
scaffolding, blowtorches, cranes, lorries, drills, and
other machinery. So it wasn't the noise that kept me
awake. Every day I went floating out over the growing city to watch, checking the avenues with a map
just for the hell of it; it looked like scum and lichen
at first with square mushrooms sprouting here and
there. But as time passed it began to take more
shape, glossy yellow sunrises would reflect off flight
after flight of glass, some of the smaller buildings

even had flags flying from their tops and people began to move in. Every hour a new sledge arrived
and furniture and boxes and people began to settle themselves back into their homes, shops, and
offices. Faces appeared at the windows to see what
the view was like from the new location. Most of
them looked disappointed for they looked out on
exactly the same bricks and barred windows of
places like West Eighty-eighth as they ever had, ad-
though one old fellow swore we had planted his
withered acacia a foot out of true because his Sia-
mese cat was used to jumping out of his fifth-floor
window onto the branch, and the first time it tried
it, it fell to its death. I was sorry about the cat but
I had to prove that the tree was correctly placed by
showing him the plan of his back yard with every
stone numbered and in its right slot including the
drain, which matched with the duplicate sewage system they had built. Actually the sewage system was
only duplicate where it joined the outer world,
down there it was completely redesigned, much
bigger and faster with a built-in rat-gassing system.
My idea of course but I had paid to have it invented. Offer enough money and people will invent
anything, in working order. So, no rats and no spilling sewers. The people of Manhattan would like
me, I thought, and even at that point they did not
seem particularly perturbed. Life for them would go
on much as usual, and if they wanted to take vaca-
tions in America rather than England they only had
to apply for free transport. I had all that worked
out; with my kind of money it was easy. Oh yes!

What I particularly liked to watch were the
spidermen working high up. They were like anti-

grav pussycats; height just did not scare them. Way
out on girders they poised with spanners and blowtorches and scorned a safe place even to eat lunch.
I floated past them and sometimes one would ac-
knowledge my presence with a grave nod of his
magnificent head. Spider's tribe didn't have to work
of course but it was in their blood and they loved it.
For hundreds of years they had spent most of their
waking hours hundreds of feet up over city streets,
why stop? There was a thrilling moment when they
had finally got the Big One (my name for the Empire State Building) right up and perfect with the
exception of the elusive eleventh floor. There was
one of those blazing sunsets and I flashed past at
about the sixtieth and got like scarlet fluorescent
blood flung in my eyes followed by a brilliant blue-
sky reflection and I instinctively reversed to take the
sight again and again, faster and faster, oh I had
been missing kicks up until then, it began to be
very real that I owned a city, red blue, red blue
went the sky off my towers of glass until the green-
ish clouds of evening came and I descended, blown
clean out of my mind with exultation. I lay in bed
that night still seeing the flash of color, and it was
something like someone was trying to get a message
through to me and my ears began to sing. I knew I
was overtired and a little disoriented; my surround-
ings were completely strange, there were bound to
be side effects. I got up before dawn and looked
out on the river. Somewhere near the island there
should have been a thing called the Statue of Liberty, but I had forgotten to include it in the deal.
Anyway, I thought, who wants sculpture that size,
I had the whole of the Guggenheim and all that

stuff to myself if I wanted Art, it all belonged to me and besides I didn't want to reopen negotiations with Spider at that point, he would think me inefficient. I was just a little depressed about the whole project around that time I must admit, but I put it down to extended impatience. Six weeks was seeming like an awful long time to realize a dream, but as Spider said:

"You don't want the Chase Manhattan in Battery Park or Penn Station under the elephants in the Natural History Museum, do you? Give us time, we'll put it together truly pretty. Nobody who lives there will know any different, it's all *organized*." And the way he said that word *organized* gave me a cool thrill of horrified admiration for him; I mean, one knew that he meant every word he said, that when he had spoken it was so.

"Okay, Chief," I murmured, and a gleam of something reached me from him. I was out-powered by Flying Spider, but I was still the one with the imagination.

"What shall we do next after this is over?" he asked me.

"How about putting the Taj Mahal on top of Ayers Rock in Australia?" He was a bit disgusted at that.

"I meant something new and original. Like we consider a merger of some kind, both our companies working together?"

I still don't know how I kept my head cool, it was fantastic. A merger! Him and me!

"Good idea, Chief," I said, and didn't sleep that night either. That was sheer happiness kept me awake though. It suddenly seemed as if I had been dreaming a dream for centuries, and it was beginning to come true.

∞

There were two days of the Competition Trip left, and she was feeling just wonderful. She wondered how she could ever have felt that the city was frightful, it must have been the shock of impact, so very many people crammed into one small island. She was with an escort in Le Mistral, which was one of New York's best restaurants, and she was slightly drunk and very happy. He was a delight to be with, charming and considerate, leading the conversation this way and that, pouring out the vintage claret that he had chosen whilst yet consulting her on his choice. She had said:

"Well, actually what I usually have at home is red plonk," and he had admitted that it could be fine stuff but he thought that night they should have something a little better. They drank it with squabs that had been stewed in a rich brown cream sauce full of olives and she marveled at the perfect crispness of the accompanying salad. In restaurants salad was usually a bit limp. This stuff was rampant with life. They talked much also about the beauty of the big city by night, and by the time they had got round to the fresh fruit salad in Kirsch and then the excellent coffee she was truly flying with well-being, happiness, joy. Her companion was stunningly handsome and beautifully bronzed, probably he took his holidays in Bermuda or somewhere fabulous like that. A noble profile, jet-black hair.

"Where did you get that wonderful tan from?" she asked him, and he smiled with no hint of acid, and explained that it was not a tan as she would see if they were in daylight, he was a full-blooded Mohawk Indian, and by day he worked as a spiderman high up on the skyscrapers, he only did the escort job at night to make extra money for his family. His wife was sick with a disease of the spleen and medical bills were steep. But, he said, they were not to talk of that, he had something wonderful to show her. The sixty-fifth floor, the Rainbow Room. Huge windows through which he indicated a fabulous view. Somehow at that moment they had become unprofessional and clasped hands, and she could hardly breathe for the shock of what she saw, it was so beautiful. The mist was below them in the canyons, moving towards them menacing and amorphous was the Empire State Building like an insect presence from Outer Space, a glittering treasure in the sky. Just coming in to land, perpetually coming nearer. She spread out her hands to it and was stunned by the mystery of architecture that is unearthly and unreal and wished a deep wish in her heart, to come one day and live in Manhattan where she felt at home and loved.

And loved! By the city of course, because she was in love with it.

"City of dreams, I love you," and maybe he heard or maybe not, but he was professional escort again, pointing out the East River with the lights on it, the bridges. But he was again holding one of her hands, to steady her, she tottered and he was rock steady, it was his job to fly high and reach ground safely.

∞

Chief Flying Spider apologized for being one day late with the goods. It was DuPont's fault, they had decided at the last minute that they wanted to come in on the move, and so the problem of how to insert their offices back into the Big One had to be solved. I came up with the unique idea of floating it all the way across the Atlantic on several layers of anti-grav sledges all inter-computerized so that there would be no hangups like the entire thing sliding down into the fathoms. DuPont resented losing working time and I wanted them in but fast so it seemed obvious to me to float the entire thing over at one blast, typewriters and computers clocking away, temporary short-wave telephones installed, elevator doors double locked. About fifteen thousand anti-grav units were fastened all the way up to the top of the Big One from the twelfth floor up and lasers sliced through the entire floor just above the ceilings of the tenth, and at the precise preset moment up it went like a plumbline sweet and perfect and in slid DuPont still yakking on the phone and hardly a drop of coffee spilled. Electricity and plumbing were put back onto permanent supply and every sliver of wood was checked for perfect fit. Mortar was injected where necessary and unbreakable steel rods slipped in like pins, down laser-bored holes full of resin which were then given an electro-magnetic charge which sealed the two joins stronger than they had originally been. All the windows were tested for warp, we didn't want glass exploding in people's faces, but there was no strain anywhere. Spider thought I was rather bright to have thought of doing it that way and I thought him pretty bright to have accomplished what I had dreamed. Together, after the merger we knew we would do things together that would shake the

world. There were then only a few things to check,
like making sure that all the commuters had been
given good homes in the surrounding English countryside. That department of the scheme was sure all
was well, but I wanted everything checked and
double checked before I declared the place officially
in working order and mine. Already the subways
were roaring and I was very pleased with those.

∞

The escort for that last night was a very nice
man who was to take her out to dinner and then the
theater. They were to see three one-act plays in an
off-Broadway theater and she looked forward to the
evening very much. She had taken especial care
with her make-up and dress. She wore a white velvet trouser-suit with trailing medieval sleeves and a
diamanté belt at high waist level, a thing she could
never have worn in East Leake. Her husband had
helped her to choose her clothes for the trip, and as
she placed a Juliet cap of rhinestones on her hair
she noticed that she pined for him less every day
and thought with horror of going back home to the
flat village and the Stir-crazies secretarial work and
the housework and having nobody interesting to
talk to . . . oh, it was going to be so dreadful—she
belonged here, in Manhattan, this was her true
home. But she told herself not to be selfish and silly,
of course she loved her husband and her home, and
the Stir-crazies were making real progress like nurs-
ery schools for children over two years, trips out
once a month, equal pay. And this was just a trip,
she was lucky, not to be greedy . . . greedy people
risked losing everything.

All during dinner she told her escort about the

previous evening when she had stood on the sixty-
fifth floor in an ecstatic condition, she rattled on all
during the excellent *crêpes* stuffed with spinach and
ham, and the coffee, and went on about the incredible beauty of New York City, Manhattan Island,
Isle of Dreams, right up until the curtain went up
on the first play. During the intervals she told her
escort about the escort of the previous evening, that
he was a Mohawk, that he was beautiful, that his
wife was sick. Her escort smiled kindly, and from
superior age and experience forbore to point out
that his lady for the evening was in love not only
with the City but with a man. If he did not say anything, then she would arrive home safely not knowing the fact herself. He took her to a soda fountain
for some iced tea, offered her lime sherbet but she
could not eat. He sent her home in a cab and there
at the door of the hotel stood her Mohawk in brown
denim overalls, moccasins, and a blue-check shirt.
She needed no telling, no prompting as to the state
of her mind, she knew what she wanted. They both
wanted the same, they talked about it in her hotel
room. They wanted to live together in Manhattan,
they wanted to forget that they had other lives.
They kissed a few times and lay back on the bed,
dizzy and reeling from the sheer delight of kissing
in a state of new love. And shocked at the impact
they would make on several lives if they went one
bit further. He spoke of his wife who would sicken
and die if she knew he made love with any other
woman, his children who would be damaged if he
left them; she spoke of her husband to whom she
felt wedded forever, she felt wedding vows were

sacred if old-fashioned, she thought about her children and saw destruction and grief looming, she thought of her house and it crumbled to dust in her vision of how it would be if she allowed herself to love this man who felt so right in her arms. He left silently and she did not weep, nor sleep either. Lay there murmuring:

"Seductive city I love you, every building, every stone, every splinter I love it all, the river round you, the great buildings, the canyons, and the smell and the taste and the feel of the hard stone sidewalk I love you so . . ." Turn the love over to inanimate objects, transmute it, somehow, make it into a memory only, so that I can live at home in peace with myself. . . .

At dawn she went out for a coffee in a drugstore unafraid of jostling and screeching tires and sirens, let them, let it, nothing can hurt me now, oh let anything try to hurt me now!

∞

Spider called me:

"It's all yours, the whole works complete with trash in the gutter and roaches. Wanna conducted tour?" I picked up the lucite block with the false eyelashes of my great-multi-great grandmother in it. I swear the damn things moved. Like crawled, or winked. Horrible but I couldn't help laughing, after all I had hardly slept for six weeks, where I got the energy from I did not know. It's amazing what a sense of accomplishment can do for the nervous system. I put the lucite block back down on some papers on my desk and told Spider no, not the conducted tour just yet, first I had a crazy thing I wanted to do, which was fly the Atlantic on an anti-grav and take a look at Manhattan Island all bleak and bare. He thought I was crazy.

"The first trip you take outside your own back yard and what do you go and see . . . it's all happening *here!* The trouble I went to make it so. . . ."

"I know, I know, it's just a feeling I have, I want to."

I hung up on him and knew I was nervous about the merger, for one thing. Our combined powers might be too much I felt, maybe we could accomplish some awful things between us, it worried me a bit. But I wasn't going to say anything, and first I had to check a few points. On the TV they were interviewing the former residents of New Jersey and places like that where all the commuters had lived who now lived on the outskirts of Leicester and Derby. Even at that it was a shorter commute and what with the inconvenience-money I was paying them they felt very happy, there was a noticeable lack of sentimentality over their homeland, the weather would be a slight problem until the weather bureau checked with Ecology to get the summers fixed without damage. I wanted it hot and humid in those New York summer streets, and they wanted the sun to ripen corn and peaches in their weekend houses. They would have it, soon, soon. Meetings were shown between old inhabitants and the new influx, and it seemed that mainly they would get on together very nicely. Both groups felt to have benefited.

"After all," said one housewife who had lived on Roulstone Crescent which was now swallowed up by the intersection of Broadway and Seventh, "it will be nice to ride into New York of an evening and go to the flicks, there warn't much choice before."

It was all set, it was mine. There would be the official company meeting to sign the merger. Before I set off for my trip I called Spider.

"By the way, what were you thinking of doing with the site of Old Manhattan?"

"I thought I might do a repro. Ancient Indian Reservation. . . ."

"See you later," I said, smiling.

∞

She stayed awake every moment until she got back home. The plane journey had been fabulous, intense blue runway lights, the lights of the city from the air, an electric storm and black silk clouds ripping on the wings, the whole sky illuminated like her sudden discovery of a new love, plunged into cloud like its loss. But then straight up to the sight of the stars, and when the air-hostess asked her if she wanted a drink she refused, saying that she wanted to be clearheaded for the dawn. Ahead into pale liquid glass containing one bright star, permitting herself one physically exploding thought of him and how it might have been and then, landing, forbidding herself ever to think of him again, because she knew that if she did something utterly dreadful might happen.

∞

I hovered about over the desolate site of Manhattan and wondered why I had come, it had been a crazy thing to do. It was utterly dreary and kind of haunted looking, the earth flat brick dust, everything flattened or filled in, all the foundations and subways, everything, smooth wreckage. Still, Spider would replant it and make it as it had been in ancient times, it would be a fine natural place one day soon. I made for home, slinging the sledge into top speed so I was back home in under two hours, round trip. I was in a state of nerves and so did not land straight away, but took a float around first. I was under the impression at first that it was my nerves and lack of sleep playing me up. The skyline was trembling. Moving around idiotically. And then I began shouting meaningless warnings. Buildings were toppling over sideways and I was only just in time to avoid the steel cupola of the Woolworth building as it glided past me like a falling rocket and exploded into scales somewhere down an abyss. I sent my sledge straight up at top speed and then began to circle, switched the controls over to automatic-avoid, and watched everything. It was the gypsum mine caving in of course, it had been roofed firm for thousands of years but this was just too much. All the engineers and consultants had said it would be fine, but dammit, they had been wrong. Maybe it was the subsonic lasers had done unseen damage, maybe it was my wanting the Big One right on top of the hill at the thinnest point of the cave roof, I don't know. The sound was softened at that height and in the closed dome, but I knew what it sounded like. All that screaming and shouting and crying out, yells of disbelief and horror, echoes of explosions as power lines hit subway cars, fires everywhere, gas leaks, whole tops of skyscrapers falling into the street and bursting like fruit, yellow cabs like beetles under bricks, flat, horns howling into silence and then the sucking

downwards, a thousand feet of sparkling white gypsum grinding against itself and spreading back miles
of surrounding yellow clay, the pressure so great
that Beacon Hill ten miles away became three feet
higher above sea level. And then I saw him, right
near the top of the Big One, outside and hanging
onto the steel fence around the parapet on the
eighty-sixth floor. He was waving to me and the
building swayed back and forth, back and forth as
its foundations worked their way down through the
crystals, crushing lower towards the thousand feet
of waiting black space. I homed in, aware of vast
winds and flashes of light, scarlet blue, scarlet blue,
explosions, sunset, dust and fire and electricity in
the air like natural forces were endorsing what was
happening. I strapped myself in and opened the
door and could hardly breathe because of gas and
dust and smoke rising and the wind full of it forcing its way into my chest and we could not hear
each other at all. I tried, I got close enough to the
parapet for it to brush me, I tried, I reached out, I
screamed at him to jump, I knew he could do it if
I hovered steady, but I had forgotten the automatic-
avoid system was still switched on. He leapt into
empty space and I zoomed out of the way of his
falling body. Down it went over and over, I stayed
to watch the island sink, like the lid of the Great Pit
was taken off, the void claiming its own again, it
was a triumphal roar, a greedy sucking, closing over
it, the Abyss eating up what was its rightful property.

∞

It was a long time ago and on Earth. I emigrated. I had no money left and no friends, no home, no choice. I don't have anything much now, no power. I didn't have any then, I have never had any. Or I would have made everything go very differently.

THE FUNERAL

KATE WILHELM

Kate Wilhelm shows us young girls deformed by the rigid expectations of their elders. She speaks to all young people betrayed, coerced, or rejected by adults who, under the guise of concern, seek instead to impose their will on the young and the future. "The Funeral" is a painful yet beautifully wrought story.

No one could say exactly how old Madam Westfall was when she finally died. At least one hundred twenty, it was estimated. At the very least. For twenty years Madam Westfall had been a shell containing the very latest products of advances made in gerontology, and now she was dead. What lay on the viewing dais was merely a painted, funereally garbed husk.

"She isn't real," Carla said to herself. "It's a doll or something. It isn't really Madam Westfall." She kept her head bowed, and didn't move her lips, but she said the words over and over. She was afraid to look at a dead person. *The second time they slaughtered all those who bore arms, unguided, mindless now, but lethal with the arms caches that they used indiscriminately.* Carla felt goose bumps along her arms and legs. She wondered if anyone else had been hearing the old Teacher's words.

The line moved slowly, all the girls in their long gray skirts had their heads bowed, their hands clasped. The only sound down the corridor was the sush-sush of slippers on plastic flooring, the occasional rustle of a skirt.

The Viewing Room had a pale green, plastic floor, frosted-green plastic walls, and floor to ceiling windows that were now slits of brilliant light from a westering sun. All the furniture had been taken from the room, all the ornamentation. There were no flowers, nothing but the dais, and the bedlike box covered by a transparent shield. And the Teachers. Two at the dais, others between the light strips, at the doors. Their white hands clasped against black garb, heads bowed, hair slicked against each head, straight parts emphasizing bilateral symmetry. The Teachers didn't move, didn't look at the dais, at the girls parading past it.

Carla kept her head bowed, her chin tucked almost inside the V of her collarbone. The serpentine line moved steadily, very slowly. "She isn't real," Carla said to herself, desperately now.

She crossed the line that was the cue to raise her head; it felt too heavy to lift, her neck seemed paralyzed. When she did move, she heard a joint crack, and although her jaws suddenly ached, she couldn't relax.

The second green line. She turned her eyes to the right and looked at the incredibly shrunken, hardly human mummy. She felt her stomach lurch and for a moment she thought she was going to vomit. "She isn't real. It's a doll. She isn't real!" The third line.

She bowed her head, pressed her chin hard against her collarbone, making it hurt. She couldn't swallow now, could hardly breathe. The line proceeded to the South Door and through it into the corridor.

She turned left at the South Door, and with her eyes downcast, started the walk back to her genetics class. She looked neither right nor left, but she could hear others moving in the same direction, slippers on plastic, the swish of a skirt, and when she passed by the door to the garden she heard laughter of some Ladies who had come to observe the viewing. She slowed down.

She felt the late sun hot on her skin at the open door and with a sideways glance, not moving her head, she looked quickly into the glaring greenery, but could not see them. Their laughter sounded like music as she went past the opening.

"That one, the one with the blue eyes and straw-colored hair. Stand up, girl."

Carla didn't move, didn't realize she was being addressed until a Teacher pulled her from her seat.

"Don't hurt her! Turn around, girl. Raise your skirts, higher. Look at me, child. Look up, let me see your face . . ."

"She's too young for choosing," said the Teacher, examining Carla's bracelet. "Another year, Lady."

"A pity. She'll coarsen in a year's time. The fuzz is so soft right now, the flesh so tender. Oh, well . . ." She moved away, flicking a red skirt about her thighs, her red-clad legs narrowing to tiny ankles, flashing silver slippers with heels that were like icicles. She smelled . . . Carla didn't know any words to describe how she smelled. She drank in the fragrance hungrily.

"Look at me, child. Look up, let me see your face . . ." The words sang through her mind over and over. At night, falling asleep she thought of the face, drawing it up from the deep black, trying to hold it in focus: white skin, pink cheek ridges, silver eyelids, black lashes longer than she had known lashes could be, silver-pink lips, three silver spots— one at the corner of her left eye, another at the corner of her mouth, the third like a dimple in the satiny cheek. Silver hair that was loose, in waves about her face, that rippled with life of its own when she moved. If only she had been allowed to touch the hair, to run her finger over that cheek . . . The dream that began with the music of the Lady's laughter, ended with the nightmare of her other words: "She'll coarsen in a year's time . . ."

After that Carla had watched the changes take place on and within her body, and she understood what the Lady had meant. Her once smooth legs began to develop hair; it grew under her arms, and, most shameful, it sprouted as a dark, coarse bush under her belly. She wept. She tried to pull the hairs out, but it hurt too much, and made her skin sore and raw. Then she started to bleed, and she lay down and waited to die, and was happy that she would die. Instead, she was ordered to the infirmary and was forced to attend a lecture on feminine hygiene. She watched in stony-faced silence while the Doctor added the new information to her bracelet. The Doctor's face was smooth and pink, her eyebrows pale, her lashes so colorless and stubby that they were almost invisible. On her chin was a brown mole with two long hairs. She wore a straight blue-gray gown that hung from her shoulders to the floor. Her drab hair was pulled back tightly from her face, fastened in a hard bun at the back of her neck. Carla hated her. She hated the Teachers. Most of all she hated herself. She yearned for maturity.

Madam Westfall had written: Maturity brings grace, beauty, wisdom, happiness. Immaturity means ugliness, unfinished beings with potential only, wholly dependent upon and subservient to the mature citizens.

There was a True-False quiz on the master screen in front of the classroom. Carla took her place quickly and touch-typed her ID number on the small screen of her machine.

She scanned the questions, and saw that they were all simple declarative statements of truth. Her stylus ran down the True column of her answer screen and it was done. She wondered why they were killing time like this, what they were waiting for. Madam Westfall's death had thrown everything off schedule.

Paperlike brown skin, wrinkled and hard, with lines crossing lines, vertical, horizontal, diagonal, leaving little islands of flesh, hardly enough to coat the bones. Cracked voice, incomprehensible: *they took away the music from the air . . . voices from the skies . . . erased pictures that move . . . boxes that sing and sob . . .* Crazy talk. And, *. . . only one left that knows. Only one.*

Madam Trudeau entered the classroom and Carla understood why the class had been personalized that period. The Teacher had been waiting for

Madam Trudeau's appearance. The girls rose hurriedly. Madam Trudeau motioned for them to be seated once more.

"The following girls attended Madam Westfall during the past five years." She read from a list. Carla's name was included on her list. On finishing it, she asked, "Is there anyone who attended Madam Westfall whose name I did not read?"

There was a rustle from behind Carla. She kept her gaze fastened on Madam Trudeau. "Name?" the Teacher asked.

"Luella, Madam."

"You attended Madam Westfall? When?"

"Two years ago, Madam. I was a relief for Sonya, who became ill suddenly."

"Very well." Madam Trudeau added Luella's name to her list. "You will all report to my office at 8 A.M. tomorrow morning. You will be excused from classes and duties at that time. Dismissed." With a bow she excused herself to the class Teacher and left the room.

∞

Carla's legs twitched and ached. Her swim class was at eight each morning and she had missed it, had been sitting on the straight chair for almost two hours, when finally she was told to go into Madam Trudeau's office. None of the other waiting girls looked up when she rose and followed the attendant from the anteroom. Madam Trudeau was seated at an oversized desk that was completely bare, with a mirrorlike finish. Carla stood before it with her eyes downcast, and she could see Madam Trudeau's face reflected from the surface of the desk. Madam Trudeau was looking at a point over

Carla's head, unaware that the girl was examining her features.

"You attended Madam Westfall altogether seven times during the past four years, is that correct?"

"I think it is, Madam."

"You aren't certain?"

"I . . . I don't remember, Madam."

"I see. Do you recall if Madam Westfall spoke to you during any of those times?"

"Yes, Madam."

"Carla, you are shaking. Are you frightened?"

"No, Madam."

"Look at me, Carla."

Carla's hands tightened, and she could feel her fingernails cutting into her hands. She thought of the pain, and stopped shaking. Madam Trudeau had pasty, white skin, with peaked black eyebrows, sharp black eyes, black hair. Her mouth was wide and full, her nose long and narrow. As she studied the girl before her, it seemed to Carla that something changed in her expression, but she couldn't say what it was, or how it now differed from what it had been a moment earlier. A new intensity perhaps, a new interest.

"Carla, I've been looking over your records. Now that you are fourteen it is time to decide on your future. I shall propose your name for the Teachers' Academy on the completion of your current courses. As my protege, you will quit the quarters you now occupy and attend me in my chambers . . ." She narrowed her eyes. "What is the matter with you, girl? Are you ill?"

"No, Madam. I . . . I had hoped . . . I mean, I designated my choice last month. I thought . . ."

Madam Trudeau looked to the side of her desk where a records screen was lighted. She scanned the report, and her lips curled derisively. "A Lady. You would be a Lady!" Carla felt a blush fire her face, and suddenly her palms were wet with sweat. Madam Trudeau laughed, a sharp barking sound. She said, "The girls who attended Madam Westfall in life, shall attend her in death. You will be on duty in the Viewing Room for two hours each day, and when the procession starts for the burial services in Scranton, you will be part of the entourage. Meanwhile, each day for an additional two hours immediately following your attendance in the Viewing Room you will meditate on the words of wisdom you have heard from Madam Westfall, and you will write down every word she ever spoke in your presence. For this purpose there will be placed a notebook and a pen in your cubicle, which you will use for no other reason. You will discuss this with no one except me. You, Carla, will prepare to move to my quarters immediately, where a learning cubicle will be awaiting you. Dismissed."

Her voice became sharper as she spoke, and when she finished the words were staccato. Carla bowed and turned to leave.

"Carla, you will find that there are certain rewards in being chosen as a Teacher."

Carlo didn't know if she should turn and bow again, or stop where she was, or continue. When she hesitated, the voice came again, shorter, raspish. "Go. Return to your cubicle."

∞

The first time, they slaughtered only the leaders, the rousers, . . . would be enough to defuse the

bomb, leave the rest silent and powerless and mal-
leable . . .

Carla looked at the floor before her, trying to
control the trembling in her legs. Madam Westfall
hadn't moved, hadn't spoken. She was dead, gone.
The only sound was the sush, sush of slippers. The
green plastic floor was a glare that hurt her eyes.
The air was heavy and smelled of death. Smelled
the Lady, drank in the fragrance, longed to touch
her. Pale, silvery-pink lips, soft, shiny, with two
high peaks on the upper lip. The Lady stroked her
face with fingers that were soft and cool and gentle. . . . *when their eyes become soft with unspeak-*
able desires and their bodies show signs of woman-
hood, then let them have their duties chosen for
them, some to bear the young for the society, some
to become Teachers, some Nurses, Doctors, some to
be taken as Lovers by the citizens, some to be . . .

Carla couldn't control the sudden start that turned
her head to look at the mummy. The room seemed
to waver, then steadied again. The tremor in her
legs became stronger, harder to stop. She pressed
her knees together hard, hurting them where bone
dug into flesh and skin. Fingers plucking at the
coverlet. Plucking bones, brown bones with horny
nails.

Water. Girl, give me water. Pretty, pretty. You
would have been killed, you would have. Pretty.
The last time they left no one over ten. No one at
all. Ten to twenty-five.

Pretty. Carla said it to herself. Pretty. She visu-
alized it as p-r-i-t-y. Pity with an r. Scanning the
dictionary for p-r-i-t-y. Nothing. Pretty. *Afraid of*
shiny, pretty faces. Young, pretty faces.

The trembling was all through Carla. Two hours.
Eternity. She had stood here forever, would die here,
unmoving, trembling, aching. A sigh and the sound
of a body falling softly to the floor. Soft body crumbling so easily. Carla didn't turn her head. It must
be Luella. So frightened of the mummy. She'd had
nightmares every night since Madam Westfall's
death. What made a body stay upright, when it fell
so easily? Take it out, the thing that held it together, and down, down. Just to let go, to know
what to take out and allow the body to fall like that
into sleep. Teachers moved across her field of vision, two of them in their black gowns. Sush-sush.
Returned with Luella, or someone, between them.
No sound. Sush-sush.

∞

The new learning cubicle was an exact duplicate
of the old one. Cot, learning machine, chair, par-
titioned-off commode and washbasin. And new, the
notebook and pen. Carla had never had a notebook
and pen before. There was the stylus that was attached to the learning machine, and the lighted
square in which to write, that then vanished into
the machine. She turned the blank pages of the
notebook, felt the paper between her fingers, tore a
tiny corner off one of the back pages, examined it
closely, the jagged edge, the texture of the fragment; she tasted it. She studied the pen just as mi-
nutely; it had a pointed, smooth end, and it wrote
black. She made a line, stopped to admire it, and
crossed it with another line. She wrote very slowly,
"Carla," started to put down her number, the one
on her bracelet, then stopped in confusion. She

never had considered it before, but she had no last name, none that she knew. She drew three heavy lines over the two digits she had put down.

At the end of the two hours of meditation she had written her name a number of times, had filled three pages with it, in fact, and had written one of the things that she could remember hearing from the gray lips of Madam Westfall: "Non-citizens are the property of the state."

∞

The next day the citizens started to file past the dais. Carla breathed deeply, trying to sniff the fragrance of the passing Ladies, but they were too distant. She watched their feet, clad in shoes of rainbow colors: pointed toes, stiletto heels; rounded toes, carved heels; satin, sequinned slippers . . . And just before her duty ended for the day, the Males started to enter the room.

She heard a gasp, Luella again. She didn't faint this time, merely gasped once. Carla saw the feet and legs at the same time and she looked up to see a male citizen. He was very tall and thick, and was dressed in the blue and white clothing of a Doctor of Law. He moved into the sunlight and there was a glitter from gold at his wrists, and his neck, and the gleam of a smooth polished head. He turned past the dais and his eyes met Carla's. She felt herself go light-headed and hurriedly she ducked her head and clenched her hands. She thought he was standing still, looking at her, and she could feel her heart thumping hard. Her relief arrived then and she crossed the room as fast as she could without appearing indecorous.

Carla wrote: "Why did he scare me so much?

Why have I never seen a Male before? Why does everyone else wear colors while the girls and the Teachers wear black and gray?"

She drew a wavering line-figure of a man, and stared at it, and then Xed it out. Then she looked at the sheet of paper with dismay. Now she had four ruined sheets of paper to dispose of.

Had she angered him by staring? Nervously she tapped on the paper and tried to remember what his face had been like. Had he been frowning? She couldn't remember. Why couldn't she think of anything to write for Madam Trudeau? She bit the end of the pen and then wrote slowly, very carefully: *Society may dispose of its property as it chooses, following discussion with at least three members, and following permission which is not to be arbitrarily denied.*

Had Madam Westfall ever said that? She didn't know, but she had to write something, and that was the sort of thing that Madam Westfall had quoted at great length. She threw herself down on the cot and stared at the ceiling. For three days she had kept hearing the Madam's dead voice, but now when she needed to hear her again, nothing.

Sitting in the straight chair, alert for any change in the position of the ancient one, watchful, afraid of the old Teacher. Cramped, tired and sleepy. Half listening to mutterings, murmurings of exhaled and inhaled breaths that sounded like words that made no sense. . . . *Mama said hide child, hide don't move and Stevie wanted a razor for his birthday and Mama said you're too young, you're only nine and he said no Mama I'm thirteen don't you remember and Mama said hide child hide don't move at all and they came in hating pretty faces . . .*

Carla sat up and picked up the pen again, then stopped. When she heard the words, they were so clear in her head, but as soon as they ended, they faded away. She wrote: "hating pretty faces. . . . hide child. . . . only nine." She stared at the words and drew a line through them.

Pretty faces. Madam Westfall had called her pretty, pretty.

∞

The chimes for social hour were repeated three times and finally Carla opened the door of her cubicle and took a step into the anteroom where the other proteges already had gathered. There were five. Carla didn't know any of them, but she had seen all of them from time to time in and around the school grounds. Madam Trudeau was sitting on a highbacked chair that was covered with black. She blended into it, so that only her hands and her face seemed apart from the chair, dead white hands and face. Carla bowed to her and stood uncertainly at her own door.

"Come in, Carla. It is social hour. Relax. This is Wanda, Louise, Stephanie, Mary, Dorothy." Each girl inclined her head slightly as her name was mentioned. Carla couldn't tell afterward which name went with which girl. Two of them wore the black-striped overskirt that meant they were in the Teacher's Academy. The other three still wore the gray of the lower school, as did Carla, with black bordering the hems.

"Carla doesn't want to be a Teacher," Madam Trudeau said drily. "She prefers the paint box of a Lady." She smiled with her mouth only. One of the

academy girls laughed. "Carla, you are not the first
to envy the paint box and the bright clothes of the
Ladies. I have something to show you. Wanda, the
film."

The girl who had laughed touched a button on a
small table and on one of the walls a picture was
projected. Carla caught her breath. It was a Lady,
all gold and white, gold hair, gold eyelids, filmy
white gown that ended just above her knees. She
turned and smiled, holding out both hands, flashing
jeweled fingers, long, gleaming nails that came to
points. Then she reached up and took off her hair.

Carla felt that she would faint when the golden
hair came off in the Lady's hands, leaving short,
straight brown hair. She placed the gold hair on a
ball, and then, one by one, stripped off the long
gleaming nails, leaving her hands just hands, bony
and ugly. The Lady peeled off her eyelashes and
brows, and then patted a brown, thick coating of
something on her face, and, with its removal, revealed pale skin with wrinkles about her eyes, with
hard, deep lines aside her nose down to her mouth
that had also changed, had become small and mean.
Carla wanted to shut her eyes, turn away and go
back to her cubicle, but she didn't dare move. She
could feel Madam Trudeau's stare, and the gaze
seemed to burn.

The Lady took off the swirling gown, and under
it was a garment Carla never had seen before that
covered her from her breasts to her thighs. The
stubby fingers worked at fasteners, and finally got
the garment off, and there was her stomach, bigger,
bulging, with cruel red lines where the garment had
pinched and squeezed her. Her breasts drooped

almost to her waist. Carla couldn't stop her eyes, couldn't make them not see, couldn't make herself not look at the rest of the repulsive body.

Madam Trudeau stood up and went to her door. "Show Carla the other two films." She looked at Carla then and said, "I order you to watch. I shall quiz you on the contents." She left the room.

The other two films showed the same Lady at work. First with a protege, then with a male citizen. When they were over Carla stumbled back to her cubicle and vomited repeatedly until she was exhausted. She had nightmares that night.

∞

How many days, she wondered, have I been here now? She no longer trembled, but became detached almost as soon as she took her place between two of the tall windows. She didn't try to catch a whiff of the fragrance of the Ladies, or try to get a glimpse of the Males. She had chosen one particular spot in the floor on which to concentrate, and she didn't shift her gaze from it.

They were old and full of hate, and they said, let us remake them in our image, and they did.

Madam Trudeau hated her, despised her. Old and full of hate . . .

"Why were you not chosen to become a Woman to bear young?"

"I am not fit, Madam. I am weak and timid."

"Look at your hips, thin, like a Male's hips. And your breasts, small and hard." Madam Trudeau turned away in disgust. "Why were you not chosen to become a Professional, a Doctor, or a Technician?"

"I am not intelligent enough, Madam. I require

many hours of study to grasp the mathematics."

"So. Weak, frail, not too bright. Why do you weep?"

"I don't know, Madam. I am sorry."

"Go to your cubicle. You disgust me."

Staring at a flaw in the floor, a place where an indentation distorted the light, creating one very small oval shadow, wondering when the ordeal would end, wondering why she couldn't fill the notebook with the many things that Madam Westfall had said, things that she could remember here, and could not remember when she was in her cubicle with pen poised over the notebook.

Sometimes Carla forgot where she was, found herself in the chamber of Madam Westfall, watching the ancient one struggle to stay alive, forcing breaths in and out, refusing to admit death. Watching the incomprehensible dials and tubes and bottles of fluids with lowering levels, watching needles that vanished into flesh, tubes that disappeared under the bedclothes, that seemed to writhe now and again with a secret life, listening to the mumbling voice, the groans and sighs, the meaningless words.

Three times they rose against the children and three times slew them until there were none left none at all because the contagion had spread and all over ten were infected and carried radios . . .

Radios? A disease? Infected with radios, spreading it among young people?

And Mama said hide child hide and don't move and put this in the cave too and don't touch it.

Carla's relief came and numbly she walked from the Viewing Room. She watched the movement of the black border of her skirt as she walked and it

seemed that the blackness crept up her legs, en-
veloped her middle, climbed her front until it
reached her neck, and then it strangled her. She
clamped her jaws hard and continued to walk her
measured pace.

∞

The girls who had attended Madam Westfall in
life were on duty throughout the school ceremonies
after the viewing. They were required to stand in a
line behind the dais. There were eulogies to the patience and firmness of the first Teacher. Eulogies to
her wisdom in setting up the rules of the school.
Carla tried to keep her attention on the speakers,
but she was so tired and drowsy that she heard only
snatches. Then she was jolted into awareness.
Madam Trudeau was talking.

". . . a book that will be the guide to all future
Teachers, showing them the way through personal
tribulations and trials to achieve the serenity that
was Madam Westfall's. I am honored by this privi-
lege, in choosing me and my apprentices to accomplish this end . . ."

Carla thought of the gibberish that she had been
putting down in her notebook and she blinked back
tears of shame. Madam Trudeau should have told
them why she wanted the information. She would
have to go back over it all and destroy all the nonsense that she had written down.

Late that afternoon the entourage formed that
would accompany Madam Westfall to her final ceremony in Scranton, her native city, where her burial
would return her to her family.

Madam Trudeau had an interview with Carla before departure. "You will be in charge of the other

girls," she said. "I expect you to maintain order. You will report any disturbance, or any infringement of rules immediately, and if that is not possible, if I am occupied, you will personally impose order in my name."

"Yes, Madam."

"Very well. During the journey the girls will travel together in a compartment of the tube. Talking will be permitted, but no laughter, no childish play. When we arrive at the Scranton home, you will be given rooms with cots. Again you will all comport yourselves with the dignity of the office which you are ordered to fulfill at this time."

Carla felt excitement mount within her as the girls lined up to take their places along the sides of the casket. They went with it to a closed limousine where they sat knee to knee, unspeaking, hot, to be taken over smooth highways for an hour to the tube. Madam Westfall had refused to fly in life, and was granted the same rights in death, so her body was to be transported from Wilmington to Scranton by the rocket tube. As soon as the girls had accompanied the casket to its car, and were directed to their own compartment, their voices raised in a babble. It was the first time any of them had left the schoolgrounds since entering them at the age of five.

Ruthie was going to work in the infants' wards, and she turned faintly pink and soft looking when she talked about it. Luella was a music apprentice already, having shown skill on the piano at an early age. Lorette preened herself slightly and announced that she had been chosen as a Lover by a Gentleman. She would become a Lady one day. Carla stared at her curiously, wondering at her pleased look, wondering if she had not been shown the films yet. Lorette was blue-eyed, with pale hair, much the same build as Carla. Looking at her, Carla could imagine her in soft dresses, with her mouth painted, her hair covered by the other hair that was cloud soft and shiny . . . She looked at the girl's cheeks flushed with excitement at the thought of her future, and she knew that with or without the paint box, Lorette would be a Lady whose skin would be smooth, whose mouth would be soft . . .

"The fuzz is so soft now, the flesh so tender." She remembered the scent, the softness of the Lady's hands, the way her skirt moved about her red-clad thighs.

She bit her lip. But she didn't want to be a Lady. She couldn't ever think of them again without loathing and disgust. She was chosen to be a Teacher.

They said it is the duty of society to prepare its non-citizens for citizenship but it is recognized that there are those who will not meet the requirements and society itself is not to be blamed for those occasional failures that must accrue.

She took out her notebook and wrote the words in it.

"Did you just remember something else she said?" Lisa asked. She was the youngest of the girls, only ten, and had attended Madam Westfall one time. She seemed to be very tired.

Carla looked over what she had written, and then read it aloud. "It's from the school rules book," she said. "Maybe changed a little, but the same meaning. You'll study it in a year or two."

Lisa nodded. "You know what she said to me?

She said I should go hide in the cave, and never lose my birth certificate. She said I should never tell anyone where the radio is." She frowned. "Do you know what a cave is? And a radio?"

"You wrote it down, didn't you? In the notebook?"

Lisa ducked her head. "I forgot again. I remembered it once and then forgot again until now." She searched through her cloth travel bag for her notebook and when she didn't find it, she dumped the contents on the floor to search more carefully. The notebook was not there.

"Lisa, when did you have it last?"

"I don't know. A few days ago. I don't remember."

"When Madam Trudeau talked to you the last time, did you have it then?"

"No. I couldn't find it. She said if I didn't have it the next time I was called for an interview, she'd whip me. But I can't find it!" She broke into tears and threw herself down on her small heap of belongings. She beat her fists on them and sobbed. "She's going to whip me and I can't find it. I can't. It's gone."

Carla stared at her. She shook her head. "Lisa, stop that crying. You couldn't have lost it. Where? There's no place to lose it. You didn't take it from your cubicle, did you?"

The girl sobbed louder. "No. No. No. I don't know where it is."

Carla kneeled by her and pulled the child up from the floor to a squatting position. "Lisa, what did you put in the notebook? Did you play with it?"

Lisa turned chalky white and her eyes became very large, then she closed them, no longer weeping.

"So you used it for other things? Is that it? What sort of things?"

Lisa shook her head. "I don't know. Just things."

"All of it? The whole notebook?"

"I couldn't help it. I didn't know what to write down. Madam Westfall said too much. I couldn't write it all. She wanted to touch me and I was afraid of her and I hid under the chair and she kept calling me, 'Child, come here don't hide, I'm not one of them. Go to the cave and take it with you.' And she kept reaching for me with her hands. I . . . they were like chicken claws. She would have ripped me apart with them. She hated me. She said she hated me. She said I should have been killed with the others, why wasn't I killed with the others."

Carla, her hands hard on the child's shoulders, turned away from the fear and despair she saw on the girl's face. Ruthie pushed past her and hugged the child.

"Hush, hush, Lisa. Don't cry now. Hush. There, there."

Carla stood up and backed away. "Lisa, what sort of things did you put in the notebook?"

"Just things that I like. Snowflakes and flowers and designs."

"All right. Pick up your belongings and sit down. We must be nearly there. It seems like the tube is stopping."

Again they were shown from a closed compartment to a closed limousine and whisked over countryside that remained invisible to them. There was a drizzly rain falling when they stopped and got out of the car.

The Westfall house was a three-storied, pseudo-

Victorian wooden building, with balconies and cu-
polas, and many chimneys. There was scaffolding
about it, and one of the three porches had been
torn away and was being replaced as restoration of
the house, turning it into a national monument,
progressed. The girls accompanied the casket to a
gloomy, large room where the air was chilly and
damp, and scant lighting cast deep shadows. After
the casket had been positioned on the dais which
also had accompanied it, the girls followed Madam
Trudeau through narrow corridors, up narrow steps,
to the third floor where two large rooms had been
prepared for them, each containing seven cots.

Madam Trudeau showed them the bathroom that
would serve their needs, told them good-night, and
motioned Carla to follow her. They descended the
stairs to a second floor room that had black, massive
furniture: a desk, two straight chairs, a bureau with
a wavery mirror over it, and a large canopied bed.

Madam Trudeau paced the black floor silently for
several minutes without speaking, then she swung
around and said, "Carla, I heard every word that
silly little girl said this afternoon. She drew pictures
in her notebook! This is the third time the word
cave has come up in reports of Madam Westfall's
mutterings. Did she speak to you of caves?"

Carla's mind was whirling. How had she heard
what they had said? Did maturity also bestow magical abilities? She said, "Yes, Madam, she spoke of
hiding in a cave."

"Where is the cave, Carla? Where is it?"

"I don't know, Madam. She didn't say."

Madam Trudeau started to pace once more. Her
pale face was drawn in lines of concentration that

carved deeply into her flesh, two furrows straight
up from the inner brows, other lines at the sides of
her nose, straight to her chin, her mouth tight and
hard. Suddenly she sat down and leaned back in
the chair. "Carla, in the last four or five years
Madam Westfall became childishly senile; she was
no longer living in the present most of the time, but
was reliving incidents in her past. Do you understand what I mean?"

Carla nodded, then said hastily, "Yes, Madam."

"Yes. Well, it doesn't matter. You know that I have
been commissioned to write the biography of
Madam Westfall, to immortalize her writings and
her utterances. But there is a gap, Carla. A large
gap in our knowledge, and until recently it seemed
that the gap never would be filled in. When Madam
Westfall was found as a child, wandering in a dazed
condition, undernourished, almost dead from exposure, she did not know who she was, where she
was from, anything about her past at all. Someone
had put an identification bracelet on her arm, a steel
bracelet that she could not remove, and that was the
only clue there was about her origins. For ten years
she received the best medical care and education
available, and her intellect sparkled brilliantly, but
she never regained her memory."

Madam Trudeau shifted to look at Carla. A trick
of the lighting made her eyes glitter like jewels.
"You have studied how she started her first school
with eight students, and over the next century
developed her teaching methods to the point of
perfection that we now employ throughout the nation, in the Males' school as well as the Females'.
Through her efforts Teachers have become the most

respected of all citizens and the schools the most powerful of all institutions." A mirthless smile crossed her face, gone almost as quickly as it formed, leaving the deep shadows, lines, and the glittering eyes. "I honored you more than you yet realize when I chose you for my protege."

The air in the room was too close and dank, smelled of moldering wood and unopened places. Carla continued to watch Madam Trudeau, but she was feeling light-headed and exhausted and the words seemed interminable to her. The glittering eyes held her gaze and she said nothing. The thought occurred to her that Madam Trudeau would take Madam Westfall's place as head of the school now.

"Encourage the girls to talk, Carla. Let them go on as much as they want about what Madam Westfall said, lead them into it if they stray from the point. Written reports have been sadly deficient." She stopped and looked questioningly at the girl. "Yes? What is it?"

"Then . . . I mean after they talk, are they to write . . . ? Or should I try to remember and write it all down?"

"There will be no need for that," Madam Trudeau said. "Simply let them talk as much as they want."

"Yes, Madam."

"Very well. Here is a schedule for the coming days. Two girls on duty in the Viewing Room at all times from dawn until dark, yard exercise in the enclosed garden behind the building if the weather permits, kitchen duty and so on. Study it, and direct the girls to their duties. On Saturday afternoon everyone will attend the burial, and on Sunday we return to the school. Now go."

Carla bowed, and turned to leave. Madam Trudeau's voice stopped her once more. "Wait, Carla. Come here. You may brush my hair before you leave."

Carla took the brush in numb fingers and walked obediently behind Madam Trudeau, who was loosening hair clasps that restrained her heavy black hair. It fell down her back like a dead snake, uncoiling slowly. Carla started to brush it.

"Harder, girl. Are you so weak that you can't brush hair?"

She plied the brush harder until her arm became heavy and then Madam Trudeau said, "Enough. You are a clumsy girl, awkward and stupid. Must I teach you everything, even how to brush one's hair properly?" She yanked the brush from Carla's hand and now there were two spots of color on her cheeks and her eyes were flashing. "Get out. Go! Leave me! On Saturday immediately following the funeral you will administer punishment to Lisa for scribbling in her notebook. Afterward report to me. And now get out of here!"

Carla snatched up the schedule and backed across the room, terrified of the Teacher who seemed demoniacal suddenly. She bumped into the other chair and nearly fell down. Madam Trudeau laughed shortly and cried, "Clumsy, awkward! You would be a Lady! You?"

Carla groped behind her for the doorknob and finally escaped into the hallway, where she leaned against the wall trembling too hard to move on. Something crashed into the door behind her and

she stifled a scream and ran. The brush. Madam
had thrown the brush against the door.

∞

Madam Westfall's ghost roamed all night, chasing
shadows in and out of rooms, making the floors
creak with her passage, echoes of her voice drifting
in and out of the dorm where Carla tossed restlessly.
Twice she sat upright in fear, listening intently, not
knowing why. Once Lisa cried out and she went to
her and held her hand until the child quieted again.
When dawn lighted the room Carla was awake and
standing at the windows looking at the ring of
mountains that encircled the city. Black shadows
against the lesser black of the sky, they darkened,
and suddenly caught fire from the sun striking their
tips. The fire spread downward, went out and became merely light on the leaves that were turning
red and gold. Carla turned from the view, unable to
explain the pain that filled her. She awakened the
first two girls who were to be on duty with Madam
Westfall and after their quiet departure, returned
to the window. The sun was all the way up now,
but its morning light was soft; there were no hard
outlines anywhere. The trees were a blend of colors
with no individual boundaries, and rocks and earth
melted together and were one. Birds were singing
with the desperation of summer's end and winter's
approach.

"Carla?" Lisa touched her arm and looked up at
her with wide, fearful eyes. "Is she going to whip
me?"

"You will be punished after the funeral," Carla
said, stiffly. "And I should report you for touching
me, you know."

The child drew back, looking down at the black border on Carla's skirt. "I forgot." She hung her head. "I'm . . . I'm so scared."

"It's time for breakfast, and after that we'll have a walk in the gardens. You'll feel better after you get out in the sunshine and fresh air."

"Chrysanthemums, dahlias, marigolds. No, the small ones there, with the brown fringes . . ." Luella pointed out the various flowers to the other girls. Carla walked in the rear, hardly listening, trying to keep her eye on Lisa, who also trailed behind. She was worried about the child. She had not slept well, had eaten no breakfast, and was so pale and wan that she didn't look strong enough to take the short garden walk with them.

Eminent personages came and went in the gloomy old house and huddled together to speak in lowered voices. Carla paid little attention to them. "I can change it after I have some authority," she said to a still inner self who listened and made no reply. "What can I do now? I'm property. I belong to the state, to Madam Trudeau and the school. What good if I disobey and am also whipped? Would that help any? I won't hit her hard." The inner self said nothing, but she thought she could hear a mocking laugh come from the mummy that was being honored.

They had all those empty schools, miles and miles of school halls where no feet walked, desks where no students sat, books that no students scribbled up, and they put the children in them and they could see immediately who couldn't keep up, couldn't learn the new ways and they got rid of them. Smart. Smart of them. They were smart and had the goods

*and the money and the hatred. My God, they hated.
That's who wins, who hates most. And is more
afraid. Every time.*

Carla forced her arms not to move, her hands to
remain locked before her, forced her head to stay
bowed. The voice now went on and on and she
couldn't get away from it.

*. . . rained every day, cold freezing rain and
Daddy didn't come back and Mama said, hide child,
hide in the cave where it's warm, and don't move no
matter what happens, don't move. Let me put it on
your arm, don't take it off, never take it off show it
to them if they find you show them make them
look. . . .*

Her relief came and Carla left. In the wide hallway that led to the back steps she was stopped by
a rough hand on her arm. "Damme, here's a likely
one. Come here, girl. Let's have a look at you." She
was spun around and the hand grasped her chin and
lifted her head. "Did I say it! I could spot her all
the way down the hall, now couldn't I. Can't hide
what she's got with long skirts and that skinny
hairdo, now can you? Didn't I spot her!" He
laughed and turned Carla's head to the side and
looked at her in profile, then laughed even louder.

She could see only that he was red faced, with
bushy eyebrows and thick gray hair. His hand holding her chin hurt, digging into her jaws at each side
of her neck.

"Victor, turn her loose," the cool voice of a female
said then. "She's been chosen already. An apprentice Teacher."

He pushed Carla from him, still holding her chin,

and he looked down at the skirts with the broad black band at the bottom. He gave her a shove that sent her into the opposite wall. She clutched at it for support.

"Whose pet is she?" he said darkly.

"Trudeau's."

He turned and stamped away, not looking at Carla again. He wore the blue and white of a Doctor of Law. The female was a Lady in pink and black.

"Carla. Go upstairs." Madam Trudeau moved from an open doorway and stood before Carla. She looked up and down the shaking girl. "Now do you understand why I apprenticed you before this trip? For your own protection."

They walked to the cemetery on Saturday, a bright, warm day with golden light and the odor of burning leaves. Speeches were made, Madam Westfall's favorite music was played, and the services ended. Carla dreaded returning to the dormitory. She kept a close watch on Lisa who seemed but a shadow of herself. Three times during the night she had held the girl until her nightmares subsided, and each time she had stroked her fine hair and soft cheeks and murmured to her quieting words, and she knew it was only her own cowardice that prevented her saying that it was she who would administer the whipping. The first shovelful of earth was thrown on top the casket and everyone turned to leave the place, when suddenly the air was filled with raucous laughter, obscene chants, and wild music. It ended almost as quickly as it started, but the group was frozen until the mountain air became unnaturally still. Not even the birds were making a sound following the maniacal outburst.

Carla had been unable to stop the involuntary look that she cast about her at the woods that circled the cemetery. Who? Who would dare? Only a leaf or two stirred, floating downward on the gentle air effortlessly. Far in the distance a bird began to sing again, as if the evil spirits that had flown past were now gone.

∞

"Madam Trudeau sent this up for you," Luella said nervously, handing Carla the rod. It was plastic, three feet long, thin, flexible. Carla looked at it and turned slowly to Lisa. The girl seemed to be swaying back and forth.

"I am to administer the whipping," Carla said. "You will undress now."

Lisa stared at her in disbelief, and then suddenly she ran across the room and threw herself on Carla, hugging her hard, sobbing. "Thank you, Carla. Thank you so much. I was so afraid, you don't know how afraid. Thank you. How did you make her let you do it? Will you be punished too? I love you so much, Carla." She was incoherent in her relief and she flung off her gown and underwear and turned around.

Her skin was pale and soft, rounded buttocks, dimpled just above the fullness. She had no waist yet, no breasts, no hair on her baby body. Like a baby she had whimpered in the night, clinging tightly to Carla, burying her head in the curve of Carla's breasts.

Carla raised the rod and brought it down, as

easily as she could. Anything was too hard. There was a red welt. The girl bowed her head lower, but didn't whimper. She was holding the back of a chair and it jerked when the rod struck.

It would be worse if Madam Trudeau was doing it, Carla thought. She would try to hurt, would draw blood. Why? Why? The rod was hanging limply, and she knew it would be harder on both of them if she didn't finish it quickly. She raised it and again felt the rod bite into flesh, sending the vibration into her arm, through her body.

Again. The girl cried out, and a spot of blood appeared on her back. Carla stared at it in fascination and despair. She couldn't help it. Her arm wielded the rod too hard and she couldn't help it. She closed her eyes a moment, raised the rod and struck again. Better. But the vibrations that had begun with the first blow increased, and she felt dizzy, and couldn't keep her eyes off the spot of blood that was trailing down the girl's back. Lisa was weeping now, her body was shaking. Carla felt a responsive tremor start within her.

Eight, nine. The excitement that stirred her was unnameable, unknowable, never before felt like this. Suddenly she thought of the Lady who had chosen her once, and scenes of the film she had been forced to watch flashed through her mind. . . . *remake them in our image.* She looked about in that moment frozen in time, and she saw the excitement on some of the faces, on others fear, disgust and revulsion. Her gaze stopped on Helga, who had her eyes closed, whose body was moving rhythmically. She raised the rod and brought it down as hard as she could, hitting the chair with a noise that brought everyone out of her own kind of trance. A sharp, cracking noise that was a finish.

"Ten!" she cried and threw the rod across the room.

Lisa turned and through brimming eyes, red, swollen, ugly with crying, said, "Thank you, Carla. It wasn't so bad."

Looking at her Carla knew hatred. It burned through her, distorted the image of what she saw. Inside her body the excitement found no outlet, and it flushed her face, made her hands numb, and filled her with hatred. She turned and fled.

Before Madam Trudeau's door, she stopped a moment, took a deep breath, and knocked. After several moments the door opened and Madam Trudeau came out. Her eyes were glittering more than ever, and there were two spots of color on her pasty cheeks.

"It is done? Let me look at you." Her fingers were cold and moist when she lifted Carla's chin. "Yes, I see. I see. I am busy now. Come back in half an hour. You will tell me about it. Half an hour." Carla never had seen a genuine smile on the Teacher's face before, and now when it came, it was more frightening than her frown was. Carla didn't move, but she felt as if every cell in her body had tried to pull back.

She bowed and turned to leave. Madam Trudeau followed her a step and said in a low vibrant voice, "You felt it, didn't you? You know now, don't you?"

"Madam Trudeau, are you coming back?" The door behind her opened, and one of the Doctors of Law appeared there.

"Yes, of course." She turned and went back to the room.

Carla let herself into the small enclosed area between the second and third floor, then stopped. She could hear the voices of girls coming down the stairs, going on duty in the kitchen, or outside for evening exercises. She stopped to wait for them to pass, and she leaned against the wall tiredly. This space was two and a half feet square perhaps. It was very dank and hot. From here she could hear every sound made by the girls on the stairs. Probably that was why the second door had been added, to muffle the noise of those going up and down. The girls had stopped on the steps and were discussing the laughter and obscenities they had heard in the cemetery.

Carla knew that it was her duty to confront them, to order them to their duties, to impose proper silence on them in public places, but she closed her eyes and pressed her hand hard on the wood behind her for support and wished they would finish their childish prattle and go on. The wood behind her started to slide.

She jerked away. A sliding door? She felt it and ran her finger along the smooth paneling to the edge where there was now a six-inch opening as high as she could reach down to the floor. She pushed the door again and it slid easily, going between the two walls. When the opening was wide enough she stepped through it. The cave! She knew it was the cave that Madam Westfall had talked about incessantly.

The space was no more than two feet wide, and very dark. She felt the inside door and there was a knob on it, low enough for children to reach. The door slid as smoothly from the inside as it had from the outside. She slid it almost closed and the voices were cut off, but she could hear other voices, from the room on the other side of the passage. They were not clear. She felt her way farther, and almost fell over a box. She held her breath as she realized that she was hearing Madam Trudeau's voice:

". . . be there. Too many independent reports of the old fool's babbling about it for there not to be something to it. Your men are incompetent."

"Trudeau, shut up. You scare the living hell out of the kids, but you don't scare me. Just shut up and accept the report. We've been over every inch of the hills for miles, and there's no cave. It was over a hundred years ago. Maybe there was one that the kids played in, buit it's gone now. Probably collapsed."

"We have to be certain, absolutely certain."

"What's so important about it anyway? Maybe if you would give us more to go on we could make more progress."

"The reports state that when the militia came here, they found only Martha Westfall. They executed her on the spot without questioning her first. Fools! When they searched the house, they discovered that it was stripped. No jewels, no silver, diaries, papers. Nothing. Steve Westfall was dead. Dr. Westfall dead. Martha. No one has ever found the articles that were hidden, and when the child again appeared, she had true amnesia that never yielded to attempts to penetrate it."

"So, a few records, diaries. What are they to you?" There was silence, then he laughed. "The money!

He took all his money out of the bank, didn't he."

"Don't be ridiculous. I want records, that's all. There's a complete ham radio, complete. Dr. Westfall was an electronics engineer as well as a teacher. No one could begin to guess how much equipment he hid before he was killed."

Carla ran her hand over the box, felt behind it. More boxes.

"Yeah, yeah. I read the reports, too. All the more reason to keep the search nearby. For a year before the end a close watch was kept on the house. They had to walk to wherever they hid the stuff. And I can just say again that there's no cave around here. It fell in."

"I hope so," Madam Trudeau said.

Someone knocked on the door, and Madam Trudeau called, "Come in."

"Yes, what is it? Speak up, girl."

"It is my duty to report, Madam, that Carla did not administer the full punishment ordered by you."

Carla's fists clenched hard. Helga.

"Explain," Madam Trudeau said sharply.

"She only struck Lisa nine times, Madam. The last time she hit the chair."

"I see. Return to your room."

The man laughed when the girl closed the door once more. "Carla is the golden one, Trudeau? The one who wears a single black band?"

"The one you manhandled earlier, yes."

"Insubordination in the ranks, Trudeau? Tut, tut. And your reports all state that you never have any rebellion. Never."

Very slowly Madam Trudeau said, "I have never had a student who didn't abandon any thoughts of

rebellion under my guidance. Carla will be obedi-
ent. And one day she will be an excellent Teacher.
I know the signs."

∞

Carla stood before the Teacher with her head
bowed and her hands clasped together. Madam
Trudeau walked around her without touching her,
then sat down and said, "You will whip Lisa every
day for a week, beginning tomorrow."

Carla didn't reply.

"Don't stand mute before me, Carla. Signify your
obedience immediately."

"I . . . I can't, Madam."

"Carla, any day that you do not whip Lisa, I will.
And I will also whip you double her allotment. Do
you understand?"

"Yes, Madam."

"You will inform Lisa that she is to be whipped
every day, by one or the other of us. Immediately."

"Madam, please . . ."

"You speak out of turn, Carla!"

"I, Madam, please don't do this. Don't make me
do this. She is too weak . . ."

"She will beg you to do it, won't she, Carla. Beg
you with tears flowing to be the one, not me. And
you will feel the excitement and the hate and every
day you will feel it grow strong. You will want to
hurt her, want to see blood spot her bare back. And
your hate will grow until you won't be able to look
at her without being blinded by your own hatred.
You see, I know, Carla. I know all of it."

Carla stared at her in horror. "I won't do it. I
won't."

"I will."

They were old and full of hatred for the shiny young faces, the bright hair, the straight backs and strong legs and arms. They said: let us remake them in our image and they did.

Carla repeated Madam Trudeau's words to the girls gathered in the two sleeping rooms on the third floor. Lisa swayed and was supported by Ruthie. Helga smiled.

That evening Ruthie tried to run away and was caught by two of the blue-clad Males. The girls were lined up and watched as Ruthie was stoned. They buried her without a service on the hill where she had been caught.

After dark, lying on the cot open-eyed, tense, Carla heard Lisa's whisper close to her ear. "I don't care if you hit me, Carla. It won't hurt like it does when she hits me."

"Go to bed, Lisa. Go to sleep."

"I can't sleep. I keep seeing Ruthie. I should have gone with her. I wanted to, but she wouldn't let me. She was afraid there would be Males on the hill watching. She said if she didn't get caught, then I should try to follow her at night." The child's voice was flat, as if shock had dulled her sensibilities.

Carla kept seeing Ruthie too. Over and over she repeated to herself: I should have tried it. I'm cleverer than she was. I might have escaped. I should have been the one. She knew it was too late now. They would be watching too closely.

An eternity later she crept from her bed and dressed quietly. Soundlessly she gathered her own belongings, and then collected the notebooks of the other girls, and the pens, and she left the room. There were dim lights on throughout the house as she made her way silently down stairs and through corridors. She left a pen by one of the outside doors, and very cautiously made her way back to the tiny space between the floors. She slid the door open and deposited everything else she carried inside the cave. She tried to get to the kitchen for food, but stopped when she saw one of the Officers of Law. She returned soundlessly to the attic rooms and tiptoed among the beds to Lisa's cot. She placed one hand over the girl's mouth and shook her awake with the other.

Lisa bolted upright, terrified, her body stiffened convulsively. With her mouth against the girl's ear Carla whispered, "Don't make a sound. Come on." She half-led, half-carried the girl to the doorway, down the stairs and into the cave and closed the door.

"You can't talk here, either," she whispered. "They can hear." She spread out the extra garments she had collected and they lay down together, her arms tight about the girl's shoulders. "Try to sleep," she whispered. "I don't think they'll find us here. And after they leave, we'll creep out and live in the woods. We'll eat nuts and berries . . ."

The first day they were jubilant at their success and they giggled and muffled the noise with their skirts. They could hear all the orders being issued by Madam Trudeau: guards in all the halls, on the stairs, at the door to the dorm to keep other girls from trying to escape also. They could hear all the interrogations, of the girls, the guards who had not seen the escapees. They heard the mocking voice of the Doctor of Law deriding Madam Trudeau's boasts of absolute control.

The second day Carla tried to steal food for them, and, more important, water. There were blue-clad Males everywhere. She returned empty-handed. During the night Lisa whimpered in her sleep and Carla had to stay awake to quiet the child who was slightly feverish.

"You won't let her get me, will you?" she begged over and over.

The third day Lisa became too quiet. She didn't want Carla to move from her side at all. She held Carla's hand in her hot, dry hand and now and then tried to raise it to her face, but she was too weak now. Carla stroked her forehead.

When the child slept Carla wrote in the notebooks, in the dark, not knowing if she wrote over other words, or on blank pages. She wrote her life story, and then made up other things to say. She wrote her name over and over, and wept because she had no last name. She wrote nonsense words and rhymed them with other nonsense words. She wrote of the savages who had laughed at the funeral and she hoped they wouldn't all die over the winter months. She thought that probably they would. She wrote of the golden light through green-black pine trees and of birds' songs and moss underfoot. She wrote of Lisa lying peacefully now at the far end of the cave amidst riches that neither of them could ever have comprehended. When she could no longer write, she drifted in and out of the golden light in the forest, listening to the birds' songs, hearing the raucous laughter that now sounded so beautiful.

TIN SOLDIER

JOAN D. VINGE

Joan D. Vinge, one of the most gifted new talents in science fiction, has written a love story of the far future. The man is a cyborg, part human and part machine; the woman is a voyager in deep space. "Tin Soldier" blends science-fictional elements with one of Hans Christian Andersen's fairy tales. The result is a moving and fascinating story, possessing the power of myth as well as possible reality.

The ship drifted down the ragged light-robe of the Pleiades, dropped like a perfect pearl into the midnight water of the bay. And reemerged, to bob gently in a chain of gleaming pearls stretched across the harbor toward the port. The port's unsleeping Eye blinked once, the ship replied. New Piraeus, pooled among the hills, sent tributaries of light streaming down to the bay to welcome all comers, full of sound and brilliance and rash promise. The crew grinned, expectant, faces peering through the transparent hull; someone giggled nervously.

. . .

The sign at the heavy door flashed a red one-legged toy; TIN SOLDIER flashed blue below it. EAT. DRINK. COME BACK AGAIN. In green. And they always did, because they knew they could.

"Soldier, another round, please!" came over canned music.

The owner of the Tin Soldier, also known as Tin Soldier, glanced up from his polishing to nod and smile, reached down to set bottles out on the bar. He mixed the drinks himself. His face was ordinary, with eyes that were dark and patient, and his hair was coppery barbed wire bound with a knotted cloth. Under the curling copper, under the skin, the back of his skull was a plastic plate. The quick fingers of the hand on the goose-necked bottle were plastic, the smooth arm was prosthetic. Sometimes he imagined he heard clicking as it moved. More than half his body was artificial. He looked to be about twenty-five; he had looked the same fifty years ago.

He set the glasses on the tray and pushed, watching as it drifted across the room, and returned to his polishing. The agate surface of the bar showed cloudy permutations of color, grain-streak and whorl and chalcedony depths of mist. He had discovered it in the desert to the east—a shattered imitation tree, like a fellow traveler trapped in stasis through time. They shared the private joke with their clientele.

"—come see our living legend!'

He looked up, saw her coming in with the crew of the *Who Got Her*–709, realized he didn't know her. She hung back as they crowded around, her short ashen hair like beaten metal in the blue-glass lantern light. *New*, he thought. Maybe eighteen, with eyes of quicksilver very wide open. He smiled at her as he welcomed them, and the other women pulled her up to the agate bar. "Come on, little sister," he heard Harkané say, "you're one of us too." She smiled back at him.

"I don't know you . . . but your name should be Diana, like the silver Lady of the Moon." His voice caught him by surprise.

Quicksilver shifted. "It's not."

Very new. And realizing what he'd almost done again, suddenly wanted it more than anything. Filled with bitter joy he said, "What is your name?"

Her face flickered, but then she met his eyes and said, smiling, "My name is Brandy."

"Brandy . . ."

A knowing voice said, "Send us the usual, Soldier. Later, yes—?"

He nodded vaguely, groping for bottles under the counter ledge. Wood screeked over stone as she pulled a stool near and slipped onto it, watching him pour. "You're very neat." She picked nuts from a bowl.

"*Long* practice."

She smiled, missing the joke.

He said, "Brandy's a nice name. And I think somewhere I've heard it—"

"The whole thing is Branduin. My mother said it was very old."

He was staring at her. He wondered if she could see one side of his face blushing. "What will you drink?"

"Oh . . . do you have any—brandy? It's a wine, I think; nobody's ever had any. But because it's my name, I always ask."

He frowned. "I don't . . . hell, I do! Stay there."

He returned with the impossible bottle, carefully wiped away its gray coat of years and laid it gleaming on the bar. Glintings of maroon speared their eyes. "All these years, it must have been waiting. That's where I heard it . . . genuine vintage brandy, from Home."

"From Terra—really? Oh, thank you!" She touched the bottle, touched his hand. "I'm going to be lucky."

Curving glasses blossomed with wine; he placed one in her palm. "*Ad astra*." She lifted the glass.

"*Ad astra;* to the stars." He raised his own, adding silently, *Tonight* . . .

They were alone. Her breath came hard as they climbed up the newly cobbled streets to his home, up from the lower city where the fluorescent lamps were snuffing out one by one.

He stopped against a low stone wall. "Do you want to catch your breath?" Behind him in the empty lot a weedy garden patch wavered with the popping street lamp.

"Thank you." She leaned downhill against him, against the wall. "I got lazy on my training ride. There's not much to do on a ship; you're supposed to exercise, but—" Her shoulder twitched under the quilted blue-silver. He absorbed her warmth.

Her hand pressed his lightly on the wall. "What's your name? You haven't told me, you know."

"Everyone calls me Soldier."

"But that's not your name." Her eyes searched his own, smiling.

He ducked his head, his hand caught and tightened around hers. "Oh . . . no, it's not. It's Maris." He looked up. "That's an old name, too. It *means* 'soldier,' consecrated to the god of war. I never liked it much."

"From 'Mars'? Sol's fourth planet, the god of war." She bent back her head and peered up into the darkness. Fog hid the stars.

"Yes."

"Were you a soldier?"

"Yes. Everyone was a soldier—every man—where I came from. War was a way of life."

"An attempt to reconcile the blow to the masculine ego?"

He looked at her.

She frowned in concentration. " 'After it was determined that men were physically unsuited to spacing, and women came to a new position of dominance as they monopolized this critical area, the Terran cultural foundation underwent severe strain. As a result, many new and not always satisfactory cultural systems are evolving in the galaxy. . . . One of these is what might be termed a backlash of exaggerated *machismo—'* "

" '—and the rebirth of the warrior/chattel tradition.' "

"You've read that book too." She looked crestfallen.

"I read a lot. *New Ways for Old*, by Ebert Ntaka?"

"Sorry . . . I guess I got carried away. But, I just read it—"

"No." He grinned. "And I agree with old Ntaka, too. Glatte—what a sour name—was an unhealthy planet. But that's why I'm here, not there."

"Ow—!" She jerked loose from his hand. "Ohh, oh . . . God, you're strong!" She put her fingers in her mouth.

He fell over apologies; but she shook her head, and shook her hand. "No, it's all right . . . really, it just surprised me. Bad memories?"

He nodded, mouth tight.

She touched his shoulder, raised her fingers to his lips. "Kiss it, and make it well?" Gently he caught her hand, kissed it; she pressed against him. "It's very late. We should finish climbing the hill . . . ?"

"No." Hating himself, he set her back against the wall.

"No? But I thought—"

"I know you did. Your first space, I asked your name, you wanted me to; tradition says you lay the guy. But I'm a cyborg, Brandy. . . . It's always good for a laugh on the poor greenie, they've pulled it a hundred times."

"A cyborg?" The flickering gray eyes raked his body.

"It doesn't show with my clothes on."

"Oh . . ." Pale lashes were beating very hard across the eyes now. She took a breath, held it. "Do —you always let it get this far? I mean—"

"No. Hell, I don't know why I . . . I owe you another apology. Usually I never ask the name. If I slip, I tell them right away; nobody's ever held to it. I don't count." He smiled weakly.

"Well, why? You mean you can't—"

"I'm not all plastic." He frowned, numb fingers

rapping stone. "God, I'm not. Sometimes I wish I was, but I'm not."

"No one? They never want to?"

"Branduin"—he faced the questioning eyes—"you'd better go back down. Get some sleep. Tomorrow laugh it off, and pick up some flashy Tail in the bar and have a good time. Come see me again in twenty-five years, when you're back from space, and tell me what you saw." Hesitating, he brushed her cheek with his true hand; instinctively she bent her head to the caress. "Good-bye." He started up the hill.

"Maris—"

He stopped, trembling.

"Thank you for the brandy . . ." She came up beside him and caught his belt. "You'll probably have to tow me up the hill."

He pulled her to him and began to kiss her, hands touching her body incredulously.

"It's getting—very, very late. Let's hurry."

Maris woke, confused, to the sound of banging shutters. Raising his head he was struck by the colors of dawn, and the shadow of Brandy standing bright-edged at the window. He left the rumpled bed and crossed cold tiles to join her. "What are you doing?" He yawned.

"I wanted to watch the sun rise, I haven't seen anything but night for months. Look, the fog's lifting already: the sun burns it up, it's on fire, over the mountains—"

He smoothed her hair, pale gold under a corona of light. "And embers in the canyon."

She looked down across ends of gray mist slowly

reddening; then back. "Good morning." She began to laugh. "I'm glad you don't have any neighbors down there!" They were both naked.

He grinned, "That's what I like about the place," and put his arms around her. She moved close in the circle of coolness and warmth.

They watched the sunrise from the bed.

In the evening she came into the bar with the crew of the *Kiss And Tell*–736. They waved to him, nodded to her and drifted into blue shadows; she perched smiling before him. It struck him suddenly that nine hours was a long time.

"That's the crew of my training ship. They want some white wine, please, any kind, in a bottle."

He reached under the bar. "And one brandy, on the house?" He sent the tray off.

"Hi, Maris . . ."

"Hi, Brandy."

"To misty mornings." They drank together.

"By the way"—she glanced at him slyly—"I passed it around that people have been missing something. You."

"Thank you," meaning it. "But I doubt if it'll change any minds."

"Why not?"

"You read Ntaka—xenophobia; to most people in most cultures cyborgs are unnatural, the next thing up from a corpse. You'd have to be a necrophile—" She frowned.

"—or extraordinary. You're the first extraordinary person I've met in a hundred years."

The smile formed, faded. "Maris—you're not exactly twenty-five, are you? How old are you?"

"More like a hundred and fifteen." He waited for the reaction.

She stared. "But, you look like twenty-five? You're real, don't you age?"

"I age. About five years for every hundred." He shrugged. "The prosthetics slow the body's aging. Perhaps it's because only half my body needs constant regeneration; or it may be an effect of the anti-rejection treatment. Nobody really understands it. It just happens sometimes."

"Oh." She looked embarrassed. "That's what you meant by 'come back and see me' . . . and they meant—Will you really live a thousand years?"

"Probably not. Something vital will break down in another three or four centuries, I guess. Even plastic doesn't last forever."

"Oh . . ."

"Live longer and enjoy it less. Except for today. What did you do today? Get any sleep?"

"No—" She shook away disconcertion. "A bunch of us went out and gorged. We stay on wake-ups when we're in port, so we don't miss a minute; you don't need to sleep. Really they're for emergencies, but everybody does it."

Quick laughter almost escaped him; he hoped she'd missed it. Serious, he said, "You want to be careful with those things. They can get to you."

"Oh, they're all right." She twiddled her glass, annoyed and suddenly awkward again, confronted by the Old Man.

Hell, it can't matter—He glanced toward the door.

"Brandy! There you are." And the crew came in. "Soldier, you must come sit with us later; but right now we're going to steal Brandy away from you."

He looked up with Brandy to the brown face, brown eyes, and salt-white hair of Harkané, Best Friend of the Mactav on the *Who Got Her–709*. Time had woven deep nets of understanding around her eyes; she was one of his oldest customers. Even the shape of her words sounded strange to him now: "Ah, Soldier, you make me feel young, always . . . Come, little sister, and join your family; share her, Soldier."

Brandy gulped brandy; her boots clattered as she dropped off the stool. "Thank you for the drink," and for half a second the smile was real. "Guess I'll be seeing you—Soldier." And she was leaving, ungracefully, gratefully.

Soldier polished the agate bar, ignoring the disappointed face it showed him. And later watched her leave, with a smug, black-eyed Tail in velvet knee pants.

Beyond the doorway yellow-green twilight seeped into the bay, the early crowds began to come together with the night. "H'lo, Maris . . . ?" Silver dulled to lead met him in a face gone hollow; thin hands trembled, clenched, trembled in the air.

"Brandy—"

"What've you got for an upset stomach?" She was expecting laughter.

"Got the shakes, huh?" He didn't laugh.

She nodded. "You were right about the pills, Maris. They make me sick. I got tired, I kept taking them . . ." Her hands rattled on the counter.

"And that was pretty dumb, wasn't it?" He poured her a glass of water, watched her trying to drink, pushed a button under the counter. "Listen,

I just called you a ride—when it comes, I want you to go to my place and go to bed."

"But—"

"I won't be home for hours. Catch some sleep and then you'll be all right, right? This is my door lock." He printed large numbers on a napkin. "Don't lose this."

She nodded, drank, stuffed the napkin up her sleeve. Drank some more, spilling it. "My mouth is numb." An abrupt chirp of laughter escaped; she put up a shaky hand. "I—won't lose it."

Deep gold leaped beyond the doorway, sunlight on metal. "Your ride's here."

"Thank you, Maris." The smile was crooked but very fond. She tacked toward the doorway.

She was still there when he came home, snoring gently in the bedroom in a knot of unmade blankets. He went silently out of the room, afraid to touch her, and sank into a leather-slung chair. Filled with rare and uneasy peace he dozed, while the starlit mist of the Pleiades' nebulosity passed across the darkened sky toward morning.

"Maris, why didn't you wake me up? You didn't have to sleep in a *chair* all night." Brandy stood before him wrestling with a towel, eyes puffy with sleep and hair flopping in sodden plumb-bobs from the shower. Her feet made small puddles on the braided rug.

"I didn't mind. I don't need much sleep."

"That's what I told *you*."

"But I meant it. I never sleep more than three hours. You needed the rest, anyway."

"I know . . . damn—" She gave up and wrapped

the towel around her head. "You're a fine guy, Maris."

"You're not so bad yourself."

She blushed. "Glad you approve. Ugh, your rug— I got it all wet." She disappeared into the bedroom.

Maris stretched unwillingly, stared up into ceiling beams bronzed with early sunlight. He sighed faintly. "You want some breakfast?"

"Sure, I'm starving! Oh, wait—" A wet head reappeared. "Let me make you breakfast? Wait for me."

He sat watching as the apparition in silver-blue flightsuit ransacked his cupboards. "You're kind of low on raw materials."

"I know." He brushed crumbs off the table. "I eat instant breakfasts and frozen dinners; I hate to cook."

She made a face.

"Yeah, it gets pretty old after half a century . . . they've only had them on Oro for half a century. They don't get any better, either."

She stuck something into the oven. "I'm sorry I was so stupid about it."

"About what?"

"About . . . a hundred years. I guess it scared me. I acted like a bitch."

"No, you didn't."

"Yes, I did! I know I did." She frowned.

"Okay, you did . . . I forgive you. When do we eat?"

They ate, sitting side by side.

"Cooking seems like an odd spacer's hobby." Maris scraped his plate appreciatively. "When can you cook on a ship?"

"Never. It's all prepared and processed. So we can't overeat. That's why we love to eat and drink when we're in port. But I can't cook now either— no place. So it's not really a hobby, I guess, any more. I learned how from my father, he loved to cook . . ." She inhaled, eyes closed.

"Is your mother dead?"

"No—" She looked startled. "She just doesn't like to cook."

"She wouldn't have liked Glatte, either." He scratched his crooked nose.

"Calicho—that's my home, it's seven light years up the cube from this corner of the Quadrangle— it's . . . a pretty nice place. I guess Ntaka would call it 'healthy,' even . . . there's lots of room, like space; that helps. Cold and not very rich, but they get along. My mother and father always shared their work . . . they have a farm." She broke off more bread.

"What did they think about you becoming a spacer?"

"They never tried to stop me; but I don't think they wanted me to. I guess when you're so tied to the land it's hard to imagine wanting to be so free. . . . It made them sad to lose me—it made me sad to lose them; but, I had to go . . ."

Her mouth began to quiver suddenly. "You know, I'll never get to see them again, I'll never have time, our trips take so long, they'll grow old and die. . . ." Tears dripped onto her plate. "And I miss my h-home—" Words dissolved into sobs, she clung to him in terror.

He rubbed her back helplessly, wordlessly, left

unequipped to deal with loneliness by a hundred years alone.

"M-Maris, can I come and see you always, will you always, always be here when I need you, and be my friend?"

"Always . . ." He rocked her gently. "Come when you want, stay as long as you want, cook dinner if you want, I'll always be here. . . ."

∞

. . . Until the night, twenty-five years later, when they were suddenly clustered around him at the bar, hugging, badgering, laughing, the crew of the *Who Got Her–709*.

"Hi, Soldier!"

"Soldier, have we—"

"Look at this, Soldier—"

"What happened to—"

"Brandy?" he said stupidly. "Where's Brandy?"

"Honestly, Soldier, you really never *do* forget a face, do you?"

"Ah-ha, I bet it's not her *face* he remembers!"

"She was right with us." Harkané peered easily over the heads around her. "Maybe she stopped off somewhere."

"Maybe she's caught a Tail *already?*" Nilgiri was impressed.

"She could if anybody could, the little rascal." Wynmet rolled her eyes.

"Oh, just send us the usual, Soldier. She'll be along eventually. Come sit with us when she does." Harkané waved a rainbow-tipped hand. "Come, sisters, gossip is not tasteful before we've had a drink."

"That little rascal."

Soldier began to pour drinks with singleminded precision, until he noticed that he had the wrong bottle. Cursing, he drank them himself, one by one.

"Hi, Maris."

He pushed the tray away.

"*Hi*, Maris." Fingers appeared in front of his face; he started. "Hey."

"Brandy!"

Patrons along the bar turned to stare, turned away again.

"Brandy—"

"Well, sure; weren't you expecting me? Everybody else is already here."

"I know. I thought—I mean, they said . . . maybe you were out with somebody already," trying to keep it light, "and—"

"Well, really, Maris, what do you take me for?" She was insulted. "I just wanted to wait till everybody else got settled, so I could have you to myself. Did you think I'd forget you? Unkind." She hefted a bright mottled sack onto the bar. "Look, I brought you a present!" Pulling it open, she dumped heaping confusion onto the counter. "Books, tapes, buttons, all kinds of things to look at. You said you'd read out the library five times; so I collected everywhere, some of them should be new . . . Don't you like them?"

"I . . ." he coughed, "I'm crazy about them! I'm—overwhelmed. Noboody ever brought me anything before. Thank you. Thanks very much. And welcome back to New Piraeus!"

"Glad to be back!" She stretched across the bar, hugged him, kissed his nose. She wore a new belt of metal inlaid with stones. "You're just like I remembered."

"You're more beautiful."

"Flatterer." She beamed. Ashen hair fell to her breasts; angles had deepened on her face. The quicksilver eyes took all things in now without amazement. "I'm twenty-one today, you know."

"No kidding? That calls for a celebration. Will you have brandy?"

"Do you still have some?" The eyes widened slightly. "Oh, yes! We should make it a tradition, as long as it lasts."

He smiled contentedly. They drank to birthdays, and to stars.

"Not very crowded tonight, is it?" Brandy glanced into the room, tying small knots in her hair. "Not like last time."

"It comes and it goes. I've always got some fisherfolk, they're heavy on tradition. . . . I gave up keeping track of ship schedules."

"We don't even believe our own; they never quite fit. We're a month late here."

"I know—happened to notice it. . . ." He closed a bent cover, laid the book flat. "So anyway, how did you like your first Quadrangle?"

"Beautiful—oh, Maris, if I start I'll never finish, the City in the Clouds on Patris, the Freeport on Sanalareta . . . and the Pleiades . . . and the depths of night, ice and fire." Her eyes burned through him toward infinity. "You can't imagine—"

"So they tell me."

She searched his face for bitterness, found none. He shook his head. "I'm a man and a cyborg; that's two League rules against me that I can't change—so why resent it? I enjoy the stories." His mouth twitched up.

"Do you like poetry?"

"Sometimes.

"Then—may I show you mine? I'm writing a cycle of poems about space, maybe someday I'll have a book. I haven't shown them to anybody else, but if you'd like—"

"I'd like it."

"I'll find them, then. Guess I should be joining the party, really, they'll think I'm antisocial"—she winced—"and they'll talk about me! It's like a small town, we're as bad as lubbers."

He laughed. "Don't—you'll disillusion me. See you later. Uh . . . listen, do you want arrangements like before? For sleeping."

"Use your place? Could I? I don't want to put you out."

"Hell, no. You're welcome to it."

"I'll cook for you—"

"I bought some eggs."

"It's a deal! Enjoy your books." She wove a path between the tables, nodding to sailor and spacer; he watched her laughing face merge and blur, caught occasional flashes of silver. Stuffing books into the sack, he set it against his shin behind the bar. And some time later, watched her go out with a Tail.

The morning of the thirteenth day he woke to find Brandy sleeping soundly in the pile of hairy cushions by the door. Curious, he glanced out into a water-gray field of fog. It was the first time she had come home before dawn. *Home?* Carefully he lifted her from the pillows; she sighed, arms found him, in her sleep she began to kiss his neck. He carried her to the bed and put her down softly, bent to . . . *No.* He turned away, left the room. He had slept with her only once. Twenty-five or three years ago, without words, she had told him they would not be lovers again. She kept the customs; a spacer never had the same man more than once.

In the kitchen he heated a frozen dinner, and ate alone.

"What's that?" Brandy appeared beside him, mummified in a blanket. She dropped down on the cushions where he sat barefoot, drinking wine and ignoring the TD.

"Three-dimensional propaganda: the Oro Morning Mine Report. You're up pretty early—it's hardly noon."

"I'm not sleepy." She took a sip of his wine.

"Got in pretty early, too. Anything wrong?"

"No . . . just—nothing happening, you know. Ran out of parties, everybody's pooped but me." She cocked her head. "What is this, anyway . . . an inquisition? 'Home awfully *early*, aren't you—?'" She glared at him and burst into laughter.

"You're crazy." He grinned.

"Whatever happened to your couch?" She prodded cushions.

"It fell apart. It's been twenty-five years, you know."

"Oh. That's too bad . . . Maris, may I read you my poems?" Suddenly serious, she produced a small, battered notebook from the folds of her blanket.

"Sure." He leaned back, watching subtle transformations occur in her face. And felt them begin to occur in himself, growing pride and a tender possessiveness.

> . . . Until, lost in darkness, we
> dance the silken star-song.

It was the final poem. "That's 'Genesis.' It's about the beginning of a flight . . . and a life." Her eyes found the world again, found dark eyes quietly regarding her.

" 'Attired with stars we shall forever sit, triumphing over Death, and Chance, and thee, O Time.' " He glanced away, pulling the tassel of a cushion. "No . . . Milton, not Maris—I could never do that." He looked back, in wonder. "They're beautiful, you are beautiful. Make a book. Gifts are meant for giving, and you are gifted."

Pleasure glowed in her cheeks. "You really think someone would want to read them?"

"Yes." He nodded, searching for the words to tell her. "Nobody's ever made me—see that way . . . as though I . . . go with you. Others would go, if they could. Home to the sky."

She turned with him to the window; they were silent. After a time she moved closer, smiling. "Do you know what I'd like to do?"

"What?" He let out a long breath.

"See your home." She set her notebook aside. "Let's go for a walk in New Piraeus. I've never really seen it by day—the real part of it. I want to see its beauty up close, before it's all gone. Can we go?"

He hesitated. "You sure you want to—?"

"Sure. Come on, lazy." She gestured him up.

And he wondered again why she had come home early.

So on the last afternoon he took her out through the stone-paved winding streets, where small white-washed houses pressed for footholds. They climbed narrow steps, panting, tasted the sea wind, bought fruit from a leathery smiling woman with a basket.

"Mmm—" Brandy licked juice from the crimson pith. "Who was that woman? She called you 'Sojer,' but I couldn't understand the rest . . . I couldn't even understand you! Is the dialect that slurred?"

He wiped his chin. "It's getting worse all the time, with all the newcomers. But you get used to everything in the lower city. . . . An old acquaintance, I met her during the epidemic, she was sick."

"Epidemic? What epidemic?"

"Oro Mines was importing workers—they started before your last visit, because of the bigger raw material demands. One of the new workers had some disease we didn't; it killed about a third of New Piraeus."

"Oh, my God—"

"That was about fifteen years ago . . . Oro's labs synthesized a vaccine, eventually, and they repopulated the city. But they still don't know what the disease was."

"It's like a trap, to live on a single world."

"Most of us have to . . . it has its compensations."

She finished her fruit, and changed the subject. "You helped take care of them, during the epidemic?"

He nodded. "I seemed to be immune, so—"

She patted his arm. "You are very good."

He laughed; glanced away. "Very plastic would be more like it."

"Don't you ever get sick?"

"Almost never. I can't even get very drunk. Someday I'll probably wake up entirely plastic."

"You'd still be very good." They began to walk again. "What did she say?"

"She said, 'Ah, Soldier, you've got a lady friend.' She seemed pleased."

"What did you say?"

"I said, 'That's right.'" Smiling, he didn't put his arm around her; his fingers kneaded emptiness.

"Well, I'm glad she was pleased . . . I don't think most people have been."

"Don't look at them. Look out there." He showed her the sea, muted greens and blues below the ivory jumble of the flat-roofed town. To the north and south mountains like rumpled cloth reached down to the shore.

"Oh, the sea—I've always loved the sea; at home we were surrounded by it, on an island. Space is like the sea, boundless, constant, constantly changing . . ."

"—spacer!" Two giggling girls made a wide circle past them in the street, dark skirts brushing their calves.

Brandy blushed, frowned, sought the sea again. "I—think I'm getting tired. I guess I've seen enough."

"Not much on up there but the new, anyway." He took her hand and they started back down. "It's just that we're a rarity up this far." A heavy man in a heavy caftan pushed past them; in his cold eyes Maris saw an alien wanton and her overaged Tail.

"They either leer, or they censure." He felt her nails mark his flesh. "What's their problem?"

"Jealousy . . . mortality. You threaten them, you spacers. Don't you ever think about it? Free and beautiful immortals—"

"They know we aren't immortal; we hardly live longer than anybody else."

"They also know you come here from a voyage of twenty-five years looking hardly older than when you left. Maybe they don't recognize you, but they *know*. And they're twenty-five years older. . . . Why do you think they go around in sacks?"

"To look ugly. They must be dreadfully repressed." She tossed her head sullenly.

"They are; but that's not why. It's because they want to hide the changes. And in their way to mimic you, who always look the same. They've done it since I can remember; you're all they have to envy."

She sighed. "I've heard on Elder they paint patterns on their skin, to hide the change. Ntaka called them 'youth-fixing,' didn't he?" Anger faded, her eyes grew cool like the sea, gray-green. "Yes, I think about it . . . especially when we're laughing at the lubbers, and their narrow lives. And all the poor panting awestruck Tails, sometimes they think they're using us, but we're always using them. . . . Sometimes I think we're very cruel."

"Very like a god—Silver Lady of the Moon."

"You haven't called me that since—that night . . . all night." Her hand tightened painfully; he said nothing. "I guess they envy a cyborg for the same things. . . ."

"At least it's easier to rationalize—and harder to imitate." He shrugged. "We leave each other alone, for the most part."

"And so we must wait for each other, we immortals. It's still a beautiful town; I don't care what they think."

He sat, fingers catching in the twisted metal of his thick bracelet, listening to her voice weave patterns through the hiss of running water. Washing away the dirty looks—Absently he reread the third paragraph on the page for the eighth time; and the singing stopped.

"Maris, do you have any—"

He looked up at her thin, shining body, naked in the doorway. "Brandy, God damn it! You're not between planets—you want to show it all to the whole damn street?"

"But I always—" Made awkward by sudden awareness, she fled.

He sat and stared at the sun-hazed windows, entirely aware that there was no one to see in. Slowly the fire died, his breathing eased.

She returned shyly, closing herself into quilted blue-silver, and sank onto the edge of a chair. "I just never think about it." Her voice was very small.

"It's all right." Ashamed, he looked past her. "Sorry I yelled at you . . . What did you want to ask me?"

"It doesn't matter." She pulled violently at her snarled hair. "Ow! Damn it!" Feeling him look at her, she forced a smile. "Uh, you know, I'm glad we picked up Mima on Treone; I'm not the little sister anymore. I was really getting pretty tired of being the greenie for so long. She's—"

"Brandy—"

"Hm?"

"Why don't they allow cyborgs on crews?"

Surprise caught her. "It's a regulation."

He shook his head. "Don't tell me 'It's a regulation,' tell me why."

"Well . . ." She smoothed wet hair-strands with her fingers. ". . . They tried it, and it didn't work out. Like with men—they couldn't endure space, they broke down, their hormonal balance was wrong. With cyborgs, stresses between the real and the artificial in the body were too severe, they broke down too. . . . At the beginning they tried cyborganics, as a way to let man keep space, like they tried altering the hormone balance. Neither worked. Physically or psychologically, there was too much strain. So finally they just made it a regulation, no men on space crews."

"But that was over a thousand years ago—cyborganics has improved. I'm healthier and live longer than any normal person. And stronger—" He leaned forward, tight with agitation.

"And slower. We don't need strength, we have artificial means. And anyway, a man would still have to face more stress, it would be dangerous."

"Are there any female cyborgs on crews?"

"No.'

"Have they ever even tried it again?"

"No—'

"You see? The League has a lock on space, they keep it with archaic laws. They don't want anyone else out there!" Sudden resentment shook his voice.

"Maybe . . . we don't." Her fingers closed, opened, closed over the soft heavy arms of the chair; her eyes were the color of twisting smoke. "Do you really blame us? Spacing is our life, it's our strength. We have to close the others out, everything changes and changes around us, there's no continuity—we only have each other. That's why we have our regulations, that's why we dress alike, look alike, act alike; there's nothing else we *can* do, and stay sane. We have to live apart, always." She pulled her hair forward, tying nervous knots. "And—that's why we never take the same lover twice, too. We have needs we have to satisfy; but we can't afford to . . . form relationships, get involved, tied. It's a danger, it's an instability. . . . You do understand that, don't you, Maris; that it's why I don't—" She broke off, eyes burning him with sorrow and, below it, fear.

He managed a smile. "Have you heard me complain?"

"Weren't you just . . .?" She lifted her head.

Slowly he nodded, felt pain start. "I suppose I was." *But I don't change.* He shut his eyes suddenly, before she read them. *But that's not the point, is it?*

"Maris, do you want me to stop staying here?"

"No— No . . . I understand, it's all right. I like the company." He stretched, shook his head. "Only, wear a towel, all right? I'm only human."

"I promise . . . that I will keep my eyes open, in the future."

He considered the future that would begin with dawn when her ship went up, and said nothing.

∞

He stumbled cursing from the bedroom to the door, to find her waiting there, radiant and wholly unexpected. "Surprise!" She laughed and hugged him, dislodging his half-tied robe.

"My God—hey!" He dragged her inside and slammed the door. "You want to get me arrested for indecent exposure?" He turned his back, making adjustments, while she stood and giggled behind him.

He faced her again, fogged with sleep, struggling to believe. "You're early—almost two weeks?"

"I know. I couldn't wait till tonight to surprise you. And I did, didn't I?" She rolled her eyes. "I heard you coming to the door!"

She sat curled on his aging striped couch, squinting out the window as he fastened his sandals. "You used to have so much room. Houses haven't filled up your canyon, have they?" Her voice grew wistful.

"Not yet. If they ever do, I won't stay to see it . . . How was your trip this time?"

"Beautiful, again . . . I can't imagine it ever being anything else. You could see it all a hundred times over, and never see it all—

> Through your crystal eye,
> Mactav, I watch the midnight's
> star turn inside out. . . .

Oh, guess what! My poems—I finished the cycle during the voyage . . . and it's going to be published, on Treone. They said very nice things about it."

He nodded smugly. "They have good taste. They must have changed, too."

" 'A renaissance in progress'—meaning they've put

on some *ver*-ry artsy airs, last decade; their Tails are really something else. . . ." Remembering, she shook her head. "It was one of them that told me about the publisher."

"You showed him your poems?" Trying not to—

"Good grief, no; he was telling me about *his*. So I thought, What have I got to lose?"

"When do I get a copy?"

"I don't know." Disappointment pulled at her mouth. "Maybe I'll never even get one; after twenty-five years they'll be out of print. 'Art is long, and Time is fleeting' . . . Longfellow had it backwards. But I made you some copies of the poems. And brought you some more books, too. There's one you should read, it replaced Ntaka years ago on the Inside. I thought it was inferior; but who are we . . . What are you laughing about?"

"What happened to that freckle-faced kid in pigtails?"

"*What?*" Her nose wrinkled.

"How old are you now?"

"Twenty-four. Oh—" She looked pleased.

"Madame Poet, do you want to go to dinner with me?"

"Oh, *food*, oh yes!" She bounced, caught him grinning, froze. "I would love to. Can we go to Good Eats?"

"It closed right after you left."

"Oh . . . the music was wild. Well, how about that seafood place, with the fish name—?"

He shook his head. "The owner died. It's been twenty-five years."

"Damn, we can never keep anything." She sighed.

"Why don't I just make us a dinner—*I'm* still here. And I'd like that."

That night, and every other night, he stood at the bar and watched her go out, with a Tail or a laughing knot of partyers. Once she waved to him; the stem of a shatterproof glass snapped in his hand; he kicked it under the counter, confused and angry.

But three nights in the two weeks she came home early. This time, pointedly, he asked her no questions. Gratefully, she told him no lies, sleeping on his couch and sharing the afternoon . . .

They returned to the flyer, moving in step along the cool jade sand of the beach. Maris looked toward the sea's edge, where frothy fingers reached, withdrew, and reached again. "You leave tomorrow, huh?"

Brandy nodded. "Uh-huh."

He sighed.

"Maris, if—"

"What?"

"Oh—nothing." She brushed sand from her boot.

He watched the sea reach, and withdraw, and reach—

"Have you ever wanted to see a ship? Inside, I mean." She pulled open the flyer door, her body strangely intent.

He followed her. "Yes."

"Would you like to see mine—the *Who Got Her*?"

"I thought that was illegal?"

" 'No waking man shall set foot on a ship of the spaceways.' It is a League regulation . . . but it's based on a superstition that's at least a thousand

years old—'Men on ships is bad luck.' Which is silly
here. Your presence on board in port isn't going to
bring us disaster."

He looked incredulous.

"I'd like you to see our life, Maris, like I see
yours. There's nothing wrong with that. And besides"—she shrugged—"no one will know; because
nobody's there right now."

He faced a wicked grin, and did his best to match
it. "I will if you will."

They got in, the flyer drifted silently from the
cove. New Piraeus rose to meet them from beyond
the ridge; the late sun struck gold from hidden
windows.

"I wish it wouldn't change—oh . . . there's another
new one. It's a skyscraper!"

He glanced across the bay. "Just finished; maybe
New Piraeus is growing up—thanks to Oro Mines.
It hardly changed over a century; after all those
years, it's a little scary."

"Even after three . . . or twenty-five?" She
pointed. "Right down there, Maris—there's our airlock."

The flyer settled on the water below the looming
semitransparent hull of the WGH–709.

Maris gazed up and back. "It's a lot bigger than
I ever realized."

"It masses twenty thousand tons, empty." Brandy
caught hold of the hanging ladder. "I guess we'll
have to go up this . . . okay?" She looked over at
him.

"Sure. Slow, maybe, but sure."

They slipped in through the lock, moved soft-footed down hallways past dim cavernous store-rooms.

"Is the whole ship transparent?" He touched a wall, plastic met plastic. "How do you get any privacy?"

"Why are you whispering?"

"I'm no— *I'm not*. Why are you?"

"*Shhh!* Because it's so *quiet*." She stopped, pride beginning to show on her face. "The whole ship can be almost transparent, like now; but usually it's not. All the walls and the hull are polarized; you can opaque them. These are just holds, anyway, they're most of the ship. The passenger stasis cubicles are up there. Here's the lift, we'll go up to the control room."

"Brandy!" A girl in red with a clipboard turned on them, outraged, as they stepped from the lift. "Brandy, what the hell do you mean by— Oh. Is that you, Soldier? God, I thought she'd brought a man on board."

Maris flinched. "Hi, Nilgiri."

Brandy was very pale beside him. "We just came out to—uh, look in on Mactav, she's been kind of moody lately, you know. I thought we could read to her. . . . What are *you* doing here?" And a whispered, "Bitch."

"Just that—checking up on Mactav. Harkané sent me out." Nilgiri glanced at the panels behind her, back at Maris, suddenly awkward. "Uh—look, since I'm already here don't worry about it, okay? I'll go down and play some music for her. Why don't you —uh, show Soldier around the ship, or something . . ." Her round face was reddening like an apple. "Bye?" She slipped past them and into the lift, and disappeared.

"*Damn*, sometimes she's such an ass."

"She didn't mean it."

"Oh, I should have—"

"—done just what you did; she *was* sorry. And at least we're not trespassing."

"God, Maris, how do you stand it? They must do it to you all the time. Don't you resent it?"

"Hell, yes, I resent it. Who wouldn't? I just got tired of getting mad. . . . And besides"—he glanced at the closed doors—"besides, nobody needs a mean bartender. Come on, show me around the ship."

Her knotted fingers uncurled, took his hand. "This way, please; straight ahead of you is our control room." She pulled him forward beneath the daybright dome. He saw a hand-printed sign above the central panel, NO-MAN'S LAND. "From here we program our computer; this area here is for the AAFAL drive, first devised by Ursula, an early spacer who—"

"What's awful about it?"

"What?"

"Every spacer I know calls the ship's drive 'awful'?"

"Oh— Not 'awful,' AAFAL: Almost As Fast As Light. Which it is. That's what we call it; there's a technical name too."

"Um." He looked vaguely disappointed. "Guess I'm used to—" Curiosity changed his face, as he watched her smiling with delight. "I—suppose it's different from antigravity?" Seventy years before she was born, he had taught himself the principles of starship technology.

"Very." She giggled suddenly. "The 'awfuls' and the 'aghs,' *hmm* . . . We do use an AG unit to leave and enter solar systems; it operates like the ones in flyers, it throws us away from the planet, and finally the entire system, until we reach AAFAL ignition speeds. With the AG you can only get fractions of the speed of light, but it's enough to concentrate interstellar gases and dust. Our force nets feed them through the drive unit, where they're converted to energy, which increases our speed, which makes the unit more efficient . . . until we're moving almost as fast as light.

"We use the AG to protect us from acceleration forces, and after deceleration to guide us into port. The start and finish can take up most of our trip time; the farther out in space you are, the less AG feedback you get from the system's mass, and the less your velocity changes. It's a beautiful time, though—you can see the AG forces through the polarized hull, wrapping you in shifting rainbow . . .

"And you are isolate"—she leaned against a silent panel and punched buttons; the room began to grow dark—"in absolute night . . . and stars." And stars appeared, in the darkness of a planetarium show; fire-gnats lighting her face and shoulders and his own. "How do you like our stars?"

"Are we in here?"

Four streaks of blue joined lights in the air. "Here . . . in space by this corner of the Quadrangle. This is our navigation chart for the Quadrangle run; see the bowed leg and brightness, that's the Pleiades. Patris . . . Sanalareta . . . Treone . . . back to Oro. The other lines zigzag too, but it doesn't show. Now come with me . . . With a flare of energy, we open our AAFAL nets in space—"

He followed her voice into the night, where flickering tracery seined motes of interstellar gas; and impossible nothingness burned with infinite energy, potential transformed and transforming. With the wisdom of a thousand years a ship of the League fell through limitless seas, navigating the shifting currents of the void, beating into the sterile winds of space. Stars glittered like snow on the curving hull, spitting icy daggers of light that moved imperceptibly into spectral blues before him, reddened as he looked behind: imperceptibly time expanded, velocity increased and with it power. He saw the haze of silver on his right rise into their path, a wall of liquid shadow . . . the Pleiades, an endless bank of burning fog, kindled from within by shrouded islands of fire. Tendrils of shimmering mists curved outward across hundreds of billions of kilometers, the nets found bountiful harvest, drew close, hurled the ship into the edge of cloud.

Nebulosity wrapped him in clinging haloes of colored light, ringed him in brilliance, as the nets fell inward toward the ship, burgeoning with energy, shielding its fragile nucleus from the soundless fury of its passage. Acceleration increased by hundredfolds, around him the Doppler shifts deepened toward cerulean and crimson; slowly the clinging brightness wove into parabolas of shining smoke, whipping past until the entire flaming mass of cloud and stars seemed to sweep ahead, shriveling toward blue-whiteness, trailing embers.

And suddenly the ship burst once more into a

void, a universe warped into a rubber bowl of brilliance stretching past him, drawing away and away before him toward a gleaming point in darkness. The shrunken nets seined near-vacuum and were filled; their speed approached $0.999c$ . . . held constant, as the conversion of matter to energy ceased within the ship . . . and in time, with a flicker of silver force, began once more to fall away. Slowly time unbowed, the universe cast off its alienness. One star grew steadily before them: the sun of Patris.

A sun rose in ruddy splendor above the City in the Clouds on Patris, nine months and seven light-years from Oro. . . . And again, Patris fell away; and the brash gleaming Freeport of Sanalareta; they crept toward Treone through gasless waste, groping for current and mote across the barren ship-wakes of half a millennium. . . . And again—

Maris found himself among fire-gnat stars, on a ship in the bay of New Piraeus. And realized she had stopped speaking. His hand rubbed the copper snarl of his hair, his eyes bright as a child's. "You didn't tell me you were a witch in your spare time."

He heard her smile, "Thank you. Mactav makes the real magic, though; her special effects are fantastic. She can show you the whole inhabited section of the galaxy, with all the trade polyhedra, like a dew-flecked cobweb hanging in the air." Daylight returned to the panel. "Mactav—that's her bank, there—handles most of the navigation, life support, all that, too. Sometimes it seems like we're almost along for the ride! But of course we're along for Mactav."

"Who or what is Mactav?" Maris peered into a darkened screen, saw something amber glimmer in its depths, drew back.

"You've never met her, neither have we—but you were staring her right in the eye." Brandy stood beside him. "She must be listening to Giri down below. . . . Okay, okay!—a Mactavia unit is the brain, the nervous system of a ship, she monitors its vital signs, calculates, adjusts. We only have to ask— sometimes we don't even have to do that. The memory is a real spacer woman's, fed into the circuits . . . someone who died irrevocably, or had reached retirement, but wanted to stay on. A human system is wiser, more versatile—and lots cheaper—than anything all-machine that's ever been done."

"Then your Mactav is a kind of cyborg."

She smiled. "Well, I guess so; in a way—"

"But the Spacing League's regulations still won't allow cyborgs in crews."

She looked annoyed.

He shrugged. "Sorry. Dumb thing to say . . . What's that red down there?"

"Oh, that's our 'stomach': the AAFAL unit, where" —she grinned—"we digest stardust into energy. It's the only thing that's never transparent, the red is the shield."

"How does it work?"

"I don't really know. I can make it go, but I don't understand why—I'm only a five-and-a-half technician now. If I was a six I could tell you." She glanced at him sidelong. "Aha! I finally impressed you!"

He laughed. "Not so dumb as you look." He had

qualified as a six half a century before, out of boredom.

"You'd better be kidding!"

"I am." He followed her back across the palely opalescing floor, looking down, and down. "Like walking on water . . . why transparent?"

She smiled through him at the sky. "Because it's so beautiful outside."

They dropped down through floors, to come out in a new hall. Music came faintly to him.

"This is where my cabin—"

Abruptly the music became an impossible agony of sound torn with screaming.

"God!" And Brandy was gone from beside him, down the hallway and through a flickering wall.

He found her inside the door, rigid with awe. Across the room the wall vomited blinding waves of color, above a screeching growth of crystal organ pipes. Nilgiri crouched on the floor, hands pressed against her stomach, shrieking hysterically. "Stop it, Mactav! Stop it! Stop it! Stop it!"

He touched Brandy's shoulder, she looked up and caught his arm; together they pulled Nilgiri, wailing, back from bedlam to the door.

"Nilgiri! Nilgiri, what happened!" Brandy screamed against her ear.

"Mactav, Mactav!"

"Why?"

"She put a . . . charge through it, she's crazy-mad . . . sh-she thinks . . . Oh, stop it, Mactav!" Nilgiri clung, sobbing.

Maris started into the room, hands over his ears. "How do you turn it off!"

"Maris, wait!"

"*How*, Brandy?"

"It's electrified, don't touch it!"

"*How?*"

"On the left, on the left, three switches—Maris, *don't*— Stop it, Mactav, stop—"

He heard her screaming as he lowered his left hand, hesitated, battered with glaring sound; sparks crackled as he flicked switches on the organ panel, once, twice, again.

"—it-it-it-it!" Her voice echoed through silent halls. Nilgiri slid down the doorjamb and sat sobbing on the floor.

"Maris, are you all right?"

He heard her dimly through cotton. Dazed with relief, he backed away from the gleaming console, nodding, and started across the room.

"*Man*," the soft hollow voice echoed echoed echoed. "What are you doing in here?"

"Mactav?" Brandy was gazing uneasily to his left.

He turned; across the room was another artificial eye, burning amber.

"Branduin, you brought him onto the ship; how could you do this thing, it is forbidden!"

"Oh, God." Nilgiri began to wail again in horror. Brandy knelt and caught Nilgiri's blistered hands; he saw anger harden over her face. "Mactav, how could you!"

"Brandy." He shook his head; took a breath, frightened. "Mactav—I'm not a man. You're mistaken."

"Maris, no . . ."

He frowned. "I'm one hundred and forty-one years old . . . half my body is synthetic. I'm hardly human, any more than you are. Scan and see." He held up his hands.

"The part of you that matters is still a man."

A smile caught at his mouth. "Thanks."

"Men are evil, men destroyed . . ."

"Her, Maris," Brandy whispered. "They destroyed her."

The smile wavered. "Something more we have in common." His false arm pressed his side.

The golden eye regarded him. "Cyborg."

He sighed, went to the door. Brandy stood to meet him, Nilgiri huddled silently at her feet, staring up.

"Nilgiri." The voice was full of pain; they looked back. "How can I forgive myself for what I've done? I will never, never do such a thing again . . . never. Please, go to the infirmary; let me help you?"

Slowly, with Brandy's help, Nilgiri got to her feet. "All right. It's all right, Mactav. I'll go on down now."

"Giri, do you want us—?"

Nilgiri shook her head, hands curled in front of her. "No, Brandy, it's okay. She's all right now. Me too—I think." Her smile quivered. "Ouch . . ." She started down the corridor toward the lift.

"Branduin, Maris, I apologize also to you. I'm— not usually like this, you know. . . ." Amber faded from her eye.

"Is she gone?"

Brandy nodded.

"That's the first bigoted computer I ever met."

And she remembered. "Your *hand*?"

Smiling, he held it out to her. "No harm; see? It's a nonconductor."

She shivered. Hands cradled the hand that ached to feel. "Mactav really isn't like that, you know. But something's been wrong lately, she gets into moods; we'll have to have her looked at when we get to Sanalareta."

"Isn't it dangerous?"

"I don't think so—not really. It's just that she has special problems; she's in there because she didn't have any choice, a strife-based culture killed her ship. She was very young, but that was all that was left of her."

"A high technology." A grimace; memory moved in his eyes.

"They were terribly apologetic, they did their best."

"What happened to them?"

"We cut contact . . . that's regulation number one. We have to protect ourselves."

He nodded, looking away. "Will they ever go back?"

"I don't know. Maybe, someday." She leaned against the doorway. "But that's why Mactav hates men; men, and war—and combined with the old taboo . . . I guess her memory suppressors weren't enough."

Nilgiri reappeared beside them. "All better." Her hands were bright pink. "Ready for anything!"

"How's Mactav acting?"

"Super-solicitous. She's still pretty upset about it, I guess."

Light flickered at the curving junctures of the walls, ceiling, floor. Maris glanced up. "Hell, it's getting dark outside. I expect I'd better be leaving;

nearly time to open up. One last night on the town?"
Nilgiri grinned and nodded; he saw Brandy hesitate.

"Maybe I'd better stay with Mactav tonight, if
she's still upset. She's got to be ready to go up tomorrow." Almost-guilt firmed resolution on her face.

"Well . . . I could stay, if you think—" Nilgiri
looked unhappy.

"No. It's my fault she's like this; I'll do it. Besides,
I've been out having a fantastic day, I'd be too tired
to do it right tonight. You go on in. Thank you,
Maris! I wish it wasn't over so soon." She turned
back to him, beginning to put her hair into braids;
quicksilver shone.

"The pleasure was all mine." The tight sense of
loss dissolved in warmth. "I can't remember a better
one either . . . or more exciting—" He grimaced.

She smiled and took his hands; Nilgiri glanced
back and forth between them. "I'll see you to the
lock."

Nilgiri climbed down through the glow to the
waiting flyer. Maris braced back from the top rung
to watch Brandy's face, bearing a strange expression, look down through whipping strands of loose
hair. "Good-bye, Maris."

"Good-bye, Brandy."

"It was a short two weeks, you know?"

"I know

"I like New Piraeus better than anywhere; I don't
know why."

"I hope it won't be too different when you get
back."

"Me too. . . . See you in three years?"

"Twenty-five."

"Oh, yeah. Time passes so quickly when you're having fun—" Almost true, almost not. A smile flowered.

"Write while you're away. Poems, that is." He began to climb down, slowly.

"I will . . . Hey, my stuff is at—"

"I'll send it back with Nilgiri." He settled behind the controls, the flyer grew bright and began to rise. He waved; so did Nilgiri. He watched her wave back, watched her in his mirror until she became the vast and gleaming pearl that was the *Who Got Her*–709. And felt the gap that widened between their lives, more than distance, more than time.

∞

"Well, now that you've seen it, what do you think?"

Late afternoon, first day, fourth visit, seventy-fifth year . . . mentally he tallied. Brandy stood looking into the kitchen. "It's—different."

"I know. It's still too new; I miss the old wood beams. They were rotting, but I miss them. Sometimes I wake up in the morning and don't know where I am. But I was losing my canyon."

She looked back at him, surprising him with her misery. "Oh . . . At least they won't reach you for a long time, out here."

"We can't walk home anymore, though."

"No." She turned away again. "All—all your furniture is built in?"

"*Um.* It's supposed to last as long as the house."

"What if you get tired of it?"

He laughed. "As long as it holds me up, I don't care what it looks like. One thing I like, though—" He pressed a plate on the wall, looking up. "The roof is polarized. Like your ship. At night you can watch the stars."

"Oh!" She looked up and back, he watched her mind pierce the high cloud-fog, pierce the day, to find stars. "How wonderful! I've never seen it anywhere else."

It had been his idea, thinking of her. He smiled.

"They must really be growing out here, to be doing things like this now." She tried the cushions of a molded chair. "Hmm . . ."

"They're up to two and a half already, they actually do a few things besides mining now. The Inside is catching up, if they can bring us this without a loss. I may even live to see the day when we'll be importing raw materials, instead of filling everyone else's mined-out guts. If there's anything left of Oro by then . . ."

"Would you stay to see that?"

"I don't know." He looked at her. "It depends. Anyway, tell me about this trip?" He stretched out on the chain-hung wall seat. "You know everything that's new with me already: one house." And waited for far glory to rise up in her eyes.

They flickered down, stayed the color of fog. "Well—some good news, and some bad news, I guess."

"Like how?" Feeling suddenly cold.

"Good news—" her smile warmed him—"I'll be staying nearly a month this time. We'll have more time to—do things, if you want to."

"How did you manage that?" He sat up.

"That's more good news. I have a chance to crew on a different ship, to get out of the Quadrangle and see things I've only dreamed of, new worlds—"

"And the bad news is how long you'll be gone."

"Yes."

"How many years?"

"It's an extended voyage, following up trade contacts; if we're lucky, we might be back in the stellar neighborhood in thirty-five years . . . thirty-five years tau—more than two hundred, here. If we're not so lucky, maybe we won't be back this way at all."

"I see." He stared unblinking at the floor, hands knotted between his knees. "It's—an incredible opportunity, all right . . . especially for your poetry. I envy you. But I'll miss you."

"I know." He saw her teeth catch her lip. "But we can spend time together, we'll have a lot of time before I go. And—well, I've brought you something, to remember me." She crossed the room to him.

It was a star, suspended burning coldly in scrolled silver by an artist who knew fire. Inside she showed him her face, laughing, full of joy.

"I found it on Treone . . . they really are in renaissance. And I liked that holo, I thought you might—"

Leaning across silver he found the silver of her hair, kissed her once on the mouth, felt her quiver as he pulled away. He lifted the woven chain, fixed it at his throat. "I have something for you, too."

He got up, returned with a slim book the color of red wine, put it in her hands.

"My poems!"

He nodded, his fingers feeling the star at his throat. "I managed to get hold of two copies—it wasn't easy. Because they're too well known now; the spacers carry them, they show them but they won't give them up. You must be known on more worlds than you could ever see."

"Oh, I hadn't even heard . . ." She laughed suddenly. "My fame preceded me. But next trip—" She looked away. "No. I won't be going that way anymore."

"But you'll be seeing new things, to make into new poems." He stood, trying to loosen the tightness in his voice.

"Yes . . . Oh, yes, I know . . ."

"A month is a long time."

A sudden sputter of noise made them look up. Fat dapples of rain were beginning to slide, smearing dust over the flat roof.

"Rain! not fog; the season's started." They stood and watched the sky fade overhead, darken, crack and shudder with electric light. The rain fell harder, the ceiling rippled and blurred; he led her to the window. Out across the smooth folded land a liquid curtain billowed, slaking the dust-dry throat of the canyons, renewing the earth and the spiny tight-leafed scrub. "I always wonder if it's ever going to happen. It always does." He looked at her, expecting quicksilver, and found slow tears. She wept silently, watching the rain.

For the next two weeks they shared the rain, and the chill bright air that followed. In the evenings she went out, while he stood behind the bar, because it was the last time she would have leave with the crew of the *Who Got Her*. But every morning he found her sleeping, and every afternoon she spent with him. Together they traced the serpentine alleyways of the shabby, metamorphosing lower city, or roamed the docks with the wind-burned fisherfolk. He took her to meet Makerrah, whom he had seen as a boy mending nets by hand, as a fishnet-clad Tail courting spacers at the Tin Soldier, as a sailor and fisherman, for almost forty years. Makerrah, now growing heavy and slow as his wood-hulled boat, showed it with pride to the sailor from the sky; they discussed nets, eating fish.

"This world is getting old. . . ." Brandy had come with him to the bar as the evening started.

Maris smiled. "But the night is young." And felt pleasure stir with envy.

"True true—" Pale hair cascaded as her head bobbed. "But, you know, when . . . if I was gone another twenty-five years, I probably wouldn't recognize this *street*. The Tin Soldier really is the only thing that doesn't change." She sat at the agate counter, face propped in her hands, musing.

He stirred drinks. "It's good to have something constant in your life."

"I know. We appreciate that too, more than anybody." She glanced away, into the dark-raftered room. "They really always do come back here first, and spend more time in here . . . and knowing that they *can* means so much: that you'll be here, young and real and remembering them." A sudden hunger blurred her sight.

"It goes both ways." He looked up.

"I know that, too. . . . You know, I always meant to ask: why did you call it the 'Tin Soldier'? I mean, I think I see . . . but why 'tin'?"

"Sort of a private joke, I guess. It was in a book of folk tales I read, *Andersen's Fairy Tales*"—he looked embarrassed—"I'd *read* everything else. It was a story about a toy shop, about a tin soldier with one leg, who was left on the shelf for years. . . . He fell in love with a toy ballerina who only loved dancing, never him. In the end, she fell into the fire, and he went after her—she burned to dust, heartless; he melted into a heart-shaped lump. . . ." He laughed carefully, seeing her face. "A footnote said sometimes the story had a happy ending; I like to believe that."

She nodded, hopeful. "Me too—Where did your stone bar come from? It's beautiful; like the edge of the Pleiades, depths of mist."

"Why all the questions?"

"I'm appreciating. I've loved it all for years, and never said anything. Sometimes you love things without knowing it, you take them for granted. It's wrong to let that happen . . . so I wanted you to know." She smoothed the polished stone with her hand.

He joined her tracing opalescences. "It's petrified wood—some kind of plant life that was preserved in stone, minerals replaced its structure. I found it in the desert."

"Desert?"

"East of the mountains. I found a whole canyon full of them. It's an incredible place, the desert."

"I've never seen one. Only heard about them, barren and deadly; it frightened me."

"While you cross the most terrible desert of them all?—between the stars."

"But it's not barren."

"Neither is this one. It's winter here now, I can

take you to see the trees, if you'd like it." He grinned. "If you dare."

Her eyebrows rose. "I dare! We could go tomorrow, I'll make us a lunch."

"We'd have to leave early, though. If you were wanting to do the town again tonight . . ."

"Oh, that's all right; I'll take a pill."

"Hey—"

She winced. "Oh, well . . . I found a kind I could take. I used them all the time at the other ports, like the rest."

"Then why—"

"Because I liked staying with you. I deceived you, now you know, true confessions. Are you mad?"

His face filled with astonished pleasure. "Hardly . . . I have to admit, I used to wonder what—"

"*Sol*-dier!" He looked away, someone gestured at him across the room. "More wine, please!" He raised a hand.

"Brandy, come on, there's a party—"

She waved. "Tomorrow morning, early?" Her eyes kept his face.

"Uh-huh. See you—"

"—later." She slipped down and was gone.

The flyer rose silently, pointing into the early sun. Brandy sat beside him, squinting down and back through the glare as New Piraeus grew narrow beside the glass-green bay. "Look, how it falls behind the hills, until all you can see are the land and the sea, and no sign of change. It's like that when the ship goes up, but it happens so fast you don't have time to savor it." She turned back to him, bright-eyed. "We go from world to world but we never see them; we're always looking up. It's good to look down, today."

They drifted higher, rising with the climbing hills, until the rumpled olive-red suede of the sea-coast grew jagged, blotched green-black and gray and blinding white.

"Is that really snow?" She pulled at his arm, pointing.

He nodded. "We manage a little."

"I've only seen snow once since I left Calicho, once it was winter on Treone. We wrapped up in furs and capes even though we didn't have to, and threw snowballs with the Tails. . . . But it was cold most of the year on our island, on Calicho—we were pretty far north, we grew special kinds of crops . . . and us kids had hairy hornbeasts to plod around on. . . ." Lost in memories, she rested against his shoulder; while he tried to remember a freehold on Glatte, and snowy walls became jumbled white-ness climbing a hill by the sea.

They had crossed the divide; the protruding bath-olith of the peaks degenerated into parched, crumbling slopes of gigantic rubble. Ahead of them the scarred yellow desolation stretched away like an infinite canvas, into mauve haze. "How far does it go?"

"It goes on forever. . . . Maybe not this desert, but this merges into others that merge into others —the whole planet is a desert, hot or cold. It's been desiccating for eons; the sun's been rising off the main sequence. The sea by New Piraeus is the only large body of free water left now, and that's dropped half an inch since I've been here. The coast is the only habitable area, and there aren't many towns there even now."

"Then Oro will never be able to change too much."

"Only enough to hurt. See the dust? Open-pit mining, for seventy kilometers north. And that's a little one."

He took them south, sliding over the eroded face of the land to twist through canyons of folded stone, sediments contorted by the palsied hands of tectonic force; or flashing across pitted flatlands lipping on pocket seas of ridged and shadowed blow-sand.

They settled at last under a steep out-curving wall of frescoed rock layered in red and green. The wide, rough bed of the sandy wash was pale in the chill glare of noon, scrunching underfoot as they began to walk. Pulling on his leather jacket, Maris showed her the kaleidoscope of ages left tumbled in stones over the hills they climbed, shouting against the lusty wind of the ridges. She cupped them in marveling hands, hair streaming like silken banners past her face; obligingly he put her chosen few into his pockets. "Aren't you cold?" He caught her hand.

"No, my suit takes care of me. How did you ever learn to know all these, Maris?"

Shaking his head, he began to lead her back down. "There's more here than I'll ever know. I just got a mining tape on geology at the library. But it made it mean more to come out here . . . where you can see eons of the planet laid open, one cycle

settling on another. To know the time it took, the
life history of an entire world: it helps my perspective, it makes me feel—young."

"We think we know worlds, but we don't, we
only see people: change and pettiness. We forget
the greater constancy, tied to the universe. It would
humble our perspective, too—" Pebbles boiled and
clattered; her hand held his strongly as his foot
slipped. He looked back, chagrined, and she
laughed. "You don't really have to lead me here,
Maris. I was a mountain goat on Calicho, and I
haven't forgotten it all."

Indignant, he dropped her hand. "You lead."

Still laughing, she led him to the bottom of the
hill.

And he took her to see the trees. Working their
way over rocks up the windless branch wash, they
rounded a bend and found them, tumbled in static
glory. He heard her indrawn breath. "Oh, Maris—"
Radiant with color and light she walked among
them, while he wondered again at the passionless
artistry of the earth. Amethyst and agate, crystal and
mimicked wood-grain, hexagonal trunks split open
to bare subtleties of mergence and secret nebulosi-
ties. She knelt among the broken bits of limb, choosing colors to hold up to the sun.

He sat on a trunk, picking agate pebbles.
"They're sort of special friends of mine; we go down
in time together, in strangely familiar bodies. . . ."
He studied them with fond pride. "But they go
with more grace."

She put her colored chunks on the ground. "No
. . . I don't think so. They had no choice."

He looked down, tossing pebbles.

"Let's have our picnic here."

They cleared a space and spread a blanket, and picnicked with the trees. The sun warmed them in the windless hollow, and he made a pillow of his jacket; satiated, they lay back head by head, watching the cloudless green-blue sky.

"You pack a good lunch."

"Thank you. It was the least I could do"—her hand brushed his arm; quietly his fingers tightened on themselves—"to share your secrets; to learn that the desert isn't barren, that it's immense, timeless, full of—mysteries. But no life?"

"No—not anymore. There's no water, nothing can live. The only things left are in or by the sea, or they're things we've brought. Across our own lifeless desert-sea."

" 'Though inland far we be, our souls have sight of that immortal sea which brought us hither.' " Her hand stretched above him, to catch the sky.

"Wordsworth. That's the only thing by him I ever liked much."

They lay together in the warm silence. A piece of agate came loose, dropped to the ground with a clink; they started.

"Maris—"

"*Hmm?*"

"Do you realize we've known each other for three-quarters of a century?"

"Yes. . . ."

"I've almost caught up with you, I think. I'm twenty-seven. Soon I'm going to start passing you. But at least—now you'll never have to see it show." Her fingers touched the rusty curls of his hair.

"It would never show. You couldn't help but be beautiful."

"Maris . . . sweet Maris."

He felt her hand clench in the soft weave of his shirt, move in caresses down his body. Angrily he pulled away, sat up, half his face flushed. "Damn—!"

Stricken, she caught at his sleeve. "No, no—" Her eyes found his face, gray filled with grief. "No . . . Maris . . . I—want you." She unsealed her suit, drew blue-silver from her shoulders, knelt before him. "I want you."

Her hair fell to her waist, the color of warm honey. She reached out and lifted his hand with tenderness; slowly he leaned forward, to bare her breasts and her beating heart, felt the softness set fire to his nerves. Pulling her close, he found her lips, kissed them long and longingly; held her against his own heart beating, lost in her silken hair. "Oh, God, Brandy . . ."

"I love you, Maris . . . I think I've always loved you." She clung to him, cold and shivering in the sunlit air. "And it's wrong to leave you and never let you know."

And he realized that fear made her tremble, fear bound to her love in ways he could not fully understand. Blind to the future, he drew her down beside him and stopped her trembling with his joy.

In the evening she sat across from him at the bar, blue-haloed with light, sipping brandy. Their faces were bright with wine and melancholy bliss.

"I finally got some more brandy, Brandy . . . a couple of years ago. So we wouldn't run out. If we

don't get to it, you can take it with you." He set
the dusty red-splintered bottle carefully on the bar.

"You could save it, in case I do come back, as
old as your grandmaw, and in need of some
warmth. . . ." Slowly she rotated her glass, watching red leap up the sides. "Do you suppose by
then my poems will have reached Home? And maybe somewhere Inside, Ntaka will be reading *me*."

"The Outside will be the Inside by then. . . . Besides, Ntaka's probably already dead. Been dead
for years."

"Oh. I guess." She pouted, her eyes growing dim
and moist. "Damn, I wish . . . I wish."

"Branduin, you haven't joined us yet tonight. It
is our last together." Harkané appeared beside
her, lean dark face smiling in a cloud-mass of blued
white hair. She sat down with her drink.

"I'll come soon." Clouded eyes glanced up, away.

"Ah, the sadness of parting keeps you apart? I
know." Harkané nodded. "We've been together so
long; it's hard, to lose another family." She regarded Maris. "And a good bartender must share
everyone's sorrows, yes, Soldier—? But bury his own.
Oh—they would like some more drinks—"

Sensing dismissal, he moved aside; with long-
practiced skill he became blind and deaf, pouring
wine.

"Brandy, you are so unhappy—don't you want to
go on this other voyage?"

"Yes, I do—! But . . ."

"But you don't. It is always so when there is
choice. Sometimes we make the right choice, and
though we're afraid we go on with it anyway. And
sometimes we make the wrong choice, and go on

with it anyway because we're afraid not to. Have you changed your mind?"

"But I can't change—"

"Why not? We will leave them a message. They will go on and pick up their second compatible."

"Is it really that easy?"

"No . . . not quite. But we can do it, if you want to stay."

Silence stretched; Maris sent a tray away, began to wipe glasses, fumbled.

"But I *should*."

"Brandy. If you go only out of obligation, I will tell you something. I want to retire. I was going to resign this trip, at Sanalareta; but if I do that, Mactav will need a new Best Friend. She's getting old and cantankerous, just like me; these past few years her behavior has begun to show the strain she is under. She must have someone who can feel her needs. I was going to ask you, I think you understand her best; but I thought you wanted this other thing more. If not, I ask you now to become the new Best Friend of the *Who Got Her*."

"But Harkané, you're not old—"

"I am eighty-six. I'm too old for the sporting life anymore; I will become a Mactav; I've been lucky, I have an opportunity."

"Then . . . yes—I do want to stay! I accept the position."

In spite of himself Maris looked up, saw her face shining with joy and release. "Brandy—?"

"Maris, I'm not going!"

"I know!" He laughed, joined them.

"Soldier." He looked up, dark met dark, Harkané's eyes that saw more than surfaces. "This will be the last time that I see you; I am retiring, you know. You have been very good to me all these years, helping me be young; you are very kind to us all. . . . Now, to say good-bye, I do something in return." She took his hand, placed it firmly over Brandy's, shining with rings on the counter. "I give her back to you. Brandy—join us soon, we'll celebrate." She rose mildly and moved away into the crowded room.

Their hands twisted, clasped tight on the counter.

Brandy closed her eyes. "God, I'm so glad!"

"So am I."

"Only the poems . . ."

"Remember once you told me, 'you can see it all a hundred times, and never see it all'?"

A quicksilver smile. "And it's true. . . . Oh, Maris, now this is my last night! And I have to spend it with them, to celebrate."

"I know. There's—no way I can have you forever, I suppose. But it's all right." He grinned. "Everything's all right. What's twenty-five years, compared to two hundred?"

"It'll seem like three."

"It'll seem like twenty-five. But I can stand it—"

∞

He stood it, for twenty-four more years, looking up from the bar with sudden eagerness every time new voices and the sound of laughter spilled into the dim blue room.

"Soldier! Soldier, you're still—"

"We missed you like—"

"—two whole weeks of—"

"—want to buy a whole *sack* for my own—"

The crew of the *DOM–428* pressed around him,

their fingers proving he was real; their lips brushed
a cheek that couldn't feel and one that could, long
loose hair rippling over the agate bar. He hugged
four at a time. "Aralea! Vlasa! Elsah, what the hell
have you done to your hair now—and Ling-shan!
My God, you're pretty, like always. Cathe—" The
memory bank never forgot a shining fresh-scrubbed
face, even after thirty-seven years. Their eyes were
very bright as he welcomed them, and their hands
left loving prints along the agate bar.

"—still have your stone bar; I'm so glad, don't
ever sell it—"

"And what's new with *you*?" Elsah gasped, and
ecstatic laughter burst over him.

He shook his head, hands up, laughing too. "—go
prematurely *deaf*? First round on the house; only
one at a time, huh?"

Elsah brushed strands of green-tinged waist-
length hair back from her very green eyes. "Sorry,
Soldier. We've just said it *all* to each other, over
and over. And gee, we haven't seen you for four
years!" Her belt tossed blue-green sparks against
her green quilted flight-suit.

"Four years? Seems more like thirty-seven." And
they laughed again, appreciating, because it was
true. "Welcome back to the Tin Soldier. What's
your pleasure?"

"Why you of course, me darlin'," said black-
haired Brigit, and she winked.

His smile barely caught on a sharp edge; he
winked back. "Just the drinks are on the house,
lass." The smile widened and came unstuck.

More giggles.

"Ach, a pity!" Brigit pouted. She wore a filigree

necklace, like the galaxy strung over her dark-suited breast. "Well, then, I guess a little olive beer, for old time's sake."

"Make it two."

"Anybody want a pitcher?"

"Sure, why not?"

"Come sit with us in a while, Soldier. Have we got things to tell you!"

He jammed the clumsy pitcher under the spigot and pulled down as they drifted away, watching the amber splatter up its frosty sides.

"Alta, hi! Good timing! How are things on the *Extra Sexy Old–115?*"

"Oh, good enough; how's Chrysalis—has it changed much?"

The froth spilled out over his hand; he let the lever jerk up, licked his fingers and wiped them on his apron.

"It's gone wild this time, you should see what they're wearing for clothes. My God, you would not believe—"

He hoisted the slimy pitcher onto the bar and set octagonal mugs on a tray.

"Aralea, did you hear what happened to the—"

He lifted the pitcher again, up to the tray's edge.

"—*Who Got Her–709?*"

The pitcher teetered.

"Their Mactav had a nervous breakdown on landing at Sanalareta. Branduin died, the poet, the one who wrote—"

Splinters and froth exploded on the agate bar and slobbered over the edge, *tinkle, crash.*

Stunned blank faces turned to see Soldier, hands moving ineffectually in a puddle of red-flecked foam.

He began to brush it off onto the floor, looking like a stricken adolescent. "Sorry . . . sorry about that."

"Ach, Soldier, you really blew it!"

"Got a mop? Here, we'll help you clean it up . . . hey, you're bleeding—?" Brigit and Ling-shan were piling chunks of pitcher onto the bar.

Soldier shook his head, fumbling a towel around the one wrist that bled. "No . . . no, thanks, leave it, huh? I'll get you another pitcher . . . it doesn't matter. Go on!" They looked at him. "I'll send you a pitcher; thanks." He smiled.

They left, the smile stopped. *Fill the pitcher.* He filled a pitcher, his hand smarting. *Clean up, damn it.* He cleaned up, wiping off disaster while the floor absorbed and fangs of glass disappeared under the bar. As the agate bar-top dried he saw the white-edged shatter flower, tendrils of hairline crack shooting out a hand's-breadth on every side. He began to trace them with a rigid finger, counting softly . . . *She loved me, she loved me not, she loved me—*

"Two cepheids and a wine, Soldier!"

"Soldier, come hear what we saw on Chrysalis if you're through!"

He nodded and poured, blinking hard. *God damn sweetsmoke in here . . . God damn everything!* Elsah was going out the door with a boy in tight green pants and a star-map-tattooed body. He stared them into fluorescent blur. And remembered Brandy going out the door too many times . . .

"Hey, *Sol*-dier, what are you doing?"

He blinked himself back.

"Come sit with us?"

He crossed the room to the nearest bulky table

and the remaining crew of the *Dirty Old Man–428.*

"How's your hand?" Vlasa soothed it with a dark, ringed finger.

"It only hurts when I laugh."

"You really are screwed up!" Ling-shan's smile wrinkled. "Oh, Soldier, why look so glum?"

"I chipped my bar."

"Ohhh . . . nothing but bad news tonight. Make him laugh, somebody, we can't go on like this!"

"Tell him the joke you heard on Chrysalis—"

"—from the boy with a cat's-eye in his navel? Oh. Well, it seems there was . . ."

His fingers moved reluctantly up the laces of his patchwork shirt and began to untangle the thumb-sized star trapped near his throat. He set it free; his hand tightened across the stubby spines, feeling only dull pressure. Pain registered from somewhere else.

"—'Oh, they fired the pickle slicer too!'"

He looked up into laughter.

"It's a tech-one joke, Soldier," Ling-Shan said helpfully.

"Oh . . . I see." He laughed, blindly.

"Soldier, we took pictures of our black hole!" Vlasa pulled at his arm. "From a respectable distance, but it was bizarre—"

"Holograms—" somebody interrupted.

"And you should see the effects!" Brigit said. "When you look into them you feel like your eyes are being—"

"Soldier, another round, please?"

"Excuse me." He pushed back his chair. "Later?" Thinking, *God won't this night ever end?*

.   .   .

His hand closed the lock on the pitted tavern door at last; his woven sandal skidded as he stepped into the street. Two slim figures, one all in sea-blue, passed him and red hair flamed; he recognized Marena, intent and content arm in arm with a gaudy, laughing Tail. Their hands were in each other's back pockets. They were going uphill; he turned down, treading carefully on the time- and fog-slicked cobbles. He limped slightly. Moist wraiths of sea fog twined the curving streets, turning the street lights into dark angels under fluorescing haloes. Bright droplets formed in his hair as he walked. His footsteps scratched to dim echoes; the laughter faded, leaving him alone with memory.

The presence of dawn took him by surprise, as a hand brushed his shoulder.

"Sojer, 'tis you?"

Soldier looked up fiercely into a gray-bristled face.

"Y'all right? What'ree doin' down here at dawn, lad?"

He recognized old Makerrah the fisherman, finally. Lately it amused the old man to call him "lad."

"Nothin' . . . nothin'." He pulled away from the brine-warped rail. The sun was rising beyond the mountains, the edge of fog caught the colors of fire and was burned away. It would be a hot day. "G'bye, ol' man." He began to walk.

"Y'sure y're all right?"

Alone again he sat with one foot hanging, feeling the suck and swell of water far below the pier.

All right . . . ? When had he ever been all right?
And tried to remember into the time before he
had known her, and could find no answer.

There had never been an answer for him on his
own world, on Glatte; never even a place for him.
Glatte, with a four-point-five technology, and a neo-
feudal society, where the competition for that technology was a cultural rationale for war. All his life
he had seen his people butchered and butchering,
blindly, trapped by senseless superstition. And
hated it, but could not escape the bitter ties that
led him to his destruction. Fragments of that former
life were all that remained now, after two centuries, still clinging to the fact of his alienness. He
remembered the taste of fresh-fallen snow . . . remembered the taste of blood. And the memory
filled him of how it felt to be nineteen, and hating
war, and blown to pieces . . . to find yourself suddenly half-prosthetic, with the pieces that were
gone still hurting in your mind; and your stepfa-
ther's voice, with something that was not pride,
saying you were finally a real man. . . . Soldier
held his breath unaware. His name was Maris, consecrated to war; and when at last he understood
why, he left Glatte forever.

He paid all he had to the notorious spacer
women; was carried in stasis between the stars,
like so much baggage. He wakened to Oro, tech
one-point-five, no wars and almost no people. And
found out that now to the rest of humanity he was
no longer quite human. But he had stayed on Oro
for ninety-six years, aging only five, alone. Ninety-
six years: a jumble of whiteness climbing a hill,
constant New Piraeus; a jumble of faces in dim-

blue lantern light, patterning a new life. A pattern endlessly repeated, his smile welcoming, welcoming with the patience of the damned, all the old/ new faces that needed him but never wanted him, while he wanted and needed them all. And then she had come to Oro, and after ninety-six years the pattern was broken. Damned Tin Soldier fell in love, after too many years of knowing better, with a ballerina who danced between the stars.

He pressed his face abruptly against the rail, pain flickered. *God, still real; thought it all turned to plastic, damn, damn . . .* And shut out three times twenty-five more years of pattern, of everyone else's nights and cold, solitary mornings trying to find her face. Ninety-one hundred days to carry the ache of returned life, until she would come again, and—

"See? That's our ship. The third one in line."

Soldier listened, unwillingly. A spacer in lavender stood with her Tail where the dock angled to the right, pointing out across the bay.

"Can't we go see it?" Blue glass glittered in mesh across the boy's back as he draped himself over the rail.

"Certainly not. Men aren't allowed on ships; it's against regulations. And anyway—I'd rather stay here." She drew him into the corner; amethyst and opal wrapped her neck in light. They began to kiss, hands wandering.

Soldier got up slowly and left them, still entwined, to privacy. The sun was climbing toward noon; above him as he walked, the skyline of New Piraeus wavered in the hazed and heated air. His eyes moved up and back toward the forty-story skeleton of the Universal Bank under construction, dropped to the warehouses, the docks, his atrophying ancient lower city. Insistent through the cry of sea birds he could hear the hungry whining of heavy machinery, the belly of a changing world. *And still I triumph over Death, and Chance, and thee, O Time—*

"But I can't stand it." His hands tightened on wood. "I stood it for ninety-six years; on the shelf." Dolefully the sea birds mocked him, creaking in the gray-green twilight, *now, now—* Wind probed the openings of his shirt like the cold fingers of sorrow. *Was dead, for ninety-six years before she came.*

For hours along the rail he had watched the ships in the bay; while he watched, a new ship had come slipping down, like the sun's tear. Now they grew bright as the day ended, setting a bracelet on the black water; stiffness made him lurch as he turned away, to artificial stars clustered on the wall of night.

Choking on the past, he climbed the worn streets, where the old patterns of a new night reached him only vaguely, and his eyes found nothing that he remembered anymore. Until he reached the time-eaten door, the thick, peeling mudbrick wall beneath the neon sign. His hand fondled the slippery lock, as it had for two hundred years. TIN SOLDIER . . . loved a ballerina. His hand slammed against the lock. *No—this bar is closed tonight.*

∞

The door slid open at his touch; Soldier entered his quiet house. And stopped, hearing the hollow

mutter of the empty night, and found himself alone
for the rest of his life.

He moved through the rooms by starlight, touching nothing, until he came to the bedroom door.
Opened it, the cold latch burning his hand. And
saw her there, lying asleep under the silver robe
of the Pleiades. Slowly he closed the door, waited,
opened it once more and filled the room with light.

She sat up, blinking, a fist against her eyes and
hair falling ash-golden to her waist. She wore a
long soft dress of muted flowers, blue and green
and earth tones. "Maris? I didn't hear you, I guess
I went to sleep."

He crossed the room, fell onto the bed beside
her, caressing her, covering her face with kisses.
"They said you were dead . . . all day I thought—"

"I am." Her voice was dull, her eyes dark-ringed
with fatigue.

"No."

"I am. To them I am. I'm not a spacer anymore;
space is closed to me forever. That's what it means
to be 'dead.' To lose your life . . . Mactav—went
crazy. I never thought we'd even get to port. I was
hurt badly, in the accident." Fingers twined loops
in her hair, pulled—

"But you're all right."

She shook her head. "No." She held out her hand,
upturned; he took it, curled its fingers into his own,
flesh over flesh, warm and supple. "It's plastic,
Maris."

He turned the hand over, stroked it, folded the
long limber fingers. "It can't be—"

"It's numb. I barely feel you at all. They tell me
I may live for hundreds of years." Her hand tight-

ened into a fist. "And I *am* a whole woman, but they forbid me to go into space again! I can't be crew, I can't be a Mactav, I can only be baggage. And—I can't even say it's unfair. . . ." Hot tears burned her face. "I didn't know what to do, I didn't know— If I should come. If you'd want a . . . ballerina who'd been in fire."

"You even wondered?" He held her close again, rested her head on his shoulder, to hide his own face grown wet.

A noise of pain twisted in her throat, her arms tightened. "Oh, Maris. Help me . . . please, help me, help me. . . ."

He rocked her silently, gently, until her sobbing eased, as he had rocked a homesick teenager a hundred years before.

"How will I live . . . on one world for centuries, always remembering. How do you bear it?"

"By learning what really matters. . . . Worlds are not so small. We'll go to other worlds if you want—we could see Home. You'd be surprised how much credit you build up over two hundred years." He kissed her swollen eyes, her reddened cheeks, her lips. "And maybe in time the rules will change."

She shook her head, bruised with loss. "Oh, my Maris, my wise love—love me, tie me to the earth."

He took her prosthetic hand, kissed the soft palm and fingers. *And make it well* . . . And knowing that it would never be easy, reached to dim the lights.

THE DAY BEFORE THE REVOLUTION

URSULA K. Le GUIN

In her award-winning novel The Dispossessed, *Ursula K. Le Guin wrote of a utopian society and its conflicts with the world its founders had fled. In "The Day Before the Revolution," she shows us the early struggles of those who wanted to build this new society, giving us an unforgettable portrayal of the woman who made it possible.*

In memoriam, Paul Goodman, 1911–1972

THE speaker's voice was as loud as empty beer-trucks in a stone street, and the people at the meeting were jammed up close, cobble-stones, that great voice booming over them. Taviri was somewhere on the other side of the hall. She had to get to him. She wormed and pushed her way among the dark-clothed, close-packed people. She did not hear the words, nor see the faces: only the booming, and the bodies pressed one behind the other. She could not see Taviri, she was too short. A broad black-vested belly and chest loomed up, blocking her way. She must get through to Taviri. Sweating, she jabbed fiercely with her fist. It was

like hitting stone, he did not move at all, but the
huge lungs let out right over her head a prodigious
noise, a bellow. She cowered. Then she understood
that the bellow had not been at her. Others were
shouting. The speaker had said something, something fine about taxes or shadows. Thrilled, she
joined the shouting—"Yes! Yes!"—and shoving on,
came out easily into the open expanse of the Regi-
mental Drill Field in Parheo. Overhead the evening sky lay deep and colorless, and all around her
nodded the tall weeds with dry, white, close-flo-
reted heads. She had never known what they were
called. The flowers nodded above her head, swaying in the wind that always blew across the fields
in the dusk. She ran among them, and they whipped
lithe aside and stood up again swaying, silent. Taviri stood among the tall weeds in his good suit,
the dark grey one that made him look like a professor or a play-actor, harshly elegant. He did not
look happy, but he was laughing, and saying something to her. The sound of his voice made her cry,
and she reached out to catch hold of his hand, but
she did not stop, quite. She could not stop. "Oh,
Taviri," she said, "it's just on there!" The queer
sweet smell of the white weeds was heavy as she
went on. There were thorns, tangles underfoot,
there were slopes, pits. She feared to fall, she
stopped.

∞

Sun, bright morning-glare, straight in the eyes,
relentless. She had forgotten to pull the blind last
night. She turned her back on the sun, but the
right side wasn't comfortable. No use. Day. She
sighed twice, sat up, got her legs over the edge of

the bed, and sat hunched in her nightdress looking down at her feet.

The toes, compressed by a lifetime of cheap
shoes, were almost square where they touched each
other, and bulged out above in corns; the nails
were discolored and shapeless. Between the knob-
like ankle bones ran fine, dry wrinkles. The brief
little plain at the base of the toes had kept its deli-
cacy, but the skin was the color of mud, and knotted veins crossed the instep. Disgusting. Sad, de-
pressing. Mean. Pitiful. She tried on all the words,
and they all fit, like hideous little hats. Hideous:
yes, that one too. To look at oneself and find it
hideous, what a job! But then, when she hadn't
been hideous, had she sat around and stared at herself like this? Not much! A proper body's not an
object, not an implement, not a belonging to be
admired, it's just you, yourself. Only when it's no
longer you, but yours, a thing owned, do you worry
about it—Is it in good shape? Will it do? Will it last?

"Who cares?" said Laia fiercely, and stood up.

It made her giddy to stand up suddenly. She had
to put out her hand to the bedtable, for she dreaded
falling. At that she thought of reaching out to Taviri, in the dream.

What had he said? She could not remember.
She was not sure if she had even touched his hand.
She frowned, trying to force memory. It had been
so long since she had dreamed about Taviri; and
now not even to remember what he had said!

It was gone, it was gone. She stood there
hunched in her nightdress, frowning, one hand on
the bedtable. How long was it since she had
thought of him—let alone dreamed of him—even

thought of him, as "Taviri"? How long since she had said his name?

Asieo said. When Asieo and I were in prison in the North. Before I met Asieo. Asieo's theory of reciprocity. Oh yes, she talked about him, talked about him too much no doubt, maundered, dragged him in. But as "Asieo," the last name, the public man. The private man was gone, utterly gone. There were so few left who had even known him. They had all used to be in jail. One laughed about it in those days, all the friends in all the jails. But they weren't even there, these days. They were in the prison cemeteries. Or in the common graves.

"Oh, oh my dear," Laia said out loud, and she sank down onto the bed again because she could not stand up under the remembrance of those first weeks in the Fort, in the cell, those first weeks of the nine years in the Fort in Drio, in the cell, those first weeks after they told her that Asieo had been killed in the fighting in Capitol Square and had been buried with the Fourteen Hundred in the lime-ditches behind Oring Gate. In the cell. Her hands fell into the old position on her lap, the left clenched and locked inside the grip of the right, the right thumb working back and forth a little pressing and rubbing on the knuckle of the left first finger. Hours, days, nights. She had thought of them all, each one, each one of the Fourteen Hundred, how they lay, how the quicklime worked on the flesh, how the bones touched in the burning dark. Who touched him? How did the slender bones of the hand lie now? Hours, years.

"Taviri, I have never forgotten you!" she whis-

pered, and the stupidity of it brought her back to
morning-light and the rumpled bed. Of course she
hadn't forgotten him. These things go without saying between husband and wife. There were her
ugly old feet flat on the floor again, just as before.
She had got nowhere at all, she had gone in a circle. She stood up with a grunt of effort and disap-
proval, and went to the closet for her dressing
gown.

The young people went about the halls of the
House in becoming immodesty, but she was too
old for that. She didn't want to spoil some young
man's breakfast with the sight of her. Besides, they
had grown up in the principle of freedom of dress
and sex and all the rest, and she hadn't. All she
had done was invent it. It's not the same.

Like speaking of Asieo as "my husband." They
winced. The word she should use as a good Odonian, of course, was "partner." But why the hell did
she have to be a good Odonian?

She shuffled down the hall to the bathrooms.
Mairo was there, washing her hair in a lavatory.
Laia looked at the long, sleek, wet hank with admiration. She got out of the House so seldom now
that she didn't know when she had last seen a re-
spectably shaven scalp, but still the sight of a full
head of hair gave her pleasure, vigorous pleasure.
How many times had she been jeered at, *Longhair, Longhair,* had her hair pulled by policemen
or young toughs, had her hair shaved off down to
the scalp by a grinning soldier at each new prison?
And then had grown it all over again, through the
fuzz, to the frizz, to the curls, to the mane . . . In

the old days. For God's love, couldn't she think of anything today but the old days?

Dressed, her bed made, she went down to commons. It was a good breakfast, but she had never got her appetite back since the damned stroke. She drank two cups of herb tea, but couldn't finish the piece of fruit she had taken. How she had craved fruit as a child, badly enough to steal it; and in the Fort—oh for God's love stop it! She smiled and replied to the greetings and friendly inquiries of the other breakfasters and big Aevi who was serving the counter this morning. It was he who had tempted her with the peach. "Look at this, I've been saving it for you," and how could she refuse? Anyway she had always loved fruit, and never got enough; once when she was six or seven she had stolen a piece off a vendor's cart in River Street. But it was hard to eat when everyone was talking so excitedly. There was news from Thu, real news. She was inclined to discount it at first, being wary of enthusiasms, but after she had read the article in the paper, and read between the lines of it, she thought, with a strange kind of certainty, deep but cold, Why, this is it; it has come. And in Thu, not here. Thu will break before this country does; the Revolution will first prevail there. As if that mattered! There will be no more nations. And yet it did matter somehow, it made her a little cold and sad—envious, in fact. Of all the infinite stupidities. She did not join in the talk much, and soon got up to go back to her room, feeling sorry for herself. She could not share their excitement. She was out of it, really out of it. It's not easy, she said to herself in justification, laboriously climbing the stairs, to accept being out of it when you've been in it, in the center of it, for fifty years. Oh for God's love. Whining!

She got the stairs and the self-pity behind her, entering her room. It was a good room, and it was good to be by herself. It was a great relief. Even if it wasn't strictly fair. Some of the kids in the attics were living five to a room no bigger than this. There were always more people wanting to live in an Odonian House than could be properly accommodated. She had this big room all to herself only because she was an old woman who had had a stroke. And maybe because she was Odo. If she hadn't been Odo, but merely the old woman with a stroke, would she have had it? Very likely. After all, who the hell wanted to room with a drooling old woman? But it was hard to be sure. Favoritism, elitism, leader-worship, they crept back and cropped out everywhere. But she had never hoped to see them eradicated in her lifetime, in one generation; only Time works the great changes. Meanwhile this was a nice, large, sunny room, proper for a drooling old woman who had started a world revolution.

Her secretary would be coming in an hour to help her despatch the day's work. She shuffled over to the desk, a beautiful, big piece, a present from the Noi Cabinetmakers' Syndicate because somebody had heard her remark once that the only piece of furniture she had ever really longed for was a desk with drawers and enough room on top . . . damn, the top was practically covered with papers with notes clipped to them, mostly in Noi's small clear handwriting: Urgent. — Northern Provinces. — Consult w/R.T.?

Her own handwriting had never been the same since Asieo's death. It was odd, when you thought about it. After all, within five years after his death she had written the whole *Analogy*. And there were those letters, which the tall guard with the watery grey eyes, what was his name, never mind, had smuggled out of the Fort for her for two years. *The Prison Letters* they called them now, there were a dozen different editions of them. All that stuff, the letters which people kept telling her were so full of "spiritual strength"—which probably meant she had been lying herself blue in the face when she wrote them, trying to keep her spirits up—and the *Analogy* which was certainly the solidest intellectual work she had ever done, all of that had been written in the Fort in Drio, in the cell, after Asieo's death. One had to do something, and in the Fort they let one have paper and pens . . . But it had all been written in the hasty, scribbling hand which she had never felt was hers, not her own like the round, black scrollings of the manuscript of *Society Without Government*, forty-five years old. Taviri had taken not only her body's and her heart's desire to the quicklime with him, but even her good clear handwriting.

∞

But he had left her the Revolution.

How brave of you to go on, to work, to write, in prison, after such a defeat for the Movement, after your partner's death, people had used to say. Damn fools. What else had there been to do?

Bravery, courage—what was courage? She had never figured it out. Not fearing, some said. Fearing yet going on, others said. But what could one do but go on? Had one any real choice, ever?

To die was merely to go on in another direction.

If you wanted to come home you had to keep going on, that was what she meant when she wrote, "True journey is return," but it had never been more than an intuition, and she was farther than ever now from being able to rationalize it. She bent down, too suddenly, so that she grunted a little at the creak in her bones, and began to root in a bottom drawer of the desk. Her hand came to an age-softened folder and drew it out, recognizing it by touch before sight confirmed: the manuscript of *Syndical Organization in Revolutionary Transition*. He had printed the title on the folder and written his name under it, Taviri Odo Asieo, IX 741. There was an elegant handwriting, every letter well-formed, bold, and fluent. But he had preferred to use a voiceprinter. The manuscript was all in voiceprint, and high quality too, hesitancies adjusted and idiosyncrasies of speech normalized. You couldn't see there how he had said "o" deep in his throat as they did on the North Coast. There was nothing of him there but his mind. She had nothing of him at all except his name written on the folder. She hadn't kept his letters, it was sentimental to keep letters. Besides, she never kept anything. She couldn't think of anything that she had ever owned for more than a few years, except this ramshackle old body, of course, and she was stuck with that . . .

Dualizing again. "She" and "it." Age and illness made one dualist, made one escapist; the mind insisted, *It's not me, it's not me*. But it was. Maybe the mystics could detach mind from body, she had always rather wistfully envied them the chance, without hope of emulating them. Escape had never been her game. She had sought for freedom here, now, body and soul.

First self-pity, then self-praise, and here she still sat, for God's love, holding Asieo's name in her hand, why? Didn't she know his name without looking it up? What was wrong with her? She raised the folder to her lips and kissed the handwritten name firmly and squarely, replaced the folder in the back of the bottom drawer, shut the drawer, and straightened up in the chair. Her right hand tingled. She scratched it, and then shook it in the air, spitefully. It had never quite got over the stroke. Neither had her right leg, or right eye, or the right corner of her mouth. They were sluggish, inept, they tingled. They made her feel like a robot with a short circuit.

And time was getting on, Noi would be coming, what had she been doing ever since breakfast?

She got up so hastily that she lurched, and grabbed at the chairback to make sure she did not fall. She went down the hall to the bathroom and looked in the big mirror there. Her grey knot was loose and droopy, she hadn't done it up well before breakfast. She struggled with it a while. It was hard to keep her arms up in the air. Amai, running in to piss, stopped and said, "Let me do it!" and knotted it up tight and neat in no time, with her round, strong, pretty fingers, smiling and silent. Amai was twenty, less than a third of Laia's age. Her parents had both been members of the Movement, one killed in the insurrection of '60, the other still recruiting in the South Provinces. Amai had grown up in Odonian Houses, born to the Revolution, a true daughter of anarchy. And so quiet and free and beautiful a child, enough to make you cry when you thought: this is what we worked for, this is what we meant, this is it, here she is, alive, the kindly, lovely future.

Laia Asieo Odo's right eye wept several little tears, as she stood between the lavatories and the latrines having her hair done up by the daughter she had not borne; but her left eye, the strong one, did not weep, nor did it know what the right eye did.

She thanked Amai and hurried back to her room. She had noticed, in the mirror, a stain on her collar. Peach juice, probably. Damned old dribbler. She didn't want Noi to come in and find her with drool on her collar.

As the clean shirt went on over her head, she thought, What's so special about Noi?

She fastened the collar-frogs with her left hand, slowly.

Noi was thirty or so, a slight, muscular fellow with a soft voice and alert dark eyes. That's what was special about Noi. It was that simple. Good old sex. She had never been drawn to a fair man or a fat one, or the tall fellows with big biceps, never, not even when she was fourteen and fell in love with every passing fart. Dark, spare, and fiery, that was the recipe. Taviri, of course. This boy wasn't a patch on Taviri for brains, nor even for

looks, but there it was: she didn't want him to see
her with dribble on her collar and her hair coming
undone.

Her thin, grey hair.

Noi came in, just pausing in the open doorway
—my God, she hadn't even shut the door while
changing her shirt!—She looked at him and saw
herself. The old woman.

You could brush your hair and change your
shirt, or you could wear last week's shirt and last
night's braids, or you could put on cloth of gold
and dust your shaven scalp with diamond powder.
None of it would make the slightest difference. The
old woman would look a little less, or a little more,
grotesque.

One keeps oneself neat out of mere decency,
mere sanity, awareness of other people.

And finally even that goes, and one dribbles un-
ashamed.

"Good morning," the young man said in his gentle voice.

"Hello, Noi."

No, by God, it was *not* out of mere decency.
Decency be damned. Because the man she had
loved, and to whom her age would not have mattered—because he was dead, must she pretend she
had no sex? Must she suppress the truth, like a
damned puritan authoritarian? Even six months
ago, before the stroke, she had made men look at
her and like to look at her; and now, though she
could give no pleasure, by God she could please
herself.

When she was six years old, and Papa's friend
Gadeo used to come by to talk politics with Papa

after dinner, she would put on the gold-colored necklace that Mama had found on a trash-heap and brought home for her. It was so short that it always got hidden under her collar where nobody could see it. She liked it that way. She knew she had it on. She sat on the doorstep and listened to them talk, and knew that she looked nice for Gadeo. He was dark, with white teeth that flashed. Sometimes he called her "pretty Laia." "There's my pretty Laia!" Sixty-six years ago.

"What? My head's dull. I had a terrible night." It was true. She had slept even less than usual.

"I was asking if you'd seen the papers this morning."

She nodded.

"Pleased about Soinehe?"

Soinehe was the province in Thu which had declared its secession from the Thuvian State last night.

He was pleased about it. His white teeth flashed in his dark, alert face. Pretty Laia.

"Yes. And apprehensive."

"I know. But it's the real thing, this time. It's the beginning of the end of the Government in Thu. They haven't even tried to order troops into Soinehe, you know. It would merely provoke the soldiers into rebellion sooner, and they know it."

She agreed with him. She herself had felt that certainty. But she could not share his delight. After a lifetime of living on hope because there is nothing but hope, one loses the taste for victory. A real sense of triumph must be preceded by real despair. She had unlearned despair a long time ago. There were no more triumphs. One went on.

"Shall we do those letters today?"

"All right. Which letters?"

"To the people in the North," he said without impatience.

"In the North?"

"Parheo, Oaidun."

She had been born in Parheo, the dirty city on the dirty river. She had not come here to the capital till she was twenty-two and ready to bring the Revolution. Though in those days, before she and the others had thought it through, it had been a very green and puerile revolution. Strikes for better wages, representation for women. Votes and wages—Power and Money, for the love of God! Well, one does learn a little, after all, in fifty years.

But then one must forget it all.

"Start with Oaidun," she said, sitting down in the armchair. Noi was at the desk ready to work. He read out excerpts from the letters she was to answer. She tried to pay attention, and succeeded well enough that she dictated one whole letter and started on another. "Remember that at this stage your brotherhood is vulnerable to the threat of . . . no, to the danger . . . to . . ." She groped till Noi suggested, "The danger of leader-worship?"

"All right. And that nothing is so soon corrupted by power-seeking as altruism. No. And that nothing corrupts altruism—no. Oh for God's love you know what I'm trying to say, Noi, you write it. They know it too, it's just the same old stuff, why can't they read my books!"

"Touch," Noi said gently, smiling, citing one of the central Odonian themes.

"All right, but I'm tired of being touched. If

you'll write the letter I'll sign it, but I can't be bothered with it this morning." He was looking at her with a little question or concern. She said, irritable, "There is something else I have to do!"

∞

When Noi had gone she sat down at the desk and moved the papers about, pretending to be doing something, because she had been startled, frightened, by the words she had said. She had nothing else to do. She never had had anything else to do. This was her work: her lifework. The speaking tours and the meetings and the streets were out of reach for her now, but she could still write, and that was her work. And anyhow if she had had anything else to do, Noi would have known it; he kept her schedule, and tactfully reminded her of things, like the visit from the foreign students this afternoon.

Oh, damn. She liked the young, and there was always something to learn from a foreigner, but she was tired of new faces, and tired of being on view. She learned from them, but they didn't learn from her; they had learnt all she had to teach long ago, from her books, from the Movement. They just came to look, as if she were the Great Tower in Rodarred, or the Canyon of the Tulaevea. A phenomenon, a monument. They were awed, adoring. She snarled at them: Think your own thoughts! —That's not anarchism, that's mere obscurantism. —You don't think liberty and discipline are incompatible, do you?—They accepted their tonguelashing meekly as children, gratefully, as if she were some kind of All-Mother, the idol of the Big Sheltering Womb. She! She who had mined the ship-

yards at Seissero, and had cursed Premier Inoilte
to his face in front of a crowd of seven thousand,
telling him he would have cut off his own balls and
had them bronzed and sold as souvenirs, if he
thought there was any profit in it—she who had
screeched, and sworn, and kicked policemen, and
spat at priests, and pissed in public on the big
brass plaque in Capitol Square that said HERE WAS
FOUNDED THE SOVEREIGN NATION STATE OF A-IO ETC
ETC, psssssss to all that! And now she was everybody's grandmama, the dear old lady, the sweet old
monument, come worship at the womb. The fire's
out, boys, it's safe to come up close.

"No, I won't," Laia said out loud. "I will not."
She was not self-conscious about talking to herself,
because she always had talked to herself. "Laia's
invisible audience," Taviri had used to say, as she
went through the room muttering. "You needn't
come, I won't be here," she told the invisible audience now. She had just decided what it was she
had to do. She had to go out. To go into the streets.

It was inconsiderate to disappoint the foreign
students. It was erratic, typically senile. It was un-
Odonian. Pssssss to all that. What was the good
working for freedom all your life and ending up
without any freedom at all? She would go out for
a walk.

*"What is an anarchist? One who, choosing, ac-
cepts the responsibility of choice."*

On the way downstairs she decided, scowling,
to stay and see the foreign students. But then she
would go out.

They were very young students, very earnest:
doe-eyed, shaggy, charming creatures from the

Western Hemisphere, Benbili and the Kingdom of
Mand, the girls in white trousers, the boys in long
kilts, warlike and archaic. They spoke of their
hopes. "We in Mand are so very far from the Revolution that maybe we are near it," said one of the
girls, wistful and smiling: "The Circle of Life!"
and she showed the extremes meeting, in the circle
of her slender, dark-skinned fingers. Amai and Aevi
served them white wine and brown bread, the hos-
pitality of the House. But the visitors, unpresump-
tuous, all rose to take their leave after barely half
an hour. "No, no, no," Laia said, "stay here, talk
with Aevi and Amai. It's just that I get stiff sitting
down, you see. I have to change about. It has been
so good to meet you, will you come back to see
me, my little brothers and sisters, soon?" For her
heart went out to them, and theirs to her, and she
exchanged kisses all round, laughing, delighted by
the dark young cheeks, the affectionate eyes, the
scented hair, before she shuffled off. She was really
a little tired, but to go up and take a nap would
be a defeat. She had wanted to go out. She would
go out. She had not been alone outdoors since—
when? since winter! before the stroke. No wonder
she was getting morbid. It had been a regular jail
sentence. Outside, the streets, that's where she
lived.

She went quietly out the side door of the House,
past the vegetable patch, to the street. The narrow
strip of sour city dirt had been beautifully gar-
dened and was producing a fine crop of beans and
ceëa, but Laia's eye for farming was unenlight-
ened. Of course it had been clear that anarchist
communities, even in the time of transition, must

work towards optimal self-support, but how that
was to be managed in the way of actual dirt and
plants wasn't her business. There were farmers and
agronomists for that. Her job was the streets, the
noisy, stinking streets of stone, where she had
grown up and lived all her life, except for the fifteen years in prison.

She looked up fondly at the façade of the House.
That it had been built as a bank gave peculiar
satisfaction to its present occupants. They kept
their sacks of meal in the bombproof money-vault,
and aged their cider in kegs in safe deposit boxes.
Over the fussy columns that faced the street, carved
letters still read, NATIONAL INVESTORS AND GRAIN
FACTORS BANKING ASSOCIATION. The Movement was
not strong on names. They had no flag. Slogans
came and went as the need did. There was always
the Circle of Life to scratch on walls and pave-
ments where Authority would have to see it. But
when it came to names they were indifferent, ac-
cepting and ignoring whatever they got called,
afraid of being pinned down and penned in, unafraid of being absurd. So this best known and second oldest of all the cooperative Houses had no
name except The Bank.

It faced on a wide and quiet street, but only a
block away began the Temeba, an open market,
once famous as a center for black market psycho-
genics and teratogenics, now reduced to vegetables,
secondhand clothes, and miserable sideshows. Its
crapulous vitality was gone, leaving only half-para-
lyzed alcoholics, addicts, cripples, hucksters, and
fifth-rate whores, pawnshops, gambling dens, for-

tune-tellers, body-sculptors, and cheap hotels. Laia turned to the Temeba as water seeks its level.

She had never feared or despised the city. It was her country. There would not be slums like this, if the Revolution prevailed. But there would be misery. There would always be misery, waste, cruelty. She had never pretended to be changing the human condition, to be Mama taking tragedy away from the children so they won't hurt themselves. Anything but. So long as people were free to choose, if they chose to drink flybane and live in sewers, it was their business. Just so long as it wasn't the business of Business, the source of profit and the means of power for other people. She had felt all that before she knew anything; before she wrote the first pamphlet, before she left Parheo, before she knew what "capital" meant, before she'd been farther than River Street where she played roll-taggie kneeling on scabby knees on the pavement with the other six-year-olds, she had known it: that she, and the other kids, and her parents, and their parents, and the drunks and whores and all of River Street, were at the bottom of something—were the foundation, the reality, the source.

But will you drag civilization down into the mud? cried the shocked decent people, later on, and she had tried for years to explain to them that if all you had was mud, then if you were God you made it into human beings, and if you were human you tried to make it into houses where human beings could live. But nobody who thought he was better than mud would understand. Now, water seeking its level, mud to mud, Laia shuffled through

the foul, noisy street, and all the ugly weakness of
her old age was at home. The sleepy whores, their
lacquered hair-arrangements dilapidated and askew,
the one-eyed woman wearily yelling her vegetables to sell, the halfwit beggar slapping flies,
these were her countrywomen. They looked like
her, they were all sad, disgusting, mean, pitiful,
hideous. They were her sisters, her own people.

She did not feel very well. It had been a long
time since she had walked so far, four or five
blocks, by herself, in the noise and push and stinking summer heat of the streets. She had wanted to
get to Koly Park, the triangle of scruffy grass at
the end of the Temeba, and sit there for a while
with the other old men and women who always
sat there, to see what it was like to sit there and
be old; but it was too far. If she didn't turn back
now, she might get a dizzy spell, and she had a
dread of falling down, falling down and having to
lie there and look up at the people come to stare
at the old woman in a fit. She turned and started
home, frowning with effort and self-disgust. She
could feel her face very red, and a swimming feeling came and went in her ears. It got a bit much,
she was really afraid she might keel over. She saw
a doorstep in the shade and made for it, let herself
down cautiously, sat, sighed.

Nearby was a fruit-seller, sitting silent behind
his dusty, withered stock. People went by. Nobody
bought from him. Nobody looked at her. Odo, who
was Odo? Famous revolutionary, author of *Com-
munity, The Analogy*, etc. etc. She, who was she?
An old woman with grey hair and a red face sit-

ting on a dirty doorstep in a slum, muttering to herself.

True? Was that she? Certainly it was what anybody passing her saw. But was it she, herself, any more than the famous revolutionary, etc., was? No. It was not. But who was she, then?

The one who loved Taviri.

Yes. True enough. But not enough. That was gone; he had been dead so long.

"Who am I?" Laia muttered to her invisible audience, and they knew the answer and told it to her with one voice. She was the little girl with scabby knees, sitting on the doorstep staring down through the dirty golden haze of River Street in the heat of late summer, the six-year-old, the sixteen-year-old, the fierce, cross, dream-ridden girl, untouched, untouchable. She was herself. Indeed she had been the tireless worker and thinker, but a bloodclot in a vein had taken that woman away from her. Indeed she had been the lover, the swimmer in the midst of life, but Taviri, dying, had taken that woman away with him. There was nothing left, really, but the foundation. She had come home; she had never left home. "True voyage is return." Dust and mud and a doorstep in the slums. And beyond, at the far end of the street, the field full of tall dry weeds blowing in the wind as night came.

"Laia! What are you doing here? Are you all right?"

One of the people from the House, of course, a nice woman, a bit fanatical and always talking. Laia could not remember her name though she had

known her for years. She let herself be taken home,
the woman talking all the way. In the big cool
common-room (once occupied by tellers counting
money behind polished counters supervised by
armed guards) Laia sat down in a chair. She was
unable just as yet to face climbing the stairs,
though she would have liked to be alone. The
woman kept on talking, and other excited people
came in. It appeared that a demonstration was being planned. Events in Thu were moving so fast
that the mood here had caught fire, and something
must be done. Day after tomorrow, no, tomorrow,
there was to be a march, a big one, from Old Town
to Capitol Square—the old route. "Another Ninth
Month Uprising," said a young man, fiery and
laughing, glancing at Laia. He had not even been
born at the time of the Ninth Month Uprising, it
was all history to him. Now he wanted to make
some history of his own. The room had filled up.
A general meeting would be held here, tomorrow,
at eight in the morning. "You must talk, Laia."

"Tomorrow? Oh, I won't be here tomorrow," she
said brusquely. Whoever had asked her smiled, another one laughed, though Amai glanced round at
her with a puzzled look. They went on talking and
shouting. The Revolution. What on earth had made
her say that? What a thing to say on the eve of
the Revolution, even if it was true.

She waited her time, managed to get up, for all
her clumsiness, to slip away unnoticed among the
people busy with their planning and excitement.
She got to the hall, to the stairs, and began to
climb them one by one. "The general strike," a
voice, two voices, ten voices were saying in the

room below, behind her. "The general strike," Laia muttered, resting for a moment on the landing. Above, ahead, in her room, what awaited her? The private stroke. That was mildly funny. She started up the second flight of stairs, one by one, one leg at a time, like a small child. She was dizzy, but she was no longer afraid to fall. On ahead, on there, the dry white flowers nodded and whispered in the open fields of evening. Seventy-two years and she had never had time to learn what they were called.

FURTHER READING

NOVELS

Suzy McKee Charnas, *Walk to the End of the World* (New York, Ballantine Books, 1974).

Thomas M. Disch, *334* (New York, Avon, 1974).

Joe Haldeman, *The Forever War* (New York, St. Martin's Press, 1974).

Ursula K. Le Guin, *The Dispossessed* (New York, Harper & Row, 1974).

Ursula K. Le Guin, *The Left Hand of Darkness* (New York, Walker, 1969).

Fritz Leiber, *Conjure Wife* (New York, Twayne, 1953).

A. M. Lightner, *The Day of the Drones* (New York, Norton, 1969).

Naomi Mitchison, *Memoirs of a Spacewoman* (London, Gollancz, 1962).

Alexei Panshin, *Rite of Passage* (New York, Ace Books, 1968).

Joanna Russ, *The Female Man* (New York, Bantam Books, 1975).

Joanna Russ, *Picnic on Paradise* (New York, Ace Books, 1968).

Wilmar Shiras, *Children of the Atom* (New York, Gnome Press, 1953).

Theodore Sturgeon, *Venus Plus X* (New York, Pyramid Books, 1960).

Philip Wylie, *The Disappearance* (New York, Holt Rinehart, 1951).

ANTHOLOGIES AND COLLECTIONS

LEIGH BRACKETT, *The Halfling and Other Stories* (New York, Ace Books, 1973).

LESTER DEL REY, ed., *The Best of C. L. Moore* (New York, Ballantine Books, 1975).

CAROL EMSHWILLER, *Joy in Our Cause* (New York, Harper & Row, 1974).

VIRGINIA KIDD, ed., *Millennial Women* (New York, Delacorte, to be published).

URSULA K. LE GUIN, *The Wind's Twelve Quarters* (New York, Harper & Row, 1975).

VONDA N. MCINTYRE and SUSAN JANICE ANDERSON, eds., *Aurora: Beyond Equality* (New York, Gold Medal Books, 1976).

JUDITH MERRIL, *Survival Ship and Other Stories* (Toronto, Kakabeka Press, 1973).

KATE WILHELM, *The Infinity Box* (New York, Harper & Row, 1975).

NON-FICTION

BEVERLY FRIEND, "Virgin Territory: Women and Sex in Science Fiction," *Extrapolation*, Vol. 14, No. 1 (December 1972).

SUZANNE KELLER, "The Future Role of Women," *The Annals of the American Academy of Political and Social Science*, Vol. 408 (July 1973).

SAM MOSKOWITZ, "When Women Rule," in Sam Moskowitz, ed., *When Women Rule* (New York, Walker, 1972).

JOANNA RUSS, "The Image of Women in Science Fiction," *Vertex*, Vol. 1, No. 6 (February 1974).

———, Introduction to Mary Shelley, *Tales and Stories* (Boston, Gregg Press, 1975).

The Science Fiction of Ursula K. Le Guin, Special Issue

of *Science Fiction Studies*, #7, Vol. 2, Part 3 (November 1975).

MAGGIE TRIPP, ed., *Woman in the Year 2000* (New York, Arbor House, 1974).

Women and the Future, Special Issue of *Futures:* The Journal of Forecasting and Planning, Vol. 7, No. 5 (October 1975).

ABOUT THE AUTHORS

LEIGH BRACKETT is the author of many science fiction stories which have appeared in *Planet Stories, Astounding*, and other magazines. Her science fiction novels include *The Big Jump, The Coming of the Terrans, The Sword of Rhiannon, The Long Tomorrow*, and *The Ginger Star*. Among her non–science fiction novels are *An Eye for an Eye* and *The Tiger Amongst Us*. She has also worked as a screenwriter; her credits include *The Big Sleep* (with William Faulkner), *Rio Bravo*, and *The Long Goodbye*. She is now editing a series of anthologies for Ballantine Books, *The Best of Planet Stories*. She is married to science fiction writer Edmond Hamilton.

URSULA K. LE GUIN is the author of many award-winning short stories, among them "The Ones Who Walk Away From Omelas," "The Day Before the Revolution," and "The Word for World is Forest." Her novels *The Left Hand of Darkness* and *The Dispossessed* each won both the Hugo Award (given annually by the members of the World Science Fiction Conventions) and the Nebula Award (given annually by the members of the Science Fiction Writers of America). A fantasy novel, *The Farthest Shore*, received the National Book Award for Children's Literature; it is part of a trilogy that includes *A Wizard of Earthsea* and *The Tombs of Atuan*. She is also the author of a collection of short stories, *The Wind's Twelve Quarters*. She lives in Oregon.

C. L. Moore is the author of many short stories and no-vellas, among them "No Woman Born," "Shambleau," "Vintage Season," "Black God's Kiss," and others in-cluded in a collection of short fiction, *The Best of C.L. Moore* (edited by Lester del Rey). Among her novels are *Judgment Night* and *Doomsday Morning*. In 1940 she married science fiction writer Henry Kuttner, and the two formed one of the most successful science fiction writing teams in the history of the field; several of their works were published under the pseudonyms Law-rence O'Donnell and Lewis Padgett. After Kuttner's death, Moore wrote many television scripts for *Maverick*, *77 Sunset Strip*, and other series. She lives in California.

Joanna Russ is the author of the novels *And Chaos Died, Picnic on Paradise*, and *The Female Man*. Her short fiction has appeared in *The Magazine of Fantasy & Science Fiction, Quark, Again, Dangerous Visions, Aurora: Beyond Equality*, and several literary magazines. Her short story "When It Changed" won a Nebula Award. She is assistant professor of English at the Uni-versity of Colorado.

Josephine Saxton is the author of the novels *The Hieros Gamos of Sam and An Smith* and *Group Feast*. She has also published a short story collection, *Vector for Seven*. Her short fiction has appeared in *New Worlds, New Dimensions, Again, Dangerous Visions, Or-bit*, and other magazines and anthologies. She lives in England.

Joan D. Vinge has a degree in anthropology and has worked as a salvage archaeologist. Her short stories have appeared in *Analog, Orbit*, and the literary magazine *Centaur*. She is currently at work on a novel. She is mar-ried to science fiction author Vernor Vinge and lives in California.

KATE WILHELM is the author of short fiction published in *Quark, Orbit, The Magazine of Fantasy & Science Fiction* and several other magazines and anthologies. Her short story "The Planners" won a Nebula Award. Her novels include *The Killer Thing, Let the Fire Fall, Margaret and I, City of Cain,* and *Where Late the Sweet Birds Sang.* Her most recent short-story collection is *The Infinity Box*; other collections are *The Downstairs Room* and *The Mile-Long Spaceship.* She is also the editor of *Nebula Award Stories Nine.* She is married to science fiction author, editor, and critic Damon Knight.

ABOUT THE EDITOR

PAMELA SARGENT is the author of twenty short stories which have appeared in *The Magazine of Fantasy & Science Fiction, Universe, Fellowship of the Stars,* and other magazines and anthologies. She is also the author of a novel, *Cloned Lives* (Fawcett-Gold Medal). She is the editor of the anthologies *Women of Wonder* and *Bio-Futures* (Vintage Books). She lives in upstate New York.